FOUNDATIONS of MATHEMATICS

Workbook 11

Series Authors and Consultants

Cathy Canavan-McGrath, Hay River, Northwest Territories
Serge Desrochers, Calgary, Alberta
Hugh MacDonald, Edmonton, Alberta
Carolyn Martin, Edmonton, Alberta
Michael Pruner, Vancouver, British Columbia
Hank Reinbold, St. Albert, Alberta
Rupi Samra-Gynane, Vancouver, British Columbia
Carol Shaw, Winnipeg, Manitoba
Roger Teshima, Calgary, Alberta
Darin Trufyn, Edmonton, Alberta

NELSON EDUCATION

NELSON EDUCATION

Foundations of Mathematics 11 Workbook

Lead Educator	Series Authors	Workbook Author
Chris Kirkpatrick	Cathy Canavan-McGrath	First Folio Resource Group Inc.
	Michael Pruner	
	Carol Shaw	
	Darin Trufyn	
	Hank Reinbold	

Editorial Director
Linda Allison

Publisher, Mathematics
Colin Garnham

Managing Editor, Development
Erynn Marcus

Product Manager
Linda Krepinsky

Project Manager
Jessica Reeve

Senior Content Editor
Tom Gamblin

Developmental Editor
First Folio Resource Group Inc.

Director, Content and Media Production
Linh Vu

Content Production Editors
Natalie Russell

Copyeditor
Gerry Jenkison

Proofreader
John Green

Production Coordinator
Sharon Latta Paterson

Design Director
Ken Phipps

Interior Design
VisutronX
Eugene Lo

Cover Design
Ken Phipps

Cover Image
Randy Lincks/Photolibrary

Asset Coordinator
Suzanne Peden

Illustrators
MPS Limited, a Macmillan Company
Crowle Art Group

Compositor
MPS Limited, a Macmillan Company

Permissions Researcher
Natalie Russell

Cover Research
Debbie Yea

COPYRIGHT © 2012 by
Nelson Education Ltd.

ISBN-13: 978-0-17-651445-7
ISBN-10: 0-17-651445-7

Printed and bound in the United States
3 4 5   15 14

For more information contact
Nelson Education Ltd.,
1120 Birchmount Road, Toronto,
Ontario M1K 5G4. Or you can visit
our Internet site at
http://www.nelson.com.

For permission to use material
from this text or product, submit
all requests online at
www.cengage.com/permissions.
Further questions about
permissions can be emailed to
permissionrequest@cengage.com.

Every effort has been made to
trace ownership of all copyrighted
material and to secure permission
from copyright holders. In the
event of any question arising as
to the use of any material, we will
be pleased to make the necessary
corrections in future printings.

Table of Contents

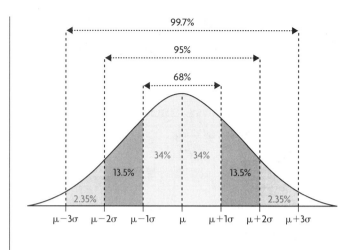

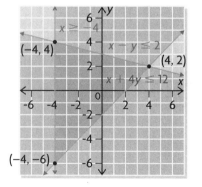

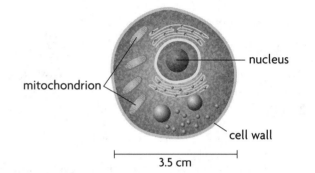

Inductive and Deductive Reasoning

Getting Started

1. Match each term with a diagram or example.

   a) equivalent form ___

   b) complementary angles ___

   c) three-digit number ___

   d) congruent shapes ___

   e) perfect cube ___

   f) prime number ___

   i)

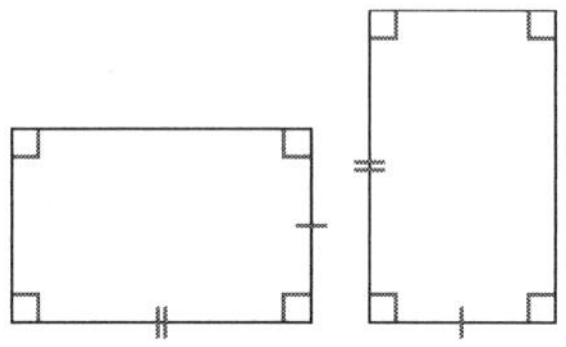

   ii)

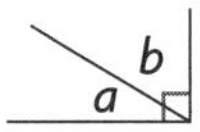

   iii) 982

   iv) 27

   v) 47

   vi) $5x - 2x = 3x$

2. Order these expressions from greatest (1) to least (4).

   a) the difference between 6^2 and 3^3 ___

   b) the sum of the first two positive even numbers ___

   c) $7^2 - 4^3 + 5^2$ ___

   d) $9^2 \div 3^3$ ___

3. Identify a number that matches each description.

   a) a multiple of 7 between 40 and 80 ___

   b) the square of an odd number ___

   c) the sum of two consecutive odd numbers ___

4. Simplify each expression. Then evaluate for $x = 5$.

   a) $x^2 - 3 + 5x + 7 - 2x$ **b)** $12 + 5(4 - x)$ **c)** $(x + 3)(x - 3) + 7$

5. Factor or expand each expression. Then evaluate for $x = -2$.

    a) $2x(4 - x)$ **b)** $9x^2 - 4$ **c)** $2x^2 - 7x - 4$

6. Solve each equation.

    a) $2x - 7 = 23$ **b)** $22 - 3x = 2x$ **c)** $3x^2 = 48$

7. Determine angles a, b, and c, without measuring.

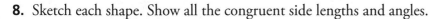

8. Sketch each shape. Show all the congruent side lengths and angles.

    a) a parallelogram that is not a rectangle   **b)** a kite that is not a rhombus

9. Examine the pattern below. Make a prediction about the next number.

$$1^2 = 1$$

$$101^2 = 10201$$

$$10101^2 = 102030201$$

$$1010101^2 = 1020304030201$$

1.1 Making Conjectures: Inductive Reasoning

YOU WILL NEED
• ruler and protractor

> **Keep in Mind**
>
> ▸ A conjecture is an unproven conclusion based on evidence.
>
> ▸ Inductive reasoning involves making a general conjecture based on specific cases by looking at patterns and recognizing properties.
>
> ▸ Additional evidence may support a conjecture but does not prove it.

Example 1

Draw a pair of intersecting lines. Measure and record the opposite angles as shown. What conjecture can you make?

Solution

Step 1. I drew two intersecting lines.

Step 2. I measured the acute angles. Each opposite angle measured 55°.

Step 3. I made this conjecture: "When two lines intersect, the opposite angles are equal."

Step 4. To support my conjecture, I measured the pair of opposite obtuse angles. They were also equal.

Example 2

Examine the pattern in the addends and their sums. What conjecture can you make?

$$1 + 3 = 4 \qquad 3 + 5 = 8 \qquad 5 + 7 = 12 \qquad 7 + 9 = 16$$

Solution

Step 1. I observed the following:

- In each case, the two addends are consecutive odd numbers.
- The sum of each pair of addends is an even number.
- Each sum is a multiple of 4.

Step 2. I made this conjecture: "The sum of two consecutive odd numbers is a multiple of 4."

Step 3. To look for more evidence to support my conjecture, I added other pairs of consecutive odd numbers.

$$35 + 37 = 72 \qquad\qquad 101 + 103 = 204$$
$$2111 + 2113 = 4224 \qquad 400\,273 + 400\,275 = 800\,548$$

In each case, the sum is a multiple of 4.

4   1.1 *Making Conjectures: Inductive Reasoning*

Copyright © 2012 by Nelson Education Ltd.

Practice

1. Anita works at a coffee shop in Canmore, Alberta. Numbers of sales for regular, medium, and large coffees were 3000, 3500, and 7000 in January. For February, Anita ordered twice as many large coffee cups as regular or medium cups. What conjecture might she have made?

2. Carol gathered the following evidence and noticed a pattern.

$$10 + 01 = 11 \qquad 24 + 42 = 66 \qquad 78 + 87 = 165$$
$$13 + 31 = 44 \qquad 39 + 93 = 132 \qquad 89 + 98 = 187$$

Carol made this conjecture: When you add a two-digit number to the number with the same digits transposed, the sum of the two numbers is a multiple of 11. Is Carol's conjecture reasonable? Provide evidence.

3. The coat of arms for Nunavut is shown. Make a conjecture about the meaning of the symbols and colours. Consider the traditions of Aboriginal peoples. (The darker areas of the central circle are blue in the coloured coat of arms, and the lighter areas are yellow.)

4. Robbie drew three different triangles. He measured the lengths of the sides and the angles in each triangle. He compared the length of the longest side with the measures of the angles in each triangle.

a) What conjecture might Robbie have made?

b) What other conjecture could he have made?

5. Draw two lines that intersect. Measure and record the four angles that are created at the point of intersection. Then make a conjecture about pairs of adjacent angles.

6. Examine the pattern in the factors and their products.

$$7(9) = 63$$

$$77(9) = 693$$

$$777(9) = 6993$$

$$7777(9) = 69\ 993$$

  a) What conjecture can you make? Provide evidence.

  b) Does a similar pattern occur with the product of nine and another factor that has repeated digits? Provide evidence to support your answer.

7. Examine this pattern in the difference of fractions. What conjecture can you make? Test your conjecture.

$$\frac{1}{1} - \frac{1}{2} = \frac{1}{2^2 - 2} \qquad \frac{1}{2} - \frac{1}{3} = \frac{1}{3^2 - 3} \qquad \frac{1}{3} - \frac{1}{4} = \frac{1}{4^2 - 4}$$

$$\frac{1}{4} - \frac{1}{5} = \frac{1}{5^2 - 5} \qquad \frac{1}{8} - \frac{1}{9} = \frac{1}{9^2 - 9} \qquad \frac{1}{11} - \frac{1}{12} = \frac{1}{12^2 - 12}$$

8. What conjecture can you make about the annual precipitation in Regina? Summarize the evidence that supports your conjecture.

Year	1998	1999	2000	2001	2002	2003	2004
Precipitation (mm)	24.70	458.00	327.00	469.60	269.50	219.20	549.00
Year	2005	2006	2007	2008	2009	2010	
Precipitation (mm)	491.40	273.80	320.00	301.90	463.80	14.60	

9. On March 11, 2011, a massive earthquake caused great damage to the northeastern coast of Japan. By some estimates, reconstruction could cost $180 billion. Suppose each Canadian were to donate $5 to the Canadian Red Cross relief efforts for Japan, by text message. Make a conjecture about the amount of time it would take for all Canadians to make a donation.

MULTIPLE CHOICE

10. What are the traits of good inductive reasoning?

   A. looking for patterns, identifying properties, gathering evidence, making a reasonable conclusion

   B. examining the data, making calculations, making guesses

   C. looking for patterns, making guesses

   D. none of the above

WRITTEN RESPONSE

11. Juice A has twice the sales of juice B, nationwide. In a televised taste test, 3 out of 4 participants preferred juice B over juice A. The manufacturers of juice B aired this test nationwide with the slogan "3 out of 4 people prefer the taste of …." Is the statement a conjecture? Explain.

1.2 Exploring the Validity of Conjectures

YOU WILL NEED
• ruler and protractor

Keep in Mind

▶ A conjecture can be supported or disproved with further evidence.

▶ You can revise a conjecture in response to new evidence.

Example 1

Are the horizontal lines in this diagram straight or curved? Make a conjecture. Then, check the validity of your conjecture.

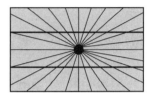

Solution

Step 1. I conjectured that the horizontal lines are straight and that the apparent curvature is an optical illusion caused by the diagonal lines.

Step 2. I put a ruler alongside each horizontal line. The lines were indeed straight.

Step 3. To verify my conjecture, I measured the distances between the horizontal lines. These distances were equal, so I knew the lines were parallel.

Example 2

Make a conjecture about this pattern. How can you check the validity of your conjecture?

$$\frac{1}{1} + \frac{1}{2} = \frac{3}{2} \qquad \frac{1}{2} + \frac{1}{3} = \frac{5}{6} \qquad \frac{1}{3} + \frac{1}{4} = \frac{7}{12} \qquad \frac{1}{5} + \frac{1}{6} = \frac{11}{30}$$

Solution

Step 1. I looked for a pattern in the denominators of the addends and the numerator of the sum.

In each case, the numerator of the sum equalled the sum of the denominators.

Step 2. I looked for a pattern in the denominators of the addends and the denominator of the sum.

In each case, the denominator of the sum equalled the product of the consecutive numbers in the denominators.

Step 3. I made this conjecture: "In the sum of two fractions with 1 in the numerator and consecutive numbers in the denominators, the numerator of the sum equals the sum of the denominators and the denominator of the sum equals the product of the denominators."

Step 4. I gathered more evidence to check the validity of my conjecture.

$$\frac{1}{6} + \frac{1}{7} = \frac{7}{42} + \frac{6}{42}, \text{ or } \frac{13}{42} \qquad \frac{1}{11} + \frac{1}{12} = \frac{12}{132} + \frac{11}{132}, \text{ or } \frac{23}{132}$$

This evidence supported my conjecture.

Practice

1. Make a conjecture about the lengths of the horizontal lines. Then check the validity of your conjecture.

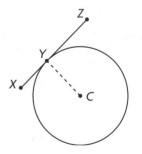

2. Examine the number pattern. Make a conjecture about the pattern. How can you determine if your conjecture is valid?

Number, x	Number of Divisors, n	Divisors	Product of Divisors	Square Root of Power, $\sqrt{x^n}$
2	2	1, 2	$1(2) = 2$	$\sqrt{2^2} = 2$
3	2	1, 3	$1(3) = 3$	$\sqrt{3^2} = 3$
4	3	1, 2, 4	$1(2)(4) = 8$	$\sqrt{4^3} = 8$
5	2	1, 5	$1(5) = 5$	$\sqrt{5^2} = 5$

3. A tangent to a circle is drawn at point Y. The centre of the circle, C, and the point of tangency, Y, are joined to create line segment CY. Make a conjecture about $\angle CYZ$. Check your conjecture by drawing several tangents to the circle and creating new angles. Is your conjecture valid?

4. Prime numbers sometimes occur as prime pairs that have a difference of 2. The prime numbers 5 and 7 form a prime pair, as do 41 and 43. There is at least one prime pair between 1 and 50, between 51 and 100, and between 101 and 150. Make a conjecture about prime pairs. Is your conjecture valid?

> **TIP**
> A prime number is a whole number greater than 1 that is divisible only by itself and 1.

Using Reasoning to Find a Counterexample to a Conjecture

YOU WILL NEED
• calculator
• ruler

Keep in Mind

▶ Gathering additional evidence can help support your conjecture, but the evidence cannot prove that your conjecture is true.

▶ A counterexample is an example or evidence that does not support your conjecture. Finding a single counterexample disproves the conjecture.

▶ Finding a counterexample will require you to revise your conjecture.

Example

Examine this pattern in the product of 11 and another two-digit number.

$$11 \times 11 = 121$$
$$12 \times 11 = 132$$
$$26 \times 11 = 286$$
$$43 \times 11 = 473$$

What conjecture can you make about the pattern?
How can you check whether your conjecture is true?

TIP

Sometimes the given evidence seems to support a conjecture, but often more evidence is needed to support the conjecture or to disprove it with a counterexample.

Solution

Step 1. I predicted that the product of 11 and a two-digit number will follow this pattern:

$$AB \times 11 = A[A + B]B$$

Step 2. To support my conjecture, I needed to gather more evidence.

Step 3. I examined several more examples.

$10 \times 11 = 110$ supports
$13 \times 11 = 143$ supports
$19 \times 11 = 209$ does not support
$28 \times 11 = 308$ does not support
$29 \times 11 = 319$ does not support
$91 \times 11 = 1001$ does not support

Step 4. I found a counterexample, so my conjecture is not true.

Step 5. I noticed that when the sum of the digits of the first factor was 10 or greater, the pattern failed. I revised my conjecture to the following: "Given a factor AB, where $A + B$ is less than 10, then the product of 11 and AB will have this form: $A[A + B]B$."

Practice

1. Show that each statement is false by finding a counterexample.

   a) If you live in Alberta, you live in a province that shares borders only with other Canadian provinces.

   b) Any animal that has wings can fly.

   c) All animals that live in the water are fish.

   d) If a quadrilateral has four right angles, then it is a square.

   e) The sum of two prime numbers is an even number.

2. Tom said that in any isosceles triangle, all three angles are acute. Do you agree or disagree? Justify your decision.

3. Belinda graphed $y = -2x + 5$, as shown. She said that x cannot have a negative value because the graph stops at (0, 5). Do you agree or disagree? Justify your decision.

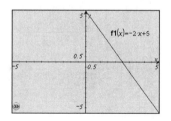

4. Consider the following conjecture. Do you agree or disagree? If you agree, say why. If you disagree, offer a counterexample and revise the conjecture to one you agree with. "When you divide two whole numbers, the quotient will be greater than the dividend."

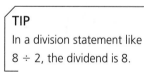

TIP

In a division statement like 8 ÷ 2, the dividend is 8.

5. Give a counterexample for each of the following conjectures.

   a) The sum of a multiple of 3 and a multiple of 6 must be odd.

   b) The difference between a multiple of 11 and a multiple of 7 is either even or divisible by 3.

   c) The farther north one goes, the colder the climate gets.

   d) If you live in Calgary, you can reach the Pacific Ocean only by travelling westward.

6. Give a counterexample, if possible, for each of the following conjectures.

   a) The sum of four consecutive numbers is equal to twice the last number.

   b) The sum of a multiple of 9 and a multiple of 27 must be a multiple of 9.

   c) If there is precipitation outside and it is May, then it must be raining.

   d) The sum of four consecutive numbers is equal to four times the first number plus 6.

7. Feather told her little sister, Star, that sheep, cattle, and hogs are all mammals. As a result, Star made this conjecture: "All mammals are raised on farms." Use a counterexample to show Star her conjecture is not valid.

MULTIPLE CHOICE

8. Which choice provides a counterexample to this conjecture? "The square of a number is always greater than the number."

   A. $0.25^2 = 0.0625$ but not $(-2)^2 = 4$

   B. $(-2)^2 = 4$ but not $0.25^2 = 0.0625$

   C. both $0.25^2 = 0.0625$ and $(-2)^2 = 4$

   D. neither $0.25^2 = 0.0625$ nor $(-2)^2 = 4$

9. Which choice provides a counterexample to the following conjecture? "All polygons with equal sides are regular hexagons." Choose the best response.

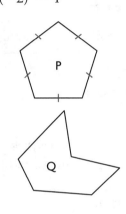

   A. Only figure P is a counterexample, because all sides are equal and it is not a regular hexagon.

   B. Figures P and Q are both counterexamples, because neither one is a regular hexagon.

   C. Only figure Q is a counterexample, because the six sides are not equal.

   D. Neither figure P nor Q is a counterexample, because P is a regular pentagon and Q does not have equal sides.

WRITTEN RESPONSE

10. Attila made the following conjecture: "The sum of two numbers is greater than the two numbers."

Do you agree or disagree with this conjecture?

   • If you agree, explain why.

   • If you disagree, explain why and offer a counterexample. Give two revisions to the conjecture for which you cannot find counterexamples.

Proving Conjectures: Deductive Reasoning

YOU WILL NEED
- calculator
- ruler

Keep in Mind

▸ A conjecture has been proved only when it has been shown to be true for every possible case or example. You do this by creating a proof that involves general cases.

▸ You can often use the transitive property in deductive reasoning. According to this property, if two things are equal to the same thing, then they are equal to each other. So, if $a = b$ and $b = c$, then $a = c$.

▸ A demonstration using an example is NOT a proof.

Example 1

Use deductive reasoning to make a conclusion from these statements:
"All koalas are marsupials. All marsupials are mammals."
"All mammals are warm-blooded. Barney is a koala."

Solution

Step 1. I drew a Venn diagram based on the statements.

Step 2. I saw from the diagram that koalas are mammals. So, Barney will have all the features of a mammal. Mammals are warm-blooded, so Barney is warm-blooded.

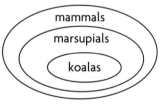

Example 2

Use deductive reasoning to prove this conjecture: "The difference of two perfect squares that are separated by one perfect square is always even."

Solution

Step 1. I let x represent any integer.

Then x^2 and $(x + 2)^2$ are two perfect squares that are separated by one perfect square.

Step 2. I calculated the difference between x^2 and $(x + 2)^2$.

$$(x + 2)^2 - x^2 = x^2 + 4x + 4 - x^2$$

$$(x + 2)^2 - x^2 = 4x + 4$$

$$(x + 2)^2 - x^2 = 2(2x + 2)$$

Step 3. The difference between x^2 and $(x + 2)^2$ will always be $2(2x + 2)$, which is even.

Practice

1. Examine each example of deductive reasoning. Why is it faulty?

   a) Given: Rain falls from the sky.

      Deduction: Skydivers are a form of rain.

   b) Given: Franco eats an apple every day at 12 noon. Franco is eating an apple now.

      Deduction: It is now 12 noon.

   c) Given: Bradley likes to play video games.

      Deduction: Lanique should not ask Bradley if he would like to play a game of tennis.

   d) Given: A television commercial shows that a person has lost 50 lb and become very fit by using an "advanced formula" tonic.

      Deduction: Everyone who buys and drinks this tonic will lose weight and become very fit.

2. Complete the conclusion for the following deductive argument: If an integer is an odd number, then its square is also odd. Seventeen is an odd number, therefore, ...

3. Complete the conclusion for the following deductive argument:

   If a perfect square is an even integer, then its square root is also an even integer. 64 is an even perfect square, therefore, ...

4. In this equation, x represents a natural number greater than 3. What does this equation prove about the sum of six consecutive natural numbers?

   $$(x - 1) + (x - 2) + (x - 3) + x + (x + 1) + (x + 2) = 3(2x - 1)$$

5. Raja wrote the following proof. What conjecture could he be trying to prove?

Let n be any integer.

$$(n + 1)(n + 1) - n^2 = n^2 + 2n + 1 - n^2$$

$$(n + 1)(n + 1) - n^2 = 2n + 1$$

6. What can you deduce about angles a, b, and c?

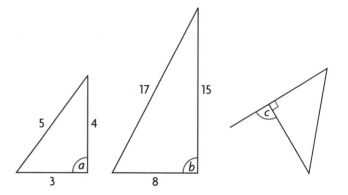

7. Try the following number trick with different numbers. Make a conjecture about the trick.

- Start with the last two digits of your birth year.
- Multiply this number by 3.
- Multiply by 7.
- Multiply by 37.
- Multiply by 13.

8. Kayenne wrote this equation, where x is an integer:

$$(x - 3) + (x - 2) + (x - 1) + x + (x + 1) + (x + 2) + (x + 3) = 7x$$

What has Kayenne proved?

9. What can you deduce about angles x and y?

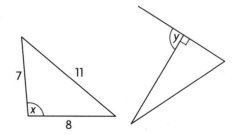

10. Nuala and Samira read the following statements:

- All frogs are amphibians.
- All amphibians are cold-blooded and have backbones.
- Mr. Dalek is Cyndi's pet frog.
- Rainbow is a cold-blooded animal with a backbone.

Nuala deduced that Mr. Dalek is cold-blooded and has a backbone.

Samira deduced that Rainbow is a frog. Who is correct?

A. Nuala only   **C.** Nuala and Samira

B. Samira only   **D.** neither Nuala nor Samira

11. Which choice uses deductive reasoning to show that the sum of two odd numbers and an even number is an even number?

A. $3 + 4 + 5 = 12$ and $5 + 10 + 11 = 26$

B. $(2x + 1) + (2y + 1) + 2z = 2(x + y + z) + 2$

C. $2x + 2y + 2z + 1 = 2(x + y + 1)$

D. none of these choices

12. Which choice uses deductive reasoning to show that the sum of two even numbers and an odd number is an odd number?

A. $4 + 6 + 9 = 19$ and $22 + 50 + 1 = 73$

B. $(2x + 1) + (2y + 1) + 2z = 2(x + y + z) + 2$

C. $2x + 2y + 1 = 2(x + y) + 1$

D. none of these choices

WRITTEN RESPONSE

13. Use deductive reasoning to show that the sum of two even numbers and an odd number is an odd number.

1.5 Proofs That Are Not Valid

Keep in Mind

▸ A single error in reasoning can destroy a deductive proof. This will result in an invalid or unsupported conclusion.

▸ Common errors include
- a false assumption or generalization
- an error in reasoning, like division by zero
- an error in calculation
- faulty logic

▸ Be careful to avoid circular reasoning; that is, assuming a result that follows from what you are trying to prove.

▸ When you write a proof, be sure that it is clear and correct. Ask someone else to read your proof to see how it can be improved.

Example 1

What type of error occurs in this deduction?

All people over 65 are retired.
Corbin is over 65, so he is retired.

Solution

I thought about the first sentence. I know some people who are over 65, and they are not retired. The error is a false assumption or generalization.

> **TIP**
>
> When looking for errors:
> - Be suspicious of any sentence that begins with "all."
> - Look for instances of division by zero.
> - Ask yourself: does the reasoning make sense?

Example 2

What type of error occurs in this deduction?

$$6 = 6$$
$$2.5(6) = 2.5(3 + 3)$$
$$2.5(6) + 1 = 2.5(3 + 3) + 1$$
$$15 + 1 = 7.5 + 4$$
$$16 = 11.5$$

Solution

Step 1. I knew that $16 \neq 11.5$, so I checked the calculations.

Step 2. There is an error in the calculation on the fourth line: $2.5(3 + 3) + 1 = 15 + 1$.

Practice

1. What type of error, if any, occurs in each deduction?

a) All people take public transit to work each day.
Lita goes to work each day.
Therefore, Lita takes public transport.

b) Suppose that: $x + y = z$
Then: $(3x - 2x) + (3y - 2y) = (3z - 2z)$
$$3x + 3y - 3z = 2x + 2y - 2z$$
$$3(x + y - z) = 2(x + y - z)$$
$$3 = 2$$

c) All runners can run for one mile without stopping.
Leif is a runner.
Therefore, Leif can run for one mile without stopping.

d) Most students do not go to public school on Sunday.
Therefore, most students should wear blue clothing on Sunday.

e)
$$2 = 2$$
$$4(2) = 4(1 + 1)$$
$$4(2) + 3 = 4(1 + 1) + 3$$
$$8 + 3 = 6 + 3$$
$$11 = 9$$

f) All the members of the girls' school soccer team practise every Wednesday after school.
Krishni is on the girls' soccer team.
Therefore, Krishni practises every Wednesday.

g) Cranberry muffin recipes call for flour and milk.
Therefore, carrot muffin recipes call for flour and milk.

h) On the first day of school last year, it was raining.
Therefore, it will rain on the first day of school next year.

2. What type of error, if any, occurs in each deduction or proof? Briefly state what the error is.

a)
$$2 = 2 + 2$$
$$4(2) = 4(2 + 2)$$
$$4(2) + 3 = 4(2 + 2) + 3$$
$$8 + 3 = 16 + 3$$
$$11 = 19$$

b)
$$3 = 3$$
$$7(3) = 7(2 + 1)$$
$$7(3) + 6 = 7(2 + 1) + 6$$
$$21 + 6 = 14 + 7$$
$$27 = 21$$

c) Things expand when they are heated and shrink when they are cooled. That is why days are longer in summer than in winter.

d) All music written today is rock or hip hop. The local orchestra is producing a new piece of music, so it must be rock or hip hop.

e) Pondthip is a hairdresser. Pondthip has a very good hairdo. Therefore, Pondthip is an excellent hairdresser.

MULTIPLE CHOICE

3. Bryce wrote this invalid proof. Which line contains his first error?

A. line 1 $10 = 5 + 5 + 5 - 5$

B. line 2 $10 = 5 + 5 - 5 + 5$

C. line 3 $10 = 10 - 10$

D. line 4 $10 = 0$

4. What type of error, if any, occurs in the following deduction?
Rolls Royce cars are expensive.
Jendra has an expensive car.
Therefore, Jendra has a Rolls Royce.

A. an error in reasoning

B. an error in calculation

C. a false assumption or generalization

D. There is no error in the deduction.

5. Andrea says she can prove that $12 = 13$. What is her error?

Andrea's Proof

Suppose that:	$x + y = z$
Then:	$(13x - 12x) + (13y - 12y) = (13z - 12z)$
Reorganize:	$13x + 13y - 13z = 12x + 12y - 12z$
Distribute:	$13(x + y - z) = 12(x + y - z)$
Divide by a common factor:	$13 = 12$

6. Rayleen created a number trick in which she always ended with the original number. However, when Rayleen tried to prove her trick, it did not work. What was her error? Write the correct proof.

Rayleen's Proof

n	Use n to represent any number.
$n + 2$	Add 2.
$2n + 2$	Multiply by 2.
$2n + 8$	Add 6.
$n + 4$	Divide by 2.
$n - 1$	Subtract 5.

7. G'Shaw says he can prove that 1 m = 1 cm. What is his error?

G'Shaw's Proof

1 m = 100 cm

$100 = (10)^2$

10 cm = one-tenth of a metre

$(0.1)^2 = 0.01$

One-hundredth of a metre is one centimetre, so 1 m = 1 cm.

1.6 Reasoning to Solve Problems

YOU WILL NEED
• calculator

Keep in Mind

▶ In solving problems, be prepared to use inductive reasoning, deductive reasoning, or both.

▶ Inductive reasoning involves solving a simpler problem, observing patterns, and drawing a logical conclusion from your observations.

▶ Deductive reasoning involves using known facts or assumptions in an argument that is then used to draw a logical conclusion.

Example 1

Ten cards, numbered from 0 to 9, are divided among five envelopes, with two cards in each envelope. Each envelope shows the sum of the cards inside it.

- The envelope marked 10 contains the 6 card.
- The envelope marked 14 contains the 5 card.

What pairs of cards does each envelope contain? Explain.

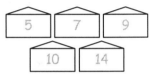

Solution

Step 1. I used deductive reasoning. I listed all of the possible pairs of numbers that each envelope could hold.

Step 2. I eliminated different possibilities.

Since the 14 envelope contained 5, it also contained 9, and therefore could not contain 6 or 8. Also, the 5 envelope could not contain 0 or 5; the 7 envelope could not contain 2 or 5; and the 9 envelope could not contain 0, 4, 5, or 9. The 10 envelope could not contain 1 or 9. Since the 10 envelope contained 6, it also contained 4, and therefore did not contain 2, 3, 7, or 8. Also, the 5 envelope did not contain 1 or 4. The 7 envelope did not contain 1, 3, 4, or 6. The 9 envelope did not contain 3 or 6. The numbers in the 7 envelope must be 0 and 7. That meant the 9 envelope could not contain 2 or 7.

Sum on Envelope	Possible Pairs of Cards
5	(0, 5), (1, 4), (2, 3)
7	(0, 7), (1, 6), (2, 5), (3, 4)
9	(0, 9), (1, 8), (2, 7), (3, 6), (4, 5)
10	(1, 9), (2, 8), (3, 7), (4, 6)
14	(5, 9), (6, 8)

Step 3. I wrote out the pairs of numbers in each envelope and checked that each number from 0 to 9 appeared once.

5: (2, 3); 7: (0, 7); 9: (1, 8); 10: (4, 6); 14: (5, 9)

Example 2

Six friends are sitting around a circular table in a noisy restaurant. Only two friends sitting next to each other can have a conversation. The friends decide to change seats at various times during the evening to make sure everyone gets a chance to talk to everyone else. What is the least number of times the friends have to change seats?

Solution

Step 1. I knew that each person had to talk to 5 different friends. I also knew that each person could talk to 2 different friends without changing places: the friends on either side of him or her. So there had to be at least 2 changes.

Step 2. I needed to check whether 2 changes would be enough. I started to create diagrams to show the conversations. The first diagram was just in alphabetical order. For the second diagram, I just had everyone switch to the other neighbour, without changing seats.

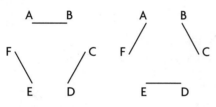

Step 3. For the third diagram, I made the first change of seating. I kept A still and put two new friends on either side. I used the same idea of new friends to finish the circle. My fourth diagram was like the second.

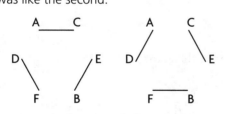

Step 4. For my last diagram, I made the second change of seating. I looked at which pairs of friends had not yet sat next to each other. I was able to complete this diagram, so I knew that the least number of seat changes was 2.

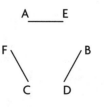

Practice

1. Does each statement show inductive or deductive reasoning?

   a) A certain tree has produced oranges each year for the past six years. Therefore, the tree will produce oranges this year.

   b) All reptiles have scales. Iguanas are reptiles. Therefore, iguanas have scales.

   c) Every multiple of 6 has a factor of 3. 24 is a multiple of 6. Therefore, 24 has a factor of 3.

   d) The unknown term in this pattern is 64: 1, 4, 16, ___, 256, 1024

   e) Every Tuesday at 10:00 p.m., the news is broadcast on television. Today is Tuesday; therefore, the news will be broadcast tonight at 10:00 p.m.

   f) Every high school student in western Canada must take English. You are a high school student in western Canada; therefore, you must take English.

2. For each set of figures, write the correct number in the centre of the fourth figure. Explain your reasoning.

   a)

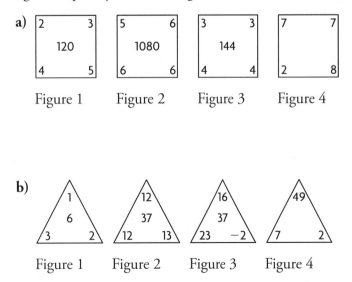

   Figure 1   Figure 2   Figure 3   Figure 4

   b)

   Figure 1   Figure 2   Figure 3   Figure 4

3. Barry, Cheryl, Devon, and Eva all go to the same high school. One likes history the best, one likes math the best, one likes computer science the best, and one likes English the best.

- Barry and Devon eat lunch with the student who likes computer science.
- Eva likes history the best.

Who likes computer science the best?

4. Harwinder, Isaac, James, and Kenneth swam a race. Early in the race, Isaac led Kenneth by 3 m, and James led Harwinder by the same amount. Kenneth was 1 m behind James. By the halfway point, James and Isaac had swapped places but were the same distance apart. Kenneth had caught up to Isaac, and Harwinder was running second. Over the last part of the race, Kenneth swapped places with Harwinder, as Isaac faded badly. Who finished third?

TIP
For each part of the race, use the information to decide what order the swimmers are in. If possible, also note how far apart they are.

5. Sadie, Tristan, Ursula, and Tawfik all live on the same street. One is a firefighter, one is a doctor, one is a lawyer, and one is a travel agent.

- Tawfik and Ursula eat lunch with the lawyer.
- Sadie and Tristan carpool with the firefighter.
- Ursula watches tennis on television with the firefighter and the lawyer.

Who is the firefighter?

6. Determine the unknown term in the pattern. Explain your reasoning.

2, 5, 9, ___, 20, 27

TIP
Look at each pair of terms. Is there a pattern in their sums? their differences? their ratios?

7. Each letter in the sentence about mathematics below represents a different letter of the alphabet. Use reasoning to decipher the quote.

Clue 1: J → M and C → T.

Clue 2: One word in the first sentence of this question appears in the quote.

J K C R O J K C B F M   B N   J K N O   L A   A B A C Z   G O I F O E C

A L I J K D K M,   A B A C Z   G O I F O E C   G I L L A M,   K E N

A B A C Z   G O I F O E C   B J K U B E X C B L E

NUMERICAL RESPONSE

8. Determine the unknown term in each pattern.

a) 15, 45, 135, _____, 1215, 3645

b) 18, 9, 4.5, _____, 1.125, 0.5625

c) 2, 2, 4, 6, _____, 16, 26, 42, 68, 110

9. a) Substitute numbers for the letters to create an addition problem with a correct solution.

$$
\begin{array}{r}
a \\
bbb \\
bbb \\
+\,bbb \\
\hline
abbb
\end{array}
$$

$a = \underline{}$ $b = \underline{}$

b) How many solutions are possible? ___

WRITTEN RESPONSE

10. a) Is the following sentence true or false? Explain your thinking.

"This sentence is false."

b) Is it possible that the sentence in part a) is meaningless? Why or why not?

11. Is the following sentence true, false, or meaningless? Explain your thinking.

"This sentence is either false or meaningless."

12. A set of nine cards, numbered from 1 to 9, is divided between two bags. The sum of the cards in the red bag is twice the sum of the cards in the white bag. The red bag contains four cards. Which bag contains the number 6? Explain.

13. Miriam had a deck of coloured cards. One-fifth of the cards are blue on both sides, and the rest have different colours on each side. Miriam laid out the cards. There were 5 blue cards, 8 yellow, and 2 red. When she flipped the cards over, she saw 6 blue cards, 5 red, and 4 yellow. How many cards are blue on one side and yellow on the other? Explain your answer.

1.7 Analyzing Puzzles and Games

YOU WILL NEED
• counters or coins

> ### Keep in Mind
>
> ▶ Inductive and deductive reasoning are useful for solving a puzzle or creating a winning game strategy.
>
> ▶ Inductive reasoning is useful for games and puzzles that require recognizing patterns or creating a particular order.
>
> ▶ Deductive reasoning is useful for games and puzzles that require inquiry and discovery to complete.

Example 1

What numbers go in squares A and B of this Sudoku puzzle?

To solve a Sudoku puzzle:

• Fill in each empty square with a number from 1 to 9.

• A number cannot appear twice in a column, row, or 3 × 3 block square.

9	6			1			2	4
		1	2	7	3	4		
		5				7		
		4	5	9	1	2		A
1	4				6		5	8
			4	5	9			
2							B	6

Solution

Step 1. I looked at the row, column, and 3 × 3 block square that A was in.

The row contained 1, 2, 4, 5, and 9, so A could not be any of those numbers. It could only be 3, 6, 7, or 8.

The column contained 6 and 8, so A could not be either of those numbers. It could only be 3 or 7.

The 3-by-3 block contained 7, so A could not be 7. A must be 3. That is, 3 must go in square A, since no other number can.

Step 2. Several numbers could go in square B, including 1, 3, 4, 7, and 9. I could not eliminate them using my reasoning from step 1. I realized that 4 could not go in any other square in the bottom row. Since 4 cannot go anywhere else, it must go in square B.

Example 2

Solve this Kakuro puzzle:

• Fill in each empty square with a number from 1 to 9.

• Each row must add up to the circled number on the left.

• Each column must add up to the circled number above.

• A number cannot appear twice in the same row or column.

	⑦	⑨	
④	A	B	⑤
⑥	C	D	E
⑪	F	G	H

Solution

Step 1. I looked at each circled number and how many squares were in the row or column. I knew A must be 1 or 3, because A and B sum to 4. It could not be 3, because only 1, 2, and 4 sum to 7. That meant A was 1 and B was 3.

Step 2. F had to be 4, because 4 has to go somewhere in the 7 column but could not be C. That meant C must be 2.

Step 3. Only 1, 2, and 3 sum to 6, so D had to be 1, which meant that E had to be 3.

Step 4. From there, I calculated that G was 5 and H was 2.

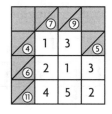

Example 3

In the Prisoner's Dilemma, two prisoners are being held by the authorities in separate interrogation rooms. Each prisoner has the same options: he or she can *cooperate* with the other prisoner by remaining silent, or *defect*, confessing to the authorities. The results of cooperating or defecting depend on what both prisoners do.

- If both prisoners cooperate, they are each sentenced to 1 year in prison.

- If both prisoners defect, they are each sentenced to 3 years.

- If one prisoner cooperates and the other defects, the defector is sentenced to 6 months and the cooperative prisoner is sentenced to 10 years.

a) What would be the best thing for the prisoners to do, and what sentence would they get, if each knew the other's decision?

b) What do you think the prisoners will actually do, and what sentence will they get, given that they do not know the other's decision?

Solution

Step 1. If each knew the other's decision, the best thing would be for them to cooperate with each other, as they both get only a 1-year sentence.

Step 2. I thought about what one of the prisoners would do.

If she cooperates, she could get either 1 year or 10 years in prison, depending on what the other prisoner does. So it is risky for her to cooperate.

If she defects, she could get either 6 months or 3 years. This is the safer option, so I reasoned that she would take it.

Step 3. The other prisoner would have exactly the same choices, so he should make the same decision. Therefore, both prisoners would defect, each getting a 3-year sentence.

Practice

1. Solve each Sudoku puzzle.

a)

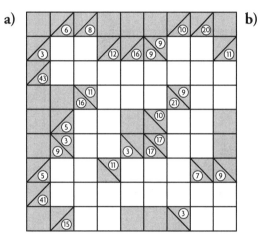

	3						4	
	8	4	6		2	7	9	
5			4		1			3
		6	1		5	4		
		1	8		6	2		
4			5		8			2
	6	3	9		7	5	1	
	2						8	

b)

4								1
			8	3	4			
9	6			1			2	4
		1	2	7	3	4		
		5				7		
		4	5	9	1	2		
1	4			6			5	8
			4	5	9			
2								6

TIP

Notice which numbers are missing from a row, a column, or a block. Are there any blank spaces into which you can put only one of those missing numbers?

2. Solve each Kakuro puzzle.

a)

b)

TIP

If the sum is 41 and there are 8 numbers, then the missing number must be 45 − 41 = 4.

If the sum is 41 and there are 7 numbers, then the two missing numbers must be 1 and 3.

You can use a similar strategy for other large numbers.

3. A taxi is travelling 3 blocks south and 3 blocks east. If the driver does not turn north or west at any point, how many routes may she choose? Explain.

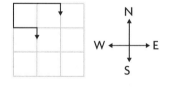

4. a) Place the numbers 22 to 26 in a V-shape, as shown, so the two arms of the V have the same total.

b) How many different solutions are there to this puzzle?

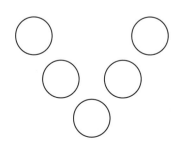

Copyright © 2012 by Nelson Education Ltd.

5. Two sisters, Jenna and Kira, find themselves playing a version of the Prisoner's Dilemma with their parents every time they get caught doing something wrong. In this dilemma, each sister has to choose between two options:

- She can cooperate with the other sister by saying nothing to her parents.

- She can defect by blaming it all on her sister.

If both sisters cooperate, they each get grounded for 1 week. If both defect, they each get grounded for 3 weeks. If only one sister cooperates, she gets grounded for 6 weeks and the other sister is not punished. Usually, both sisters defect, to be on the safe side.

a) Jenna is tired of always being grounded for 3 weeks and decides to play a tit-for-tat strategy. Each time the sisters are caught out by their parents, Jenna will cooperate with Kira, unless Kira defected the previous time. Will Jenna's strategy likely benefit either her or Kira? Explain.

b) After a while, Kira figures out Jenna's new strategy and decides that she will also play tit-for-tat. Predict what will happen.

6. Explain, using diagrams, why tic-tac-toe can always be played to stalemate (that is, neither player wins).

dart in this ring scores triple points

dart in this ring scores double points

dart in inner bull scores 50 points (the inner bull also counts as a double)

dart in outer bull scores 25 points

7. Tom and Bob are playing darts. Tom has a score of 65. To win, he must reduce his score to zero and have his last counting dart be a double. Which of the following scores on the dartboard, in order, would make him the winner?

A. double 15, 20, 15

C. 20, 15, double 15

B. 0, 5, triple 20

D. double 20, 15, 10

8. Rahim and Jessica are playing darts. Jessica has a score of 57. To win, she must reduce her score to zero and have her last counting dart be a double. How many ways can she win if she scores a double 18 with her first dart?

A. 2

C. 6

B. 5

D. 10

9. In a leapfrog puzzle, coloured counters are moved along a space on a board.

Board at start:

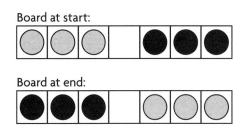

Board at end:

• A counter can move into an empty space.

• A counter can leapfrog over another counter into an empty space.

What is the minimum number of moves needed to exchange 8 red counters with 8 blue counters?

A. 64   **B.** 80   **C.** 48   **D.** 78

10. This 4 × 4 KenKen puzzle must be solved using only the numbers 1 to 4. Do not repeat a number in any row or column. The darkly outlined sets of squares are cages. The numbers in each cage must combine in any order to produce the target number, using the operation shown. What number goes in the shaded square?

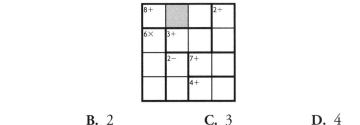

A. 1   **B.** 2   **C.** 3   **D.** 4

11. Solve each puzzle.

a)

5	3		2		9		8	4
	8	9		6		7	2	
			1		8			
4		8				3		9
			4		3			
	2	7		4		5	9	
6	5		9		7		4	2

b)

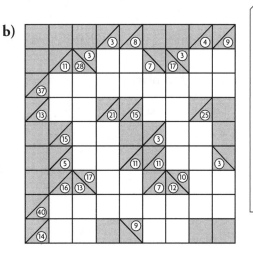

12. a) Place the numbers 50 to 56 in a V-shape, as shown, so the two arms of the V have the same total.

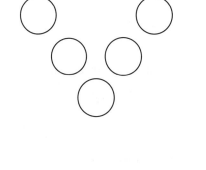

b) How many different solutions are there to this puzzle?

13. In chess, a knight moves in an L-shape: two squares in one direction (vertically or horizontally), then one square at right angles to that direction. It is possible to make a "knight's tour" of an otherwise empty chessboard, with the knight landing on each square exactly once. To do this, it is helpful to know how many moves a knight can make from any given position on the board.

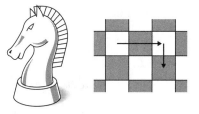

How many moves can a knight make from each of the starting points shown on this grid?

a) ___   **c)** ___   **e)** ___

b) ___   **d)** ___   **f)** ___

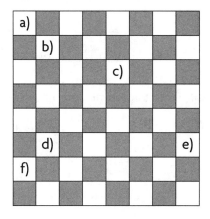

Complete the following to summarize the important ideas from this chapter.

Q: What does inductive reasoning involve?

A: • Inductive reasoning starts with specific _____.

    • Identifying _____ and observing _____ may lead
to a general _____. This _____ can then be stated
as a _____.

NEED HELP?
• See Lesson 1.1

Q: What role does evidence play in supporting conjectures?

A: • Finding _____ evidence supporting a conjecture makes it _____ likely
true.

    • Evidence can also show a conjecture to be _____ but can suggest
ways to _____ the conjecture.

NEED HELP?
• See Lessons 1.1, 1.2

Q: What is a counterexample, and how does it relate to a conjecture?

A: • A counterexample is an example that _____ a conjecture. This
means that the conjecture is _____.

    • If you cannot find a counterexample, you _____ be certain a
counterexample does not exist.

    • If you do find a counterexample, the conjecture must be _____.
However, you may be able to _____ the conjecture.

NEED HELP?
• See Lesson 1.3

Conjecture:
All prime numbers are odd. ✗

2 is prime.

Q: What does deductive reasoning involve?

A: • Deductive reasoning starts with general _____ known to be true.

    • _____ reasoning then leads to a specific _____.

    • A _____ of a conjecture must involve _____ cases.

NEED HELP?
• See Lesson 1.4

Q: What are some common errors in proofs?

A: • _____ by zero is an example of a(n) _____ in
reasoning.

    • A false _____ or _____ can lead to _____
reasoning; that is, "proving" something that you began by assuming.

NEED HELP?
• See Lesson 1.5

MULTIPLE CHOICE

1. Which conjecture about the product of three odd integers seems most reasonable?

    A. It will be an even integer. **C.** It will be negative.

    B. It will be an odd integer. **D.** It is not possible to make a conjecture.

2. Which conjecture about the interior angles in a hexagon seems most reasonable?

    A. Their sum is always 180°. **C.** Their sum is always 720°.

    B. Their sum is always 360°. **D.** It is not possible to make a conjecture.

3. Rainfeather noticed the following:

    $$\frac{432\,432}{7} = 61\,776, \quad \frac{432\,432}{11} = 39\,312, \quad \frac{432\,432}{13} = 33\,264, \quad \text{and}$$

    $$\frac{172\,172}{7} = 24\,596, \quad \frac{172\,172}{11} = 15\,652, \quad \frac{172\,172}{13} = 13\,244$$

    Which conjecture might Rainfeather make from this evidence? Is this conjecture reasonable?

    A. Any six-digit number composed of three repeating digits is divisible by 7, 11, and 13; yes, this is reasonable.

    B. Any six-digit number is divisible by 7, 11, and 13; no, this is not reasonable.

    C. Any odd number is divisible by 7, 11, and 13; yes, this is reasonable.

    D. It is not possible to make a conjecture.

4. Which figure is a counterexample to the conjecture "All polygons with eight equal sides are regular octagons"?

    A. Figure I only **C.** Figure I and Figure II

    B. Figure II only **D.** neither Figure I nor Figure II

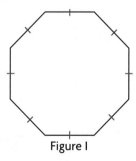

Figure I

5. Which choice provides a counterexample to the conjecture "When you divide one whole number by another whole number, the quotient will be greater than the divisor and less than the dividend"?

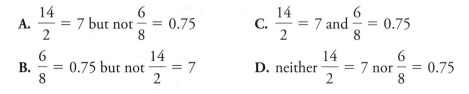

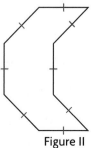

Figure II

6. All kangaroos are marsupials. All marsupials are mammals. All mammals are warm-blooded. Ginger Jack is a kangaroo. What can be deduced about Ginger Jack?

    A. Ginger Jack is warm-blooded but is not a mammal.

    B. Ginger Jack is a mammal but is not warm-blooded.

    C. Ginger Jack is warm-blooded and a mammal.

    D. Ginger Jack is neither warm-blooded nor a mammal.

7. What type of error, if any, occurs in the following deduction?

"All people who work do so from 9 a.m. to 5 p.m., with one hour for lunch. Bill works, so he works from 9 a.m. to 5 p.m."

    A. a false assumption or generalization

    B. an error in reasoning

    C. an error in calculation

    D. There is no error in the deduction.

8. What type of error, if any, occurs in the following proof?

Suppose that:	$a + b = c$
Then:	$(4a - 3a) + (4b - 3b) = (4c - 3c)$
Reorganize:	$4a + 4b - 4c = 3a + 3b - 3c$
Using distribution:	$4(a + b - c) = 3(a + b - c)$
	$4 = 3$

    A. an error in calculation   **C.** a false assumption or generalization

    B. an error in reasoning   **D.** There is no error in the deduction.

NUMERICAL RESPONSE

9. Determine the unknown term in each pattern.

    a) 3, 12, 48, 192, _____, 3072, 12 288

    b) 12 500, 2500, _____, 100, 20, 4

    c) 14, 28, 56, 112, _____, 448, 896

10. What number should go in each square of this Sudoku puzzle?

    a) square A ___   **c)** square C ___

    b) square B ___   **d)** square D ___

2	A	6		4		3	7	
8		4			9		5	
		B	1		C			
	2							3
		8	6		7	9		
5	6						1	
		D			4			
	5		3			8		2
	7	3		6		5		1

11. Do you agree or disagree with the following conjectures? Justify your decisions with a counterexample if possible.

   a) The sum of a multiple of 5 and a multiple of 15 will be an odd number.

   b) The sum of a multiple of 5 and a multiple of 15 will be an even number.

12. In this equation, x is an integer. What does the equation prove? Support your answer with a specific example.

$$x + (x + 1) + (x + 2) + (x + 3) + (x + 4) + (x + 5) + (x + 6) = 7x + 21$$

13. Do you agree or disagree with the following conjecture? Justify your decision with a counterexample if possible.

"Forensic scientists will always discover enough evidence to convict the guilty person, because that is what happens on television."

14. Form a conclusion based on the following statements. Explain whether your reasoning was inductive or deductive.

"All marsupials have pouches." "Kangaroos are marsupials."

15. Continue the sequence 5, 14, 23, 32, 41, … by two terms. Explain whether your reasoning was inductive or deductive.

Getting Started

1. Match each term with one or more shapes.

   a) quadrilateral   **d)** parallelogram   **g)** equilateral triangle

   b) kite   **e)** acute triangle   **h)** scalene triangle

   c) rhombus   **f)** obtuse triangle   **i)** isosceles triangle

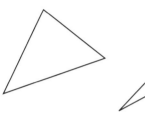

2. Draw a diagram to illustrate each term.

   a) parallel lines   **b)** supplementary angles

3. Explain how you know that each pair of triangles is similar.

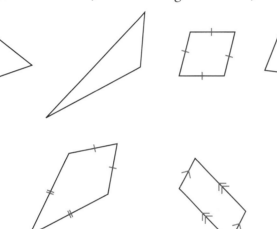

4. Determine the measures of the unknown angles.

a)

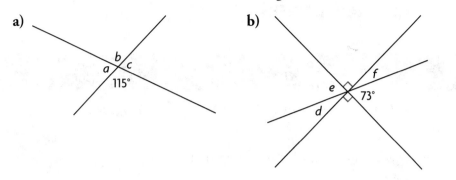

b)

5. Determine the measures of the unknown angles in terms of *x*.

a)

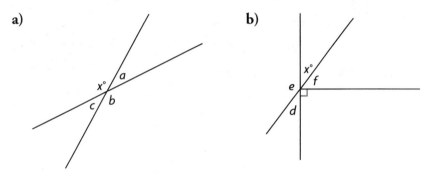

b)

6. Identify the congruent triangles.

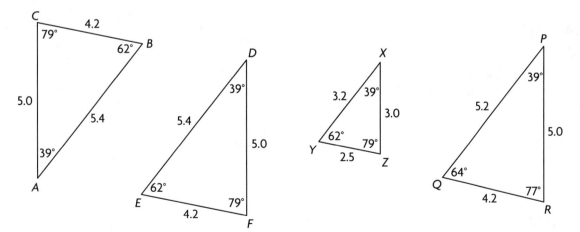

2.1 Exploring Parallel Lines

Keep in Mind

▶ A transversal is a line that intersects two or more other lines, forming corresponding angles.

- When a transversal intersects two parallel lines, the corresponding angles (e.g., ∠x and ∠y in the diagram) are equal.
- When a transversal intersects two non-parallel lines, the corresponding angles (e.g., ∠p and ∠q in the diagram) are not equal.

▶ Other angles are also formed when a transversal intersects two parallel lines:

- Interior angles lie between, or inside, the parallel lines (e.g., ∠y and ∠p).
- Exterior angles lie outside the parallel lines (e.g., ∠x and ∠q).

▶ When a transversal intersects a pair of lines and creates equal corresponding angles, the pair of lines is parallel.

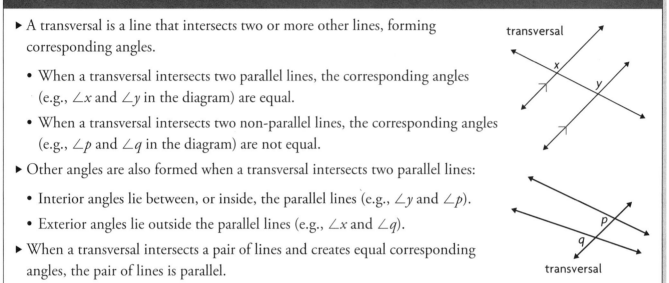

Example

Identify the transversal and the corresponding angles in this diagram. Are the corresponding angles equal? How do you know?

Solution

Step 1. I looked at the diagram. A transversal goes through two or more lines, so *EF* must be the transversal.

Step 2. There are four pairs of corresponding angles: *a* and *e*, *b* and *f*, *c* and *g*, and *d* and *h*.

Step 3. *AB* and *CD* are parallel. So, each pair of corresponding angles is equal.

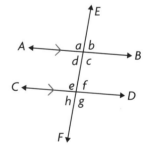

Practice

1. Identify the transversal and corresponding angles in each diagram. Also identify the interior and exterior angles, if they exist.

a)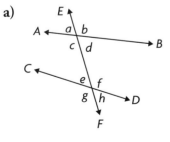

transversal: _____

corresponding angles:

_____

_____

interior angles: _____

exterior angles: _____

b)

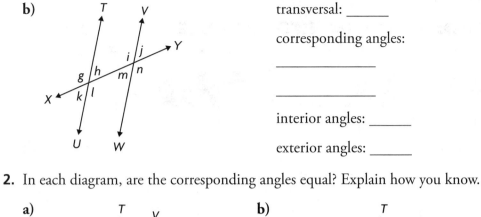

transversal: _____

corresponding angles:

_____

_____

interior angles: _____

exterior angles: _____

2. In each diagram, are the corresponding angles equal? Explain how you know.

a)

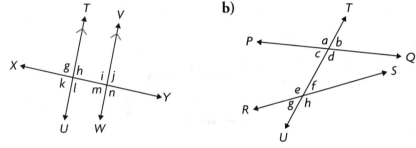

b)

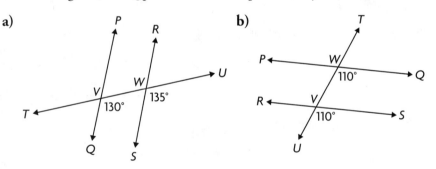

3. In each diagram, is *PQ* parallel to *RS*? Explain how you know.

a)

b)

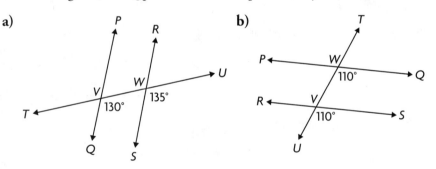

MULTIPLE CHOICE

4. In which figure, or figures, are interior angles marked?

A. Figure I only   **C.** Figure I and Figure II

B. Figure II only   **D.** neither Figure I nor Figure II

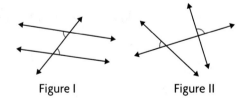

Figure I   Figure II

WRITTEN RESPONSE

5. Joan made this conjecture: If a transversal intersects two or more lines, then those lines are parallel. Do you agree? Support your answer with a diagram and/or a counterexample.

2.2 Angles Formed by Parallel Lines

YOU WILL NEED
• protractor

Keep in Mind

▶ When a transversal intersects two parallel lines:

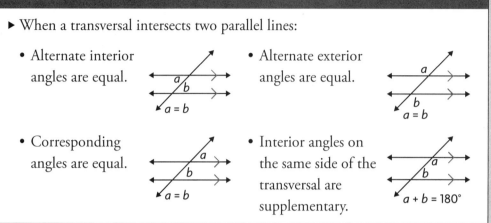

- Alternate interior angles are equal.

  $a = b$

- Alternate exterior angles are equal.

  $a = b$

- Corresponding angles are equal.

  $a = b$

- Interior angles on the same side of the transversal are supplementary.

  $a + b = 180°$

Example

Determine the measures of angles a, b, c, and d. Give reasons for your answers.

Solution

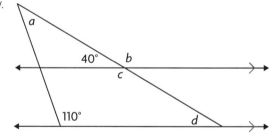

Step 1. $\angle c + 40° = 180°$ The 40° angle and $\angle c$ are supplementary.
$\angle c = 140°$

Step 2. $\angle b = \angle c$ Angles b and c are vertically opposite angles.
$\angle b = 140°$

Step 3. $\angle d = 40°$ Angle d and the 40° angle are corresponding angles between parallel lines.

Step 4. $\angle a + 110° + \angle d = 180°$ The sum of the interior angles
$\angle a + 110° + 40° = 180°$ in a triangle is 180°.
$\angle a = 30°$

Practice

1. How do you know that the solid lines in each diagram are parallel?

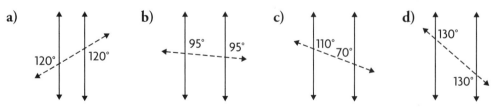

a)
120° 120°

b)
95° 95°

c)
110° 70°

d)
130° 130°

2. Determine the measures of angles x, y, and z. Give reasons.

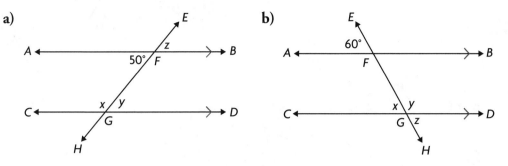

a)

b)

3. Determine the measures of angles a, b, c, and d in the Example on page 42, using a different method. Give reasons.

4. Joelle wrote this proof that $AB \parallel YZ$. Identify and correct her errors.

$$\angle AXY + \angle YXZ + \angle BXY = 180° \qquad \text{supplementary angles}$$

$$\angle AXY + 85° + 35° = 180°$$

$$\angle AXY = 60°$$

$$\angle AXY = \angle YXZ \qquad \text{corresponding angles}$$

Therefore, $AB \parallel YZ$.

5. Is this quadrilateral a trapezoid? Explain how you know.

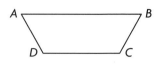

6. Determine the measures of angles *w*, *x*, *y*, and *z*.

a)

c)

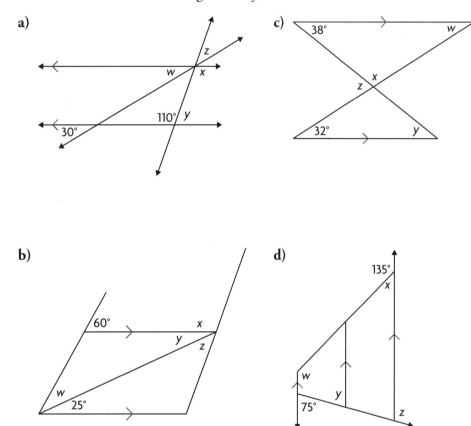

b)

d)

7. *WXYZ* is a trapezoid. Determine the measures of angles *a*, *b*, *c*, *d*, and *e*.

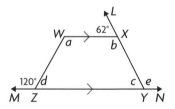

8. Determine the measures of all of the unknown angles in figure *ABCDE*.

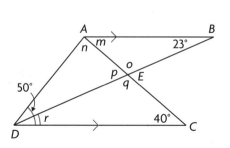

9. Lee made this design. He claims that triangles *ADE* and *ABC* are similar. Maria says they are not. Who is correct and why?

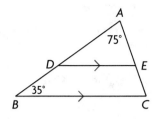

10. Label the diagram with the missing angle measures.

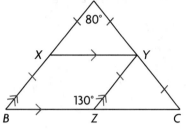

11. Terence is creating a stained-glass panel. He will use coloured triangles to form the panel. He assembled this quadrilateral. Is it a parallelogram? Explain how you know.

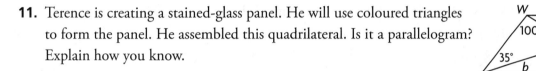

MULTIPLE CHOICE

12. Which angles does the diagram show? Choose the best answer.

    A. alternate interior angles   **C.** interior angles

    B. corresponding angles   **D.** all of these choices

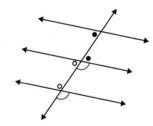

WRITTEN RESPONSE

13. Show that $\angle d = 97°$.

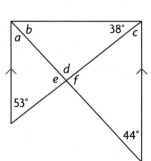

2.3 Angle Properties in Triangles

Keep in Mind

► The measures of the interior angles in a triangle sum to 180°.

$$\angle A + \angle B + \angle C = 180°$$

► The measure of an exterior angle of a triangle is equal to the sum of the two interior angles that are not adjacent to the exterior angle.

$$\angle DBA = \angle BAC + \angle ACB$$

Example 1

Determine the measures of angles *a*, *b*, and *c*.

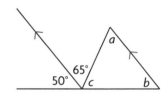

Solution

Step 1. $\angle a = 65°$ Alternate interior angles between parallel lines are equal.

Step 2. $\angle a + \angle b = 50° + 65°$ The exterior angle equals the sum of the two

$65° + \angle b = 115°$ non-adjacent interior angles.

$\angle b = 50°$

Step 3. $\angle a + \angle b + \angle c = 180°$ The interior angles sum to 180°.

$65° + 50° + \angle c = 180°$

$\angle c = 65°$

Example 2

In $\triangle ACD$, $AC = AD$. Prove that $\angle ACB = \angle ADE$.

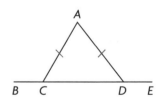

Solution

$\angle ACD = \angle ADC$ property of isosceles triangle

$\angle ACB + \angle ACD = \angle ADC + \angle ADE$ supplementary angles, both sides = 180°

$\angle ACB + \angle ADC = \angle ADC + \angle ADE$ substitution

$\angle ACB = \angle ADE$

Practice

1. Determine the measures of the interior angles of △*CDE*.

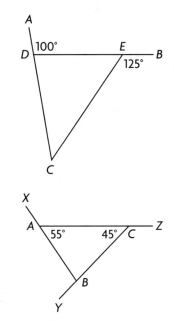

2. Determine the measures of ∠*XAZ*, ∠*YBX*, and ∠*YCZ*.

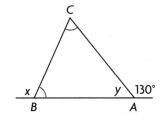

3. Determine the angles in Example 1, on page 46 using a different method.

4. Triangle *ABC* is isosceles, with *AB* = *AC*. Determine the measures of angles *x* and *y*.

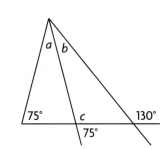

5. Determine the measures of angles *a*, *b*, and *c*.

6. Determine the measures of ∠OJK, ∠JKO, and ∠JOK.

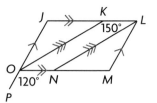

7. Determine the measure of ∠DAC. Show your work.

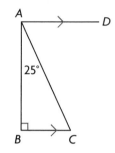

8. In △EFG, GI bisects ∠FGH.

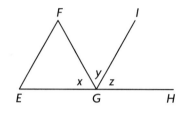

   a) If ∠E = ∠y, then prove that EF ∥ GI.

   b) If ∠F = ∠z, then prove that EF ∥ GI.

9. Prove that AB ∥ CD.

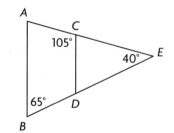

10. Determine the measures of the exterior angles of an isosceles triangle where the non-base angle is 70°. Explain your reasoning and include a diagram.

11. Prove that $\triangle ABC$ is similar to $\triangle DCE$.

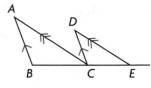

MULTIPLE CHOICE

12. With which set of properties can you solve for angles x, y, and z?

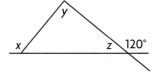

    A. supplementary angles, exterior angle, sum of angles in triangle

    B. supplementary angles, alternate interior angles, sum of angles in triangle

    C. supplementary angles, corresponding angles, exterior angle

    D. none of these choices

WRITTEN RESPONSE

13. Determine the measures of angles in trapezoid $ABCD$.

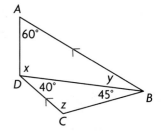

2.4 Angle Properties in Polygons

▸ A convex polygon has all interior angle measures less than 180°.

▸ The exterior angles of a convex polygon sum to 360°.

▸ For a convex polygon with n sides, the sum of the measures of the interior angles is $180°(n - 2)$.

▸ For a regular polygon (any polygon with equal side lengths) with n sides, the measure of each interior angle is $\dfrac{180°(n - 2)}{n}$.

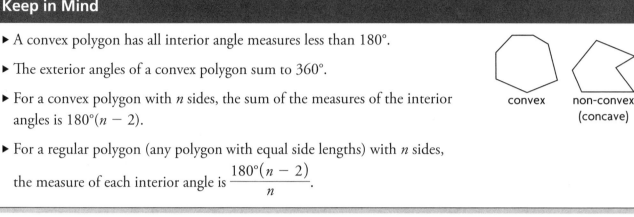

convex non-convex
(concave)

Example 1

Determine the measure of each interior angle of a regular nonagon.

Solution

Step 1. A regular nonagon has nine equal sides, so $n = 9$.

Step 2. I substituted $n = 9$ into the expression for the measure of an interior angle of a regular polygon:

$$\frac{180°(9 - 2)}{9} = \frac{180°(7)}{9}, \text{ or } 140°$$

The measure of an interior angle of a regular nonagon is 140°.

Example 2

Rachel is tiling her bathroom floor. She is using regular hexagon and regular triangle tiles. The side length of a triangle tile is equal to the side length of a hexagon tile. Can she tile the floor without leaving any gaps between tiles?

Solution

Step 1. A hexagon has six sides, so $n = 6$. I substituted $n = 6$ into the expression for the measure of an interior angle of a regular polygon.

$$\frac{180°(6 - 2)}{6} = \frac{180°(4)}{6}, \text{ or } 120°$$

The measure of an interior angle of a regular hexagon is 120°.

Step 2. The measure of an interior angle of an equilateral triangle is 60°.

Step 3. I drew a diagram to visualize the problem.

A triangle and a hexagon fit together to form an angle that measures 120° + 60°, or 180°.

I can repeat the tiling pattern for another 180°.

This pattern tiles the floor without leaving gaps.

I can tile the floor using regular hexagon and triangle tiles without leaving any gaps.

$120° + 60° + 120° + 60° = 360°$

Practice

1. **a)** Determine the sum of the measures of the interior angles of a regular heptagon.

TIP
A heptagon has 7 sides. If you are unfamiliar with the name of a polygon, try looking it up on the Internet.

   b) Determine the measure of each interior angle of a regular heptagon, to the nearest tenth of a degree.

   c) Determine the measure of an exterior angle of a regular heptagon.

2. Determine the sum of the measures of the interior angles in a 16-sided convex polygon.

3. Kim measured one interior angle of an irregular convex pentagon. She claims that the sum of the measures of the exterior angles is 5(65°), or 325°. Is she correct? Explain.

65°

4. Kieran drew a 14-sided convex polygon. One of the interior angles measures 155°. Is it a regular polygon? Explain.

5. Which of these regular polygons will tessellate a plane surface? Complete the table.

Regular Polygon	Measure of Interior Angle	360° Evenly Divisible by Measure of Interior Angle?
triangle	60°	Yes, so it will tessellate.
square		
pentagon		
hexagon		
heptagon		
octagon		

6. The exterior angles of a convex hexagon measure 35°, 50°, 55°, and 60°. The other two angles are congruent. Determine the measures of the interior angles of the hexagon.

7. Determine the measures of angles *a*, *b*, and *c*.

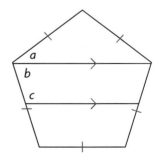

8. Cameron wants to tile the floor of his kitchen. He has tiles in the shape of squares, equilateral triangles, and regular pentagons to choose from. The side lengths of all the shapes are equal. He will use two different shapes of tiles. Which ones should he choose? Explain how you know.

Regular Polygon	Measure of Interior Angle	360° Evenly Divisible by Measure of Interior Angle?
triangle	60°	yes
square		
pentagon		

MULTIPLE CHOICE

9. Which equation gives the sum of the interior angles of a convex polygon?

   A. $S(n) = 180°(n - 1)$ **C.** $S(n) = 180°(n - 3)$

   B. $S(n) = 180°(n - 2)$ **D.** $S(n) = 180°(n)$

10. Which expression calculates the measure of an interior angle of a regular polygon?

   A. $\dfrac{180°(n - 2)}{n}$ **C.** $\dfrac{180°(n)}{n}$

   B. $\dfrac{180°(n - 1)}{n}$ **D.** $180°(n)$

WRITTEN RESPONSE

11. Determine the values of *a*, *b*, *c*, and *d*. Show your work.

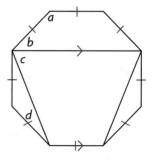

2 Test Prep

Complete the following to summarize the important ideas from this chapter.

Q: When a transversal intersects a pair of lines, what do you know?

A: • If the intersected lines are _____:

Corresponding
angles are

_____.

Alternate interior
angles are

_____.

Alternate exterior
angles are

_____.

Same-side interior
angles are

_____.

• If corresponding angles are _____, the intersected lines

are _____.

NEED HELP?
• See Lessons 2.1, 2.2

Q: What are the two key angle relationships for triangles?

A: • The _____ of the _____ angle measures

of a triangle is ___°.

$\angle A + \_\_ + \_\_ = \_\_°$

• The measure of an _____ angle is the sum of the measures

of the two _____-adjacent _____ angles.

$\angle DBA = \_\_ + \_\_$

NEED HELP?
• See Lesson 2.3

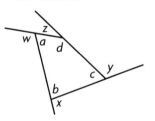

B

D   *B*

Q: What are the useful points to remember about angles of polygons?

A: • The _____ angle sum of an *n*-sided _____ polygon

is _____.

• The measure of each _____ angle of a _____ polygon

is $\dfrac{\boxed{}}{\boxed{}}$.

In the diagram, $\angle a + \_\_ + \_\_ + \_\_ = \_\_\_\_°(\_\_ - 2)$.

• The sum of the _____ angle measures of any _____

polygon is 360°. In the diagram, $\_\_ + \_\_ + \_\_ + \_\_ = 360°$.

NEED HELP?
• See Lesson 2.4

2 Chapter Test

MULTIPLE CHOICE

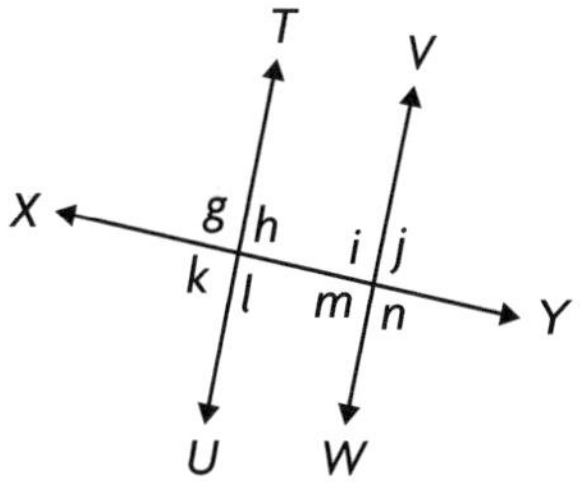

1. In the figure shown, which angles are supplementary interior angles?

   A. ∠h, ∠j   **B.** ∠g, ∠n   **C.** ∠h, ∠i   **D.** ∠h, ∠m

2. Which angles are alternate interior angles?

   A. ∠h, ∠j   **B.** ∠g, ∠n   **C.** ∠h, ∠i   **D.** ∠h, ∠m

3. Which angles are supplementary exterior angles?

   A. ∠h, ∠j   **B.** ∠g, ∠j   **C.** ∠h, ∠i   **D.** ∠h, ∠m

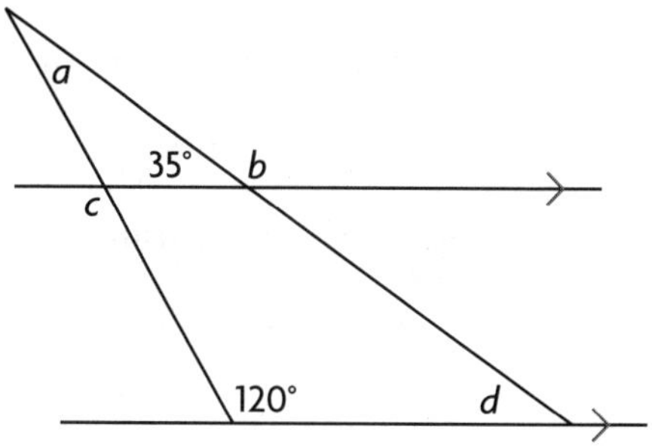

4. In the figure shown, what is the measure of ∠a?

   A. 25°   **B.** 35°   **C.** 120°   **D.** 145°

5. What is the measure of ∠c?

   A. 25°   **B.** 35°   **C.** 120°   **D.** 145°

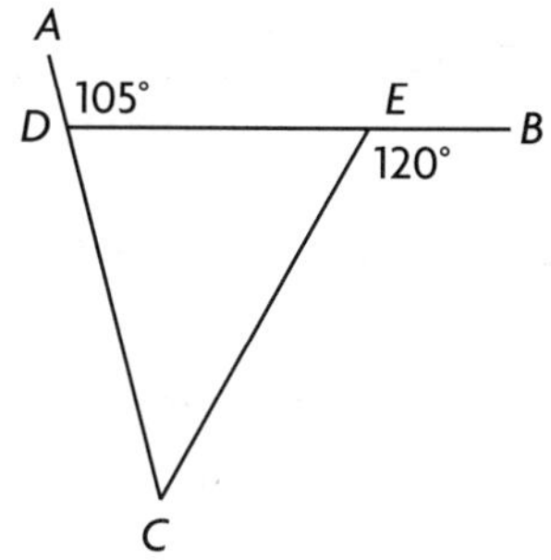

6. In the figure shown, what is the measure of ∠CDE?

   A. 75°   **B.** 60°   **C.** 120°   **D.** 45°

7. What is the measure of ∠ECD?

   A. 75°   **B.** 60°   **C.** 120°   **D.** 45°

8. What is the measure of ∠DEC?

   A. 75°   **B.** 60°   **C.** 120°   **D.** 45°

9. What is the sum of the measures of the interior angles of a polygon with 17 sides?

   A. 3060°   **B.** 2880°   **C.** 2700°   **D.** 159°

10. What is the measure of each interior angle of a regular 18-sided polygon?

   A. 180°   **B.** 175°   **C.** 160°   **D.** 150°

11. What is the measure of each exterior angle of a regular 17-sided polygon, to the nearest tenth?

   A. 25.1°   **B.** 21.2°   **C.** 10.6°   **D.** 8.1°

NUMERICAL RESPONSE

12. Determine the measures of angles a, b, c, and d.

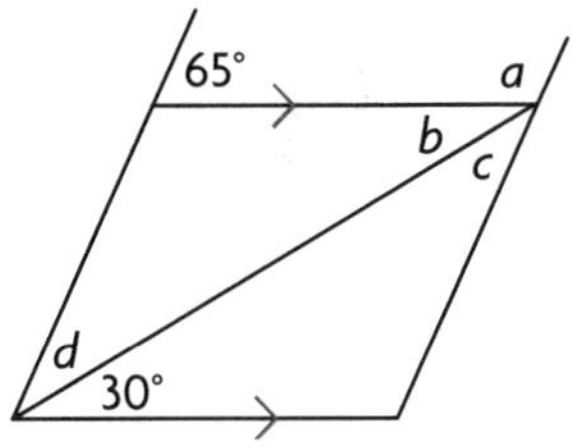

$\angle a =$ ___° $\angle b =$ ___° $\angle c =$ ___° $\angle d =$ ___°

13. Determine the measures of the unknown angles in figure *WXOYZ*.

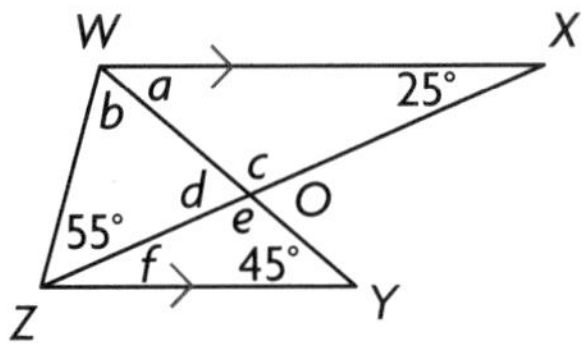

$\angle a =$ ___° $\angle b =$ ___° $\angle c =$ ___°

$\angle d =$ ___° $\angle e =$ ___° $\angle f =$ ___°

14. a) Determine the sum of the interior angles of a regular 18-sided polygon.

______°

b) Determine the measure of an interior angle of a regular 18-sided polygon, to the nearest tenth. ______°

c) Determine the measure of an exterior angle of a regular 18-sided polygon, to the nearest tenth. ______°

WRITTEN RESPONSE

15. Determine the measures of angles p, q, r, s, and t. Give reasons.

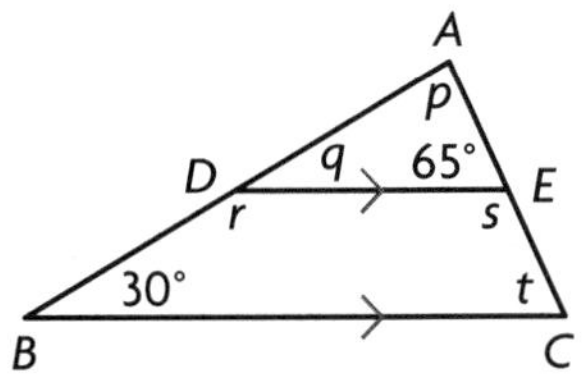

16. Prove that $PQ \parallel RS$.

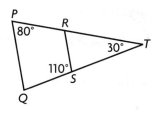

17. The sum of the measures of the interior angles of an unknown polygon is 3780°. Determine the number of sides that the polygon has. Show your work.

18. Prove that $\triangle ACD$ is isosceles.

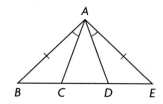

1–2 Cumulative Test

MULTIPLE CHOICE

1. Kari is studying the number of handshakes among groups of people. Based on groups of 2, 3, and 4 people with 1, 3, and 6 handshakes, she conjectures that the number of handshakes follows the sequence of triangular numbers. Kari then discovers that there are 10 handshakes among 5 people and 15 handshakes among 6 people. What can you say, based only on the new evidence, about Kari's conjecture?

   A. The conjecture is valid.

   B. The new evidence supports the conjecture.

   C. The conjecture is not valid.

   D. The new evidence does not support the conjecture.

2. Kevin claims that the midpoints of any quadrilateral, when joined, form a rhombus. Which of the following is a counterexample to Kevin's conjecture?

   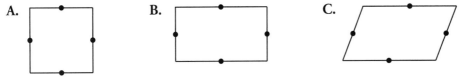

3. Which of the following is the key step in a proof that the difference of the squares of the numbers n and $n + 2$ is even?

   A. $(n + 2)^2 - n^2 = 4n + 4$

   B. The differences of $(n + 2)^2$ and $(n + 1)^2$, and of $(n + 1)^2$ and n^2, are odd.

   C. If n is even, then both squares are even; if n is odd, then both squares are odd.

   D. all of these choices

4. This proof seems to show that $4 = 2$. Where is the error?

   Let $a = 2b$, $b \neq 0$.

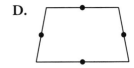

$$a^2 = 2ab$$
$$a^2 - 4b^2 = 2ab - 4b^2$$
$$(a + 2b)(a - 2b) = 2b(a - 2b)$$
$$a + 2b = 2b$$
$$4b = 2b$$
$$4 = 2$$

   A. Multiply by a.
   (Subtract $4b^2$.)

   B. Factor.

   C. Divide by $(a - 2b)$.
   (Substitute $a = 2b$.)

   D. Divide by b.

5. Which of the following pairs of angles are corresponding angles?

A. $\angle a$ and $\angle e$ B. $\angle b$ and $\angle h$ C. $\angle a$ and $\angle d$ D. $\angle b$ and $\angle c$

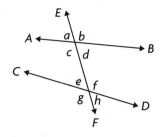

6. Which statement is true of any isosceles trapezoid?

A. Interior angles at opposite vertices are equal.

B. Interior angles at adjacent vertices are equal.

C. Interior angles at opposite vertices are supplementary.

D. Interior angles at adjacent vertices are complementary.

7. What is the measure of each interior angle of a regular nonagon?

A. 280°   B. 40°   C. 147.3°   D. 140°

NUMERICAL RESPONSE

8. A 3 × 3 magic square is a square grid in which each whole number from 1 to 9 appears once, so that the sums of each row, each column, and each diagonal are all equal.

a) What is the sum of each row, column, and diagonal of a 3 × 3 magic square? _____

b) Complete this 3 × 3 magic square.

1	5	
	7	2

c) Create a 3 × 3 magic square of your own.

d) How many different 3 × 3 magic squares are there? _____

9. A Mobius loop can be made by joining the ends of a strip of paper with a half twist. If you draw a line down the middle of a Mobius loop you will see that it has only one surface, not two like a regular loop.

a) Suppose you now make a whole twist before joining the ends.

How many surfaces does the resulting loop have? ___

b) If you make a twist and a half, how many surfaces does the resulting

loop have? ___

c) How many surfaces does a loop formed by *n* whole twists have? ___

d) How many surfaces does a loop formed by *n* whole twists, plus a half twist,

have? ___

10. Determine each angle measure.

$$\angle a = \underline{\quad}° \qquad \angle b = \underline{\quad}° \qquad \angle c = \underline{\quad}°$$

$$\angle d = \underline{\quad}° \qquad \angle e = \underline{\quad}° \qquad \angle f = \underline{\quad}°$$

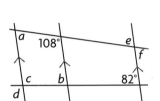

11. Determine the following angle measures in the regular pentagon *ABCDE*.

$$\angle EAB = \underline{\quad}° \qquad \angle AEF = \underline{\quad}° \qquad \angle EAF = \underline{\quad}° \qquad \angle FAB = \underline{\quad}°$$

$$\angle EFA = \underline{\quad}°$$

$$\angle AFB = \underline{\quad}° \qquad \angle EBA = \underline{\quad}° \qquad \angle DAC = \underline{\quad}° \qquad \angle ADC = \underline{\quad}°$$

$$\angle ACD = \underline{\quad}°$$

Use your results to identify two pairs of similar triangles within *ABCDEF*.

$$\triangle ACD \sim \triangle\underline{\qquad} \qquad \triangle\underline{\qquad} \sim \triangle FAB$$

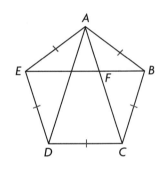

WRITTEN RESPONSE

12. You are escaping from an underground maze and encounter two guards, each standing in front of a door. A mysterious voice tells you that one door leads to freedom, the other to eternal imprisonment. The voice also tells you that one guard always tells the truth and the other always lies, but does not tell you which is which. You are allowed to ask only one question of only one guard. If you ask the right question, you will be able to escape.

a) Does it matter which guard you ask a question? Explain why or why not.

b) What question should you ask?

13. a) Make a conjecture about the sum of two consecutive perfect squares.

   b) List evidence that supports or disproves your conjecture.

   c) If possible, prove your conjecture.

14. The measure of an exterior angle of a triangle is the sum of the measures of the two non-adjacent interior angles. Use this fact and $\triangle ABC$ to prove that the sum of the interior angle measures of a triangle is 180°.

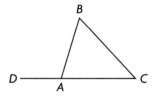

15. Can squares and equilateral triangles with the same side lengths be used to create a tessellation? Explain why or why not. Include a sketch in your explanation.

Getting Started

1. Match each term with the picture or example that best illustrates its definition.

a) tangent ratio ___

b) angle of elevation ___

c) acute triangle ___

d) opposite side ___

e) cosine ratio ___

f) sum of the angles of a triangle ___

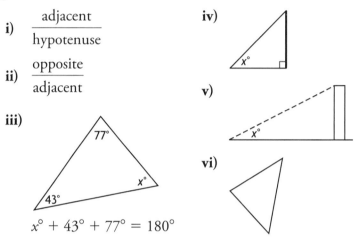

i) $\dfrac{\text{adjacent}}{\text{hypotenuse}}$

ii) $\dfrac{\text{opposite}}{\text{adjacent}}$

iii)

77°

43°

$x°$

$x° + 43° + 77° = 180°$

iv)

$x°$

v)

$x°$

vi)

2. Solve for each unknown.

a) $\dfrac{x}{7} = \dfrac{5}{14}$

b) $\dfrac{17}{3} = \dfrac{a}{12}$

c) $\dfrac{12}{p} = \dfrac{14}{5}$

3. Which is the longest side in each triangle? Which is the shortest side? Explain how you know.

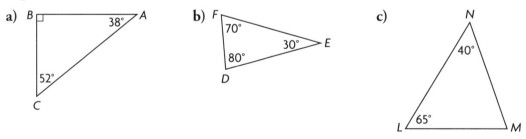

a) B 38° A 52° C

b) F 70° 30° E 80° D

c) N 40° 65° L M

4. Which is the largest angle in each triangle? Which is the smallest angle? Explain how you know.

a)
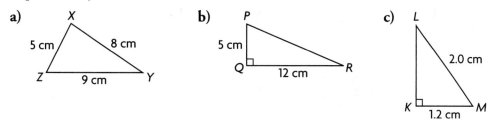

b)

c)

5. Determine the measures of the unknown angles. Give your reasons.

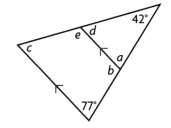

6. Determine the value of each primary trigonometric ratio. Round to four decimal places where appropriate.

a) $\sin 22° =$ _____   **b)** $\cos 60° =$ _____   **c)** $\tan 45° =$ _____

7. Determine the measure of each acute angle, to the nearest degree.

a) $\sin X = 0.4$ **b)** $\cos Y = \dfrac{3}{8}$ **c)** $\tan Z = \dfrac{5}{2}$

$\angle X =$ ___° $\angle Y =$ ___° $\angle Z =$ ___°

8. Solve $\triangle ABC$ (determine all unknown sides and values). Round each value to the nearest tenth, where appropriate.

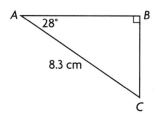

9. a) Is $\triangle PQR \sim \triangle SRT$? Explain.

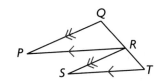

b) Are there ratios equivalent to $\dfrac{QR}{RT}$? Explain.

3.1 Exploring Side–Angle Relationships in Acute Triangles

YOU WILL NEED
• dynamic geometry software OR ruler and protractor

Keep in Mind

▶ The ratios of $\dfrac{\text{length of opposite side}}{\sin(\text{angle})}$ are equivalent for all three side–angle pairs in an acute triangle.

Example 1

Given that $\dfrac{a}{\sin 30°} = \dfrac{13}{\sin 70°}$, sketch the triangle for the situation. Then determine a, to one decimal place.

Solution

Step 1. I sketched a triangle showing side a opposite a 30° angle and a side measuring 13 opposite a 70° angle.

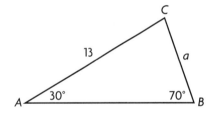

TIP

If the vertices or angles of a triangle are labelled, for example, A, B, and C, then the sides of the triangle are generally labelled a, b, and c to match. Side a is the side opposite $\angle A$, and so on.

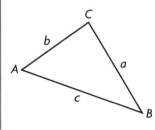

Step 2. I isolated a by multiplying both sides by sin 30°.

$$\frac{a}{\sin 30°} = \frac{13}{\sin 70°}$$

$$\sin 30°\left(\frac{a}{\sin 30°}\right) = \sin 30°\left(\frac{13}{\sin 70°}\right)$$

$$a = \sin 30°\left(\frac{13}{\sin 70°}\right)$$

Step 3. I evaluated a with my calculator.

$$a = 6.917...$$

$$a = 6.9$$

The length of a is approximately 6.9.

Example 2

Determine $\angle A$ to the nearest degree for $\dfrac{20}{\sin A} = \dfrac{13}{\sin 36°}$.

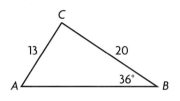

Solution

Step 1. I decided to sketch a triangle for the situation.

Step 2. I inverted the ratios so I could isolate sin A more easily.

$$\frac{\sin A}{20} = \frac{\sin 36°}{13}$$

Step 3. I isolated sin A by multiplying both sides by 20.

$$\sin A = 20\left(\frac{\sin 36°}{13}\right)$$

Step 4. I evaluated $\angle A$ using my calculator.

$$\angle A = \sin^{-1}\left(20\left(\frac{\sin 36°}{13}\right)\right)$$

$\angle A$ measures approximately 65°.

$$\angle A = 64.727...°$$

Practice

1. Sketch a triangle for each situation. Then solve for the unknown side length, to one decimal place.

   a) $\dfrac{q}{\sin 25°} = \dfrac{15}{\sin 80°}$

   d) $\dfrac{\sin 55°}{t} = \dfrac{\sin 35°}{4.1}$

   b) $\dfrac{\sin 32°}{r} = \dfrac{\sin 75°}{13}$

   e) $\dfrac{u}{\sin 50°} = \dfrac{12}{\sin 63°}$

   c) $\dfrac{\sin 60°}{s} = \dfrac{\sin 75°}{5}$

   f) $\dfrac{v}{\sin 65°} = \dfrac{6}{\sin 42°}$

2. Sketch a triangle for each situation. Then solve for the unknown angle measure, to the nearest degree.

a) $\dfrac{12}{\sin A} = \dfrac{14}{\sin 50°}$

d) $\dfrac{5.5}{\sin D} = \dfrac{3.6}{\sin 35°}$

b) $\dfrac{\sin B}{15} = \dfrac{\sin 56°}{13}$

e) $\dfrac{\sin E}{46} = \dfrac{\sin 39°}{31}$

c) $\dfrac{18}{\sin C} = \dfrac{20}{\sin 60°}$

f) $\dfrac{\sin F}{6} = \dfrac{\sin 45°}{5}$

3. For each triangle, write an equation based on two equivalent ratios for side–angle pairs. Then solve your equation for the unknown side length or angle measure. Round to the nearest tenth of a unit.

a)

b)

Copyright © 2012 by Nelson Education Ltd.

4. Which expression describes the ratios of side–angle pairs in $\triangle XYZ$?

 A. $x(\sin X) = y(\sin Y) = z(\sin Z)$

 B. $\dfrac{x}{\sin Z} = \dfrac{y}{\sin X} = \dfrac{z}{\sin Y}$

 C. $x(\sin y) = y(\sin Z) = z(\sin X)$

 D. $\dfrac{z}{\sin Z} = \dfrac{y}{\sin Y} = \dfrac{x}{\sin X}$

5. Which ratios are equivalent for all three side–angle pairs in acute triangles?

 A. $\dfrac{\sin(\text{angle})}{\text{length of opposite side}}$

 C. $\dfrac{\cos(\text{angle})}{\text{length of opposite side}}$

 B. $\dfrac{\text{length of adjacent side}}{\sin(\text{angle})}$

 D. $\dfrac{\text{length of adjacent side}}{\cos(\text{angle})}$

NUMERICAL RESPONSE

6. Solve for the unknown side length or angle measure. Round to the nearest tenth of a unit.

a) $\dfrac{c}{\sin 38°} = \dfrac{7}{\sin 73°}$

$c \doteq$ _____

b) $\dfrac{13}{\sin B} = \dfrac{11}{\sin 48°}$

$\angle B \doteq$ _____ $°$

c) $\dfrac{\sin 17°}{1.8} = \dfrac{\sin 81°}{x}$

$x \doteq$ _____

d) $\dfrac{\sin P}{3.7} = \dfrac{\sin 64°}{5.3}$

$\angle P \doteq$ _____ $°$

e) $\dfrac{2.9}{\sin 32°} = \dfrac{4.7}{\sin A}$

$\angle A \doteq$ _____ $°$

f) $\dfrac{\sin 62°}{q} = \dfrac{\sin 68°}{28}$

$q \doteq$ _____

3.2 Proving and Applying the Sine Law

YOU WILL NEED
- ruler and protractor
- calculator

Keep in Mind

▶ You can use the sine law, $\dfrac{a}{\sin A} = \dfrac{b}{\sin B} = \dfrac{c}{\sin C}$, to solve an acute triangle problem when you know

- two sides and the angle opposite a known side

- two angles and any side

or

▶ If you know the measures of two angles in a triangle, you can determine the third angle, because the angles must add to 180°.

Example

A triangle has angles measuring 75° and 60°. The side opposite the 75° angle is 14.0 m in length. Determine the length of the side opposite the 60° angle, to the nearest tenth of a metre.

Solution

Step 1. I sketched the triangle and labelled the items I knew.

Step 2. I wanted to determine the length of b. I knew a, $\angle A$, and $\angle B$, so I decided to use the sine law. I entered the values I knew.

$$\frac{b}{\sin B} = \frac{a}{\sin A}$$

$$\frac{b}{\sin 60°} = \frac{14.0}{\sin 75°}$$

Step 3. I isolated b by multiplying both sides by $\sin 60°$, then calculated its value.

$$\sin 60°\left(\frac{b}{\sin 60°}\right) = \sin 60°\left(\frac{14.0}{\sin 75°}\right)$$

$$b = 11.000...$$

Step 4. I rounded to the nearest tenth. The length of AC is about 11.0 m. It makes sense that AC is shorter than BC, because $\angle B$ measures less than $\angle A$.

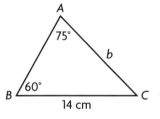

TIP

To determine side lengths, use

$$\frac{a}{\sin A} = \frac{b}{\sin B} = \frac{c}{\sin C}$$

To determine angles, use

$$\frac{\sin A}{a} = \frac{\sin B}{b} = \frac{\sin C}{c}$$

Copyright © 2012 by Nelson Education Ltd.

Practice

1. Can you use the sine law to determine the length of the indicated side or the measure of the indicated angle in each case? Explain how you know.

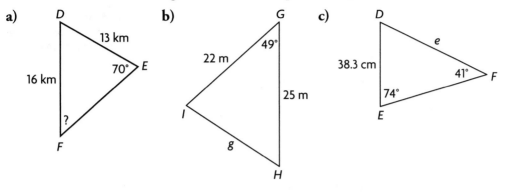

a)

b)

c)

2. Determine the indicated side length or angle measure, to one decimal place.

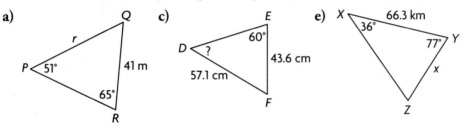

a)

c)

e)

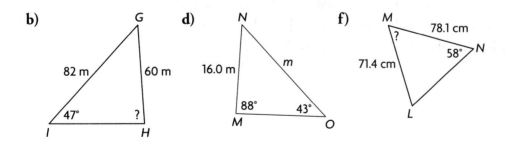

b)

d)

f)

3. a) In $\triangle DEF$, $\angle D = 61°$, $d = 23.9$ cm, and $\angle E = 38°$. Determine e, to one decimal place.

b) In $\triangle RST$, $\angle S = 54°$, $s = 91.8$ cm, and $\angle T = 64°$. Determine t, to one decimal place.

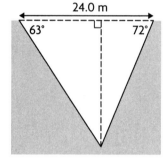

> **TIP**
> It is a good idea to begin each solution with a sketch of the triangle you are working with. This will help you avoid errors.

4. To bungee jump from a bridge safely, Jordan needs to know the depth of the gorge below the bridge. Determine the depth of the gorge, to the nearest tenth of a metre.

5. A radio mast is supported by two wires on opposite sides. On the ground, the ends of the wires are 60.0 m apart. One wire makes a 62° angle with the ground, and the other makes a 75° angle with the ground. To the nearest tenth of a metre, how long are the wires, and how tall is the mast?

6. What do you need to know about an acute triangle to use the sine law?

    A. all the angles   **C.** two angles and any side

    B. all the sides   **D.** two sides and any angle

WRITTEN RESPONSE

7. In $\triangle LMN$, $\angle M = 50°$, $m = 11.2$ cm, and $l = 9.8$ cm. Solve the triangle. Round angles to the nearest degree and sides to the nearest tenth of a centimetre.

> **TIP**
> "Solving" a triangle means determining all the unknown sides and angles.

8. A search and rescue helicopter crew completed a training exercise. The crew left the heliport and flew 15.0 km in the direction S45°E. They turned, then flew N40°E and arrived at their destination. The destination is 25.0 km from the heliport. Determine, to the nearest tenth of a kilometre, the distance the crew travelled on the second leg of their trip.

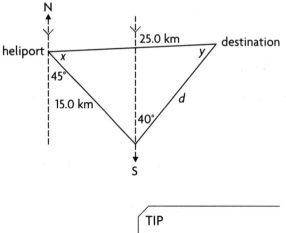

> **TIP**
> The notation N40°E means a direction 40° east of due north.

Proving and Applying the Cosine Law

YOU WILL NEED
- ruler and protractor
- calculator

Keep in Mind

▶ The cosine law: in an acute triangle *ABC*,

$$a^2 = b^2 + c^2 - 2bc \cos A$$

$$b^2 = a^2 + c^2 - 2ac \cos B$$

$$c^2 = a^2 + b^2 - 2ab \cos C$$

▶ You can use the cosine law to solve a problem that can be modelled by an acute triangle when you know

- two sides and the contained angle
- all three sides

▶ When using the cosine law to determine an angle, you can

- Substitute the known values first, and then solve for the unknown angle.

- Rearrange the formula to solve for the cosine of the unknown angle, and then substitute and evaluate.

Example 1

Determine the length of *CB*, to the nearest centimetre.

Solution

Step 1. I saw that I could not use the sine law, since I did not know the measure of an angle and its opposite side. I knew I could use the cosine law, because I knew two sides and the contained angle.

Step 2. I wrote the formula and substituted the values I knew. Then I solved for *a*.

$$a^2 = b^2 + c^2 - 2bc \cos A$$

$$a^2 = 22^2 + 36^2 - 2(22)(36) \cos 74°$$

$$a^2 = 484 + 1296 - 1584 \cos 74°$$

$$a^2 = 1507.999\ldots$$

$$a = \sqrt{1507.999\ldots}$$

$$a = 38.832\ldots$$

TIP
The contained angle is the angle between the two sides that you know.

Step 3. I rounded to the nearest centimetre.
The length of *BC* is 39 cm.

Example 2

Determine the measure of ∠A, to the nearest degree.

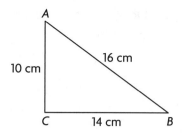

Solution

Step 1. I saw that I could not use the sine law, since I did not know any angle measures. I decided to rearrange the cosine law, so I could solve for the measure of an angle.

$$a^2 = b^2 + c^2 - 2bc \cos A$$

$$a^2 - b^2 - c^2 = -2bc \cos A$$

$$\frac{a^2 - b^2 - c^2}{-2bc} = \cos A$$

Step 2. I substituted the known values and solved for ∠A.

$$\frac{14^2 - 10^2 - 16^2}{-2(10)(16)} = \cos A$$

$$\frac{-160}{-320} = \cos A$$

$$\cos^{-1}(0.5) = ∠A$$

$$60° = ∠A$$

Step 3. I did not need to round. ∠A is exactly 60°.

Practice

1. Can you use the cosine law to determine the length of the indicated side or the measure of the indicated angle in each case? Explain how you know.

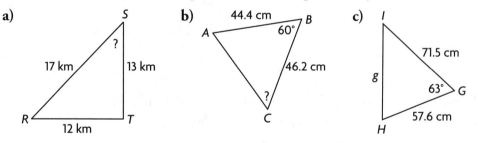

a)

b)

c)

2. Determine the length of the indicated side, to one decimal place.

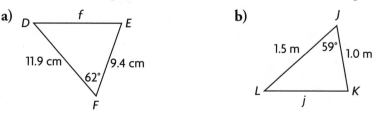

a)

b)

3. Determine the measure of the indicated angle, to the nearest degree.

a)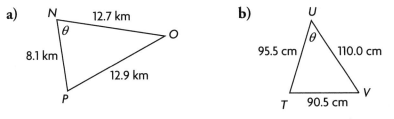

b)

4. a) In $\triangle DEF$, $d = 23.9$ cm, $e = 16.8$ cm, and $f = 27.0$ cm. Determine $\angle F$, to the nearest degree.

c) In $\triangle ABC$, $b = 15.0$ cm, $c = 18.5$ cm, and $\angle A = 75°$. Determine a, to one decimal place.

b) In $\triangle XYZ$, $x = 13.5$ cm, $y = 18.2$ cm, and $\angle Z = 60°$. Determine z, to one decimal place.

d) In $\triangle RST$, $r = 67.8$ m, $s = 60.4$ m, and $t = 89.5$ m. Determine $\angle S$, to the nearest degree.

5. What do you need to know about an acute triangle to use the cosine law?

  A. all the angles   **C.** two angles and any side

  B. all the sides   **D.** two sides and any angle

WRITTEN RESPONSE

6. Solve $\triangle TUV$, where $t = 9.5$ cm, $u = 16.0$ cm, and $\angle V = 55°$. Give angles to the nearest degree and sides to one decimal place.

7. The pendulum of a grandfather clock is 115.0 cm long. When the pendulum swings from one side to the other side, it travels a horizontal distance of 35.0 cm. Determine the angle through which the pendulum swings. Answer to the nearest tenth of a degree.

YOU WILL NEED
- ruler

▶ The sine law, the cosine law, the primary trigonometric ratios, and the sum of angles in a triangle may all be useful for solving acute triangle problems.

▶ When selecting the sine law or the cosine law, consider which sides and/or angles are given and which side or angle is to be determined.

Example

Determine the height of *AC*, to the nearest metre.

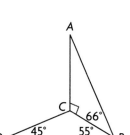

Solution

Step 1. In order to determine *AC*, I knew I would need to determine *BC* and use a primary trigonometric ratio. Based on the given information in △*DBC*, I would need to use the sine law to determine *BC*.

Step 2. I determined ∠*BCD*, using the sum of angles in a triangle. In △*DBC*,

$$\angle BCD = 180° - 55° - 45°$$

$$\angle BCD = 80°$$

Step 3. I determined *BC*, using the sine law.

$$\frac{BC}{\sin D} = \frac{BD}{\sin C}$$

$$\frac{BC}{\sin 45°} = \frac{50}{\sin 80°}$$

$$\sin 45°\left(\frac{BC}{\sin 45°}\right) = \sin 45°\left(\frac{50}{\sin 80°}\right)$$

$$BC = \sin 45°\left(\frac{50}{\sin 80°}\right)$$

$$BC = 35.900...$$

Step 4. I used the tangent ratio to write an equation with *AC*.

$$\tan 66° = \frac{AC}{BC}$$

$$\tan 66° = \frac{AC}{35.900...}$$

$$35.900...(\tan 66°) = 35.900...\left(\frac{AC}{35.900...}\right)$$

$$80.634... = AC$$

The height of *AC* is approximately 81 m.

Practice

1. Can you determine the indicated angle measure? If so, would you use the sine law or the cosine law? Explain how you know.

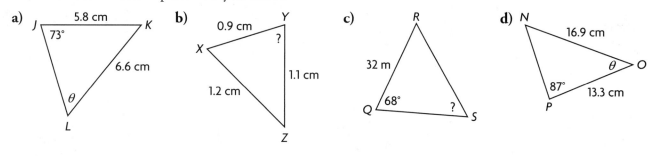

2. Determine the indicated angle measures in question 1, where possible.

3. Read each situation description. Can you determine the indicated distance or angle measure? If so, would you use the sine law or the cosine law?

   a) An engineer measures the angle of elevation to the top of a building as 65°. She then walks 25.0 m to the other side of the building, turns around, and measures the angle of elevation to the same point on the building to be 75°. She wants to determine the distance from her second location to the top of the building.

   b) A surveyor places three stakes that make a triangle with angles of 50°, 60°, and 70°. He wants to determine the perimeter of the triangle.

   c) A kayak leaves a dock on Lake Athabasca and heads due north for 2.3 km. At the same time, a second kayak travels in a direction N55°E from the dock for 1.8 km. In which direction, to the nearest degree, would the second kayak have to travel to meet the first kayak?

TIP
Drawing a clearly labelled diagram makes it easier to select a strategy for solving a problem.

4. Determine the indicated value in each part of question 3, where possible.

5. Look at the fences enclosing the pen shown.

    a) How long is the lower fence?   **b)** How long is the upper right fence?

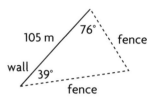

6. A hiker leaves base camp in Banff National Park and travels N20°W for 0.7 km. The hiker then travels S65°W until he is directly west of the camp. How far is the hiker from the camp, to the nearest tenth of a kilometre?

7. In a parallelogram, two adjacent sides measure 28 cm and 21 cm. The shorter diagonal is 15 cm. Determine, to the nearest degree, the smaller angle measures in the parallelogram.

MULTIPLE CHOICE

8. Is it possible to determine the indicated angle measure? If so, how?

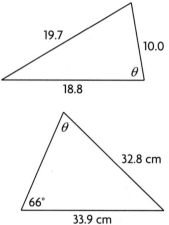

    A. yes, using the sine law   **C.** yes, using primary trigonometric ratios

    B. yes, using the cosine law   **D.** no, not possible

9. Is it possible to determine the indicated angle measure? If so, how?

    A. yes, using the sine law   **C.** yes, using primary trigonometric ratios

    B. yes, using the cosine law   **D.** no, not possible

WRITTEN RESPONSE

10. A hydro tower is supported by two wires on opposite sides. On the ground, the ends of the wire are 48 m apart. One wire makes a 62° angle with the ground. The other makes a 75° angle with the ground. Draw a diagram of the situation. Then determine the height of the tower, to the nearest tenth of a metre.

3 Test Prep

Complete the following to summarize the important ideas from this chapter.

Q: What are the two forms of the sine law for $\triangle ABC$?

NEED HELP?
• See Lessons 3.1, 3.2

A: $\dfrac{a}{\sin A} = \dfrac{\boxed{}}{\boxed{}} = \dfrac{\boxed{}}{\boxed{}}$ or $\dfrac{\sin A}{a} = \dfrac{\boxed{}}{\boxed{}} = \dfrac{\boxed{}}{\boxed{}}$

Q: How is the cosine law usually stated for $\triangle ABC$?

NEED HELP?
• See Lesson 3.3

A: $a^2 = $ _____

Q: When using the cosine law to solve for angle A in $\triangle ABC$, should you rearrange first or substitute first?

NEED HELP?
• See Lesson 3.3

A: • You can either rearrange and then _____, or substitute and then

_____.

• If you rearrange first, you will be using the _____ law in the form

$\_\_\_\_\_ A = \dfrac{\boxed{}}{\boxed{}}$

Q: When would you use the sine law or the cosine law to solve acute triangles? (Mark the triangles with the given information, like the first one.)

NEED HELP?
• See Lessons 3.2, 3.3, 3.4

A: • Given three _____, SSS, to determine an angle, use the

_____ law in the form $\cos A = \dfrac{\boxed{}}{\boxed{}}$.

• Given two _____ and the _____ opposite one of the

sides, _____, to determine another _____, use the

_____ law in the form $\dfrac{\boxed{}}{\boxed{}} = \dfrac{\boxed{}}{\boxed{}}$.

• Given two _____ and the included _____, SAS, use the

_____ law in the form $a^2 = $ _____.

• Given two _____ and a _____, ASA or _____,

to determine another side, use the sine law in the

form $\dfrac{\boxed{}}{\boxed{}} = \dfrac{\boxed{}}{\boxed{}}$.

3 Chapter Test

MULTIPLE CHOICE

Determine the measure of the indicated angle, to the nearest degree.

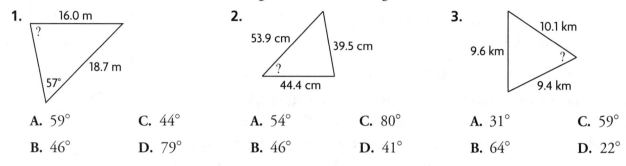

1.
- **A.** 59°
- **C.** 44°
- **B.** 46°
- **D.** 79°

2.
- **A.** 54°
- **C.** 80°
- **B.** 46°
- **D.** 41°

3.
- **A.** 31°
- **C.** 59°
- **B.** 64°
- **D.** 22°

Determine the indicated side length, to the nearest tenth of a unit.

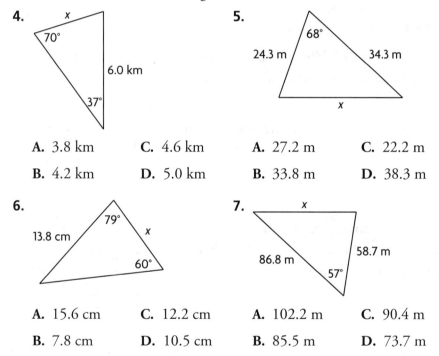

4.
- **A.** 3.8 km
- **C.** 4.6 km
- **B.** 4.2 km
- **D.** 5.0 km

5.
- **A.** 27.2 m
- **C.** 22.2 m
- **B.** 33.8 m
- **D.** 38.3 m

6.
- **A.** 15.6 cm
- **C.** 12.2 cm
- **B.** 7.8 cm
- **D.** 10.5 cm

7.
- **A.** 102.2 m
- **C.** 90.4 m
- **B.** 85.5 m
- **D.** 73.7 m

NUMERICAL RESPONSE

8. Determine the indicated side length, to the nearest tenth of a unit, or angle measure, to the nearest degree.

   a) In $\triangle ABC$, $b = 14.0$ m, $c = 9.3$ m, and $\angle A = 66°$.

   Therefore, $a = $ _____ m.

   b) In $\triangle VWX$, $v = 60$ cm, $x = 85$ cm, and $\angle W = 20°$.

   Therefore, $w = $ _____ cm.

   c) In $\triangle DEF$, $d = 42.2$ cm, $e = 47.8$ cm, and $f = 50.1$ cm.

   Therefore, $\angle D = $ ___°.

9. A canoe leaves a dock on Lake Claire and heads in a direction N71°E for 1.9 km. At the same time, a second canoe travels in a direction S28°E from the dock for 3.1 km.

The distance between the canoes is _____ km, to the nearest tenth of a kilometre.

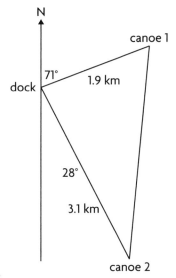

10. In a parallelogram, two adjacent sides measure 4.2 cm and 5.9 cm. The shorter diagonal is 2.6 cm.

The larger angles in the parallelogram measure ___°, to the nearest degree.

11. An atmospheric scientist is trying to determine the altitude (height above Earth's surface) of a circular cloud directly above him. The scientist measures the angle of elevation to the north end of the cloud to be 89° and the angle of elevation to the south end of the cloud to be 85°. The scientist knows that this cloud has a diameter of about 150 m.

The altitude of the cloud, to the nearest metre, is _____ m.

12. A bush pilot delivers supplies to an isolated village by flying 470 km in the direction N66°E. While at the village, the pilot decides that she must refuel at a camp located 35 km S11°E of the village.

By the time she returns to her starting point, the pilot will have flown a total distance of _____ km, to the nearest kilometre.

WRITTEN RESPONSE

13. Two airplanes leave Hay River airport at the same time. One flies at 550 km/h. The other flies at 330 km/h. About 2 h later, they are 1200 km apart. Determine the angle between their paths, to the nearest degree.

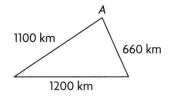

14. An airplane is spotted by two observers on opposite sides of it. On the ground, the observers are 1500 m apart. One observer's line of sight to the airplane makes an 83° angle with the ground. The other's line of sight makes a 69° angle with the ground. Determine the distance from each observer to the airplane, to the nearest metre.

15. Joanna is using a surveying instrument to determine the height of a mast. She selects two surveying positions, P and Q, to create a baseline PQ that is 48 m long. The base of the mast is at R and its tip is at S. Joanna determines the elevation of the mast from position P: $\angle RPS = 73°$. She also determines these ground-level angles: $\angle RPQ = 47°$ and $\angle RQP = 65°$.

a) How tall is the mast, to the nearest metre?

b) If Joanna had measured the elevation of the mast from position Q instead of position P, what would her measurement have been, to the nearest degree?

Getting Started

1. Match each term with the most appropriate diagram or description.

a) obtuse triangle ___

b) contained angle ___

c) sine law ___

d) side–angle pair ___

e) cosine law ___

f) acute triangle ___

i) $c^2 = a^2 + b^2 - 2ab \cos C$

ii) $\dfrac{a}{\sin A} = \dfrac{b}{\sin B} = \dfrac{c}{\sin C}$

iii)

v)

vi)

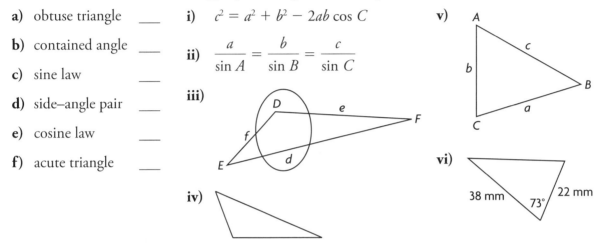

For questions 2 through 7, round answers to the nearest tenth, as appropriate.

2. Solve each right triangle (determine all unknown sides and angle measures).

a)

b)

3. For each triangle, identify the given information as *SAS* or *SSS*. Then use the cosine law to determine the indicated measure.

a)

b)

4. For each triangle, identify the given information as *ASA* or *SSA*. Then use the sine law to determine the indicated measure.

a)

b)

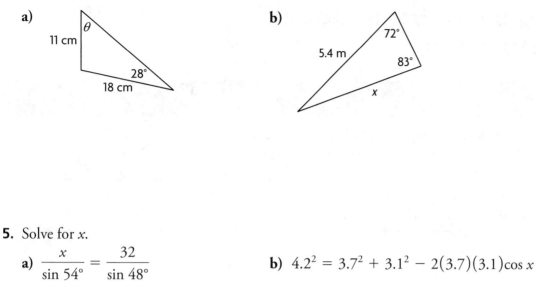

5. Solve for *x*.

a) $\dfrac{x}{\sin 54°} = \dfrac{32}{\sin 48°}$

b) $4.2^2 = 3.7^2 + 3.1^2 - 2(3.7)(3.1)\cos x$

6. Determine the indicated side length or angle measure in each triangle.

a)

b)

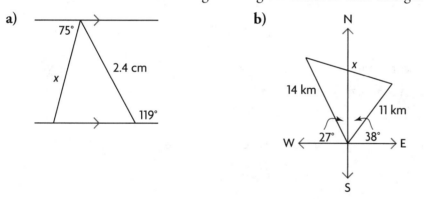

7. In $\triangle XYZ$, $x = 6.4$ cm, $\angle Y = 71°$, and $\angle Z = 28°$. Solve $\triangle XYZ$.

4.1 Exploring the Primary Trigonometric Ratios of Obtuse Angles

YOU WILL NEED
• calculator

Keep in Mind

▶ The value of a trigonometric ratio for an angle, θ, is related to the value of the same trigonometric ratio for the supplement of the angle, $180° - \theta$.

▶ For any angle θ:

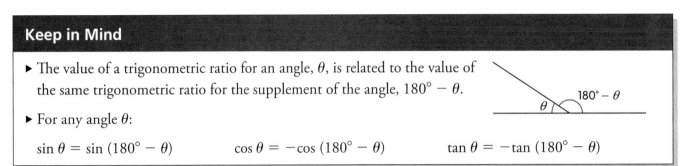

$$\sin \theta = \sin (180° - \theta) \qquad \cos \theta = -\cos (180° - \theta) \qquad \tan \theta = -\tan (180° - \theta)$$

Example

Determine the measures of two angles between $0°$ and $180°$ that have each sine ratio. Round each answer to the nearest degree.

a) 0.34

b) $\dfrac{4}{7}$

Solution

a) 0.34

Step 1. I determined the measure of the acute angle, θ, such that $\sin \theta = 0.34$.

$$\sin^{-1}(0.34) = 19.876...°$$

The acute angle measures $20°$, to the nearest degree.

Step 2. I used the relationship $\sin \theta = \sin (180° - \theta)$ to find the measure of the obtuse angle with the sine ratio 0.34.

$$180° - 19.876...° = 160.124...°$$

The obtuse angle measures $160°$, to the nearest degree.

b) $\dfrac{4}{7}$

Step 1. I determined the measure of the acute angle, θ, such that $\sin \theta = \dfrac{4}{7}$.

$$\sin^{-1}\left(\frac{4}{7}\right) = 34.849...°$$

The acute angle measures $35°$, to the nearest degree.

Step 2. I used the relationship $\sin \theta = \sin (180° - \theta)$ to determine the measure of the obtuse angle with sine ratio $\dfrac{4}{7}$.

$$180° - 34.849...° = 145.151...°$$

The obtuse angle measures $145°$, to the nearest degree.

Practice

1. Determine if each of the following equations is true. Explain your answer.

   a) $\tan 48° = \tan 132°$

   c) $\cos 30° = -\cos 60°$

   b) $\cos 20° = -\cos 160°$

   d) $\sin 100° = -\sin 80°$

2. Calculate $\sin 62°$, to four decimal places.

   Predict another angle, θ, such that $\sin \theta = \sin 62°$. Check your prediction.

3. Calculate $\tan 96°$, to four decimal places.

   Predict another angle, θ, such that $\tan \theta = -\tan 96°$. Check your prediction.

4. a) Determine an acute angle, θ, that has $\sin \theta = 0.47$.

   b) Determine the supplement of the angle from part a).

   c) Without calculating, determine the sine ratio of the angle from part b). Explain your answer.

MULTIPLE CHOICE

5. Which two angles have the sine ratio 0.63?

   A. 63°, 117°   **B.** 39°, 51°   **C.** 39°, 141°   **D.** none of these

6. Which two angles have the tangent ratio 0.45?

   A. 24°, 156°   **B.** 45°, 135°   **C.** 1°, 179°   **D.** none of these

NUMERICAL RESPONSE

7. Determine two angles between 0° and 180° that have the sine ratio 0.122.

4.2 Proving and Applying the Sine and Cosine Laws for Obtuse Triangles

YOU WILL NEED
• calculator

Example 1

Determine the measure of $\angle C$, to the nearest degree.

Solution

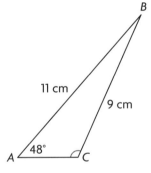

Step 1. I knew the lengths of two sides, c and a, and the measure of $\angle A$, so I used the sine law to write an equation I can use to find $\angle C$.

$$\frac{\sin A}{a} = \frac{\sin C}{c}$$

Step 2. I substituted the given sides and angle into my equation.

$$\frac{\sin 48°}{9} = \frac{\sin C}{11}$$

Step 3. I isolated sin C.

$$9 \sin C = 11 \sin 48°$$

$$\sin C = \frac{11 \sin 48°}{9}$$

TIP

Write the sine law with the angles in the numerator when you need to find the measure of an angle.

Copyright © 2012 by Nelson Education Ltd.

Step 4. I used the inverse sine to determine the measure of $\angle C$.

$$C = \sin^{-1}\left(\frac{11 \sin 48°}{9}\right)$$

$$C = 65.269...°$$

Step 5. From the diagram, $\angle C$ is obtuse. I used the relationship $\sin \theta = \sin (180° - \theta)$.

$$180° - 65.269...° = 114.730...°$$

The measure of $\angle C$ is 115°.

Example 2

Determine the measure of $\angle E$, to the nearest degree.

Solution

Step 1. I knew the lengths of all three sides, d, e, and f, so I used the cosine law.

$$e^2 = d^2 + f^2 - 2df \cos E$$

Step 2. I rearranged to isolate $\cos E$.

$$e^2 + 2df \cos E = d^2 + f^2$$

$$2df \cos E = d^2 + f^2 - e^2$$

$$\cos E = \frac{d^2 + f^2 - e^2}{2df}$$

Step 3. I substituted the known values and simplified.

$$\cos E = \frac{(9)^2 + (12)^2 - (20)^2}{2(9)(12)}$$

$$\cos E = -0.8101...$$

$$\angle E = \cos^{-1}(-0.8101...), \text{ or}$$

$$144.114...°$$

The measure of $\angle E$ is about 144°.

Practice

1. Identify and correct the errors in each solution.

a) Determine x.

$$x^2 = 8^2 + 27^2 - 2(8)(27) \cos 96°$$

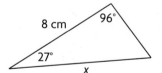

b) Determine x.

$$\sin 21° = \frac{3}{x}$$

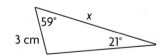

4.2 Proving and Applying the Sine and Cosine Laws for Obtuse Triangles **89**

2. For each triangle, would you use the sine law, the cosine law, both, or neither to determine the unknown side length or angle measure?

a)

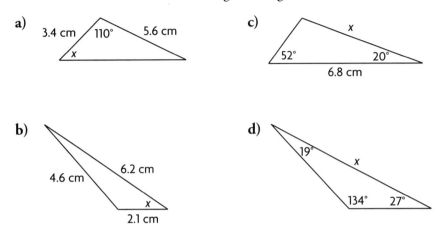

c)

b)

d)

3. Determine the unknown side length in each triangle, to the nearest tenth.

a)

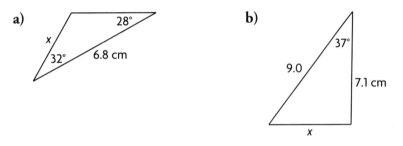

b)

4. Determine the unknown angle in each triangle, to the nearest degree.

a)

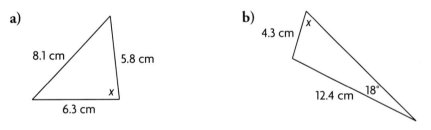

b)

5. Compare proving the sine law for acute triangles with proving the sine law for obtuse triangles. How are they the same? How are they different?

6. Compare proving the cosine law for acute triangles with proving the cosine law for obtuse triangles. How are they the same? How are they different?

7. In $\triangle ABC$, $a = 16$ m, $b = 18$ m, and $c = 10$ m. Determine the measure of each interior angle, to the nearest tenth of a degree.

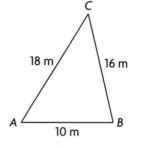

> **TIP**
>
> The sign of the cosine ratio tells you whether the angle is acute (positive cosine) or obtuse (negative cosine).

8. Solve $\triangle MNP$, given $\angle P = 125°$, $p = 26.0$ m, and $m = 17.1$ m. Round each side length or angle measure to the nearest tenth of a unit.

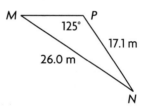

> **TIP**
>
> "Solving" a triangle means determining all the unknown sides and angles.

9. From a helicopter, the angles of depression to points A and B on opposite sides of a pond measure 27° and 46°, as shown. Determine the width of the pond, to the nearest metre.

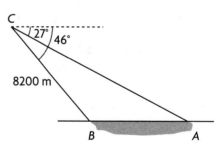

4.2 Proving and Applying the Sine and Cosine Laws for Obtuse Triangles **91**

4.3 The Ambiguous Case of the Sine Law

YOU WILL NEED
- calculator
- ruler
- protractor
- compass

Keep in Mind

▶ You must check for the ambiguous case of the sine law when you are given two side lengths and the measure of an angle opposite one of the sides: *SSA*.

▶ For any $\triangle ABC$ with height h where $h = b \sin A$, and given $\angle A$ and the lengths of a and b, check the following possibilities:

- If $\angle A$ is acute, there are four possibilities to consider:

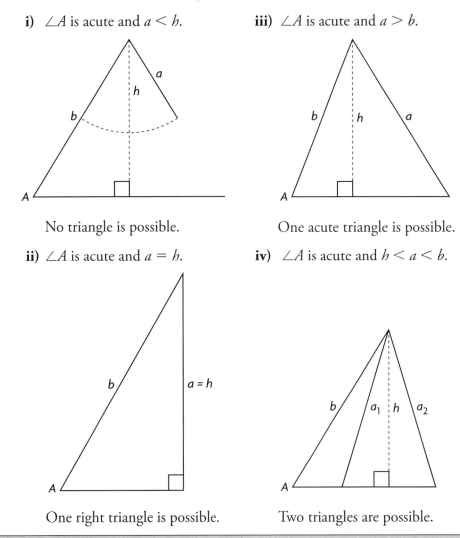

i) $\angle A$ is acute and $a < h$.

No triangle is possible.

ii) $\angle A$ is acute and $a = h$.

One right triangle is possible.

iii) $\angle A$ is acute and $a > b$.

One acute triangle is possible.

iv) $\angle A$ is acute and $h < a < b$.

Two triangles are possible.

- If $\angle A$ is obtuse, there are two possibilities to consider:

i) $\angle A$ is obtuse and $a < b$ or $a = b$.

ii) $\angle A$ is obtuse and $a > b$.

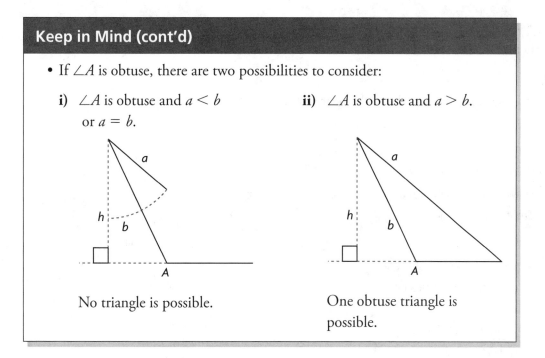

No triangle is possible.

One obtuse triangle is possible.

Example 1

In each case, determine the number of triangles that are possible.

$\triangle ABC$

$\angle A = 40°$, $a = 3$ cm, $b = 4$ cm

$\triangle DEF$

$\angle D = 120°$, $d = 2$ cm, $e = 3$ cm

Solution

Step 1. I used the given information to determine the number of triangles. For both $\triangle ABC$ and $\triangle DEF$, the situation is *SSA*.

$\triangle ABC$: Since $\angle A$ is acute and $a < b$, I needed to check $h = b \sin A$: $h = 4 \sin 40°$, or about 2.57, so $h < a < b$. There are two possible triangles.

$\triangle DEF$: Since $\angle D$ is obtuse and $d < e$, no triangle is possible.

Step 2. I checked by using a ruler and a protractor to draw the triangles.

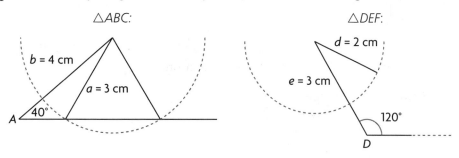

Example 2

Isha is at the starting point of two southeasterly paths at an angle measure of $25°$ to each other. She followed these directions:

- Follow the more southerly path for 10.2 km to a lookout.

- Turn due north and walk another 5.4 km to a cabin.

- Turn and walk directly back to the starting point along the more northerly path.

What is the compass direction of the return path, to the nearest degree?

Solution

Step 1. I used the given information to draw a diagram.

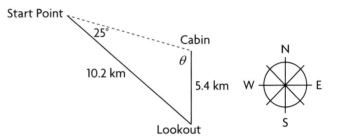

Step 2. From the diagram, I saw that the direction of the return path was approximately west northwest.

Step 3. I saw that the situation was *SSA* and that there were two side−angle pairs. I substituted the values into the sine rule and solved for θ.

$$\frac{\sin \theta}{10.2} = \frac{\sin 25°}{5.4}$$

$$10.2 \left(\frac{\sin \theta}{10.2} \right) = 10.2 \left(\frac{\sin 25°}{5.4} \right)$$

$$\sin \theta = 0.7982...$$

$$\theta = \sin^{-1}(0.7982...)$$

$$\theta = 52.966...°$$

Step 4. From my diagram, I could see that θ could not be acute. So, θ had to be the supplement of the acute angle I had found.

$$\theta = 180° - 52.966...°$$

$$\theta = 127.034...°$$

Step 5. I subtracted the measure of the angle in my triangle from 180° to determine the direction of travel.

$$180° - 127.034...° = 52.966...°$$

The compass direction of the return path is N53°W, to the nearest degree.

Practice

1. Determine whether each description of a triangle involves the *SSA* situation.

   a) In $\triangle ABC$, $\angle A = 13°$, $a = 2$ cm, and $b = 6$ cm.

   b) In $\triangle DEF$, $\angle D = 89°$, $d = 14$ cm, and $f = 11$ cm.

   c) In $\triangle PQR$, $\angle P = 38°$, $q = 27$ cm, and $r = 19$ cm.

2. For each description in question 1 that involves the *SSA* situation, determine whether zero, one, or two triangles are possible. Give your reasons.

3. Calculate the height of each triangle, to the nearest tenth of a centimetre. Determine the number of triangles that are possible. Give your reasons.

   a) In $\triangle RST$, $\angle R = 103°$, $r = 16$ cm, and $s = 9$ cm.

   b) In $\triangle XYZ$, $\angle X = 50°$, $x = 5.2$ cm, and $z = 7.1$ cm.

   c) In $\triangle ABC$, $\angle A = 74°$, $a = 28.0$ cm, and $b = 28.9$ cm.

4. Given each set of measurements for $\triangle ABC$, determine the number of triangles that are possible. Draw a diagram to support your answer.

   a) $\angle A = 110°$, $a = 4.7$ cm, and $b = 5.1$ cm

   b) $\angle A = 50°$, $a = 6.3$ cm, and $b = 8.2$ cm

5. In $\triangle XYZ$, $\angle X = 67°$, $x = 3.2$ m, and $y = 3.4$ m.

    a) Determine a possible measure for $\angle Y$, to the nearest degree.

    b) State another possible value for $\angle Y$. Give one reason why this is a possible value.

    c) Which of these possible values for $\angle Y$ corresponds to a possible triangle? Explain.

MULTIPLE CHOICE

6. In $\triangle MNP$, $n = 4.5$ cm and $\angle M = 35°$.

    What is the height of the triangle from base p?

    A. 4.5 cm   **B.** 3.7 cm   **C.** 2.6 cm   **D.** 0.4 cm

7. In $\triangle PQR$, $\angle P = 108°$, $q = 4.9$ m, and $p = 4.5$ m.

    Which statement is true for this set of measurements?

    A. This is not an *SSA* situation.

    B. This is an *SSA* situation; no triangle is possible.

    C. This is an *SSA* situation; only one triangle is possible.

    D. This is an *SSA* situation; two triangles are possible.

8. Which set of measurements can produce two possible triangles?

    A. $\angle A = 62°$, $a = 3.2$ m, $b = 4.0$ m

    B. $\angle A = 52°$, $a = 6.8$ m, $b = 7.4$ m

    C. $\angle A = 102°$, $a = 6.2$ m, $b = 9.0$ m

    D. none of these

9. In obtuse $\triangle ABC$, $\angle B = 24°$, $b = 18$ cm, and $a = 22$ cm. Calculate the measure of $\angle A$, to the nearest degree. Is there more than one possible answer? Explain how you know.

10. In $\triangle DEF$, $\angle D = 97°$, $d = 5.3$ cm, and $e = 4.8$ cm. Calculate the measure of $\angle E$, to the nearest degree. Is there more than one possible answer? Explain how you know.

11. Gail works as an aerial photographer. On one trip she takes off from the airport and flies for 52 km on a bearing of N50°E. Then she turns and flies southwest for 38 km, until she is due east of the airport.

a) Sketch a diagram of Gail's flight.

b) Explain how this situation could be ambiguous, and why it is not.

c) How far is Gail from the airport when she is due east of it?

4.4 Solving Problems Using Obtuse Triangles

YOU WILL NEED
• calculator

Keep in Mind

▶ You can use the following decision tree to help choose a strategy when solving problems that involve trigonometry.

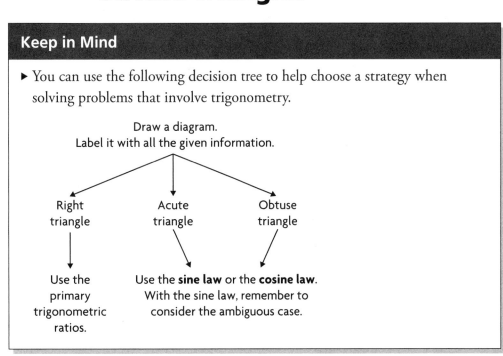

Example 1

An aerial cable car takes passengers across a 74 m wide gorge. At one point in the crossing, the angles of depression of the cable supporting the cable car measure 43° and 37°. Determine the length of the cable, to the nearest tenth of a metre.

Solution

Step 1. I drew a diagram to represent the situation. The cable runs from *A* to *C* to *B*. The cable car is at *C*.

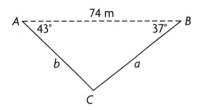

Step 2. I know the sum of the angle measures in a triangle is 180°. I used this fact to calculate the measure of ∠C in the triangle.

$$\angle C = 180° - (43° + 37°)$$

$$\angle C = 100°$$

Step 3. I used the sine law to determine the lengths of *a* and *b*. The sum *a* + *b* represents the length of the cable.

$$\frac{a}{\sin 43°} = \frac{74}{\sin 100°} \qquad\qquad \frac{b}{\sin 37°} = \frac{74}{\sin 100°}$$

$$a = \frac{74 \sin 43°}{\sin 100°} \qquad\qquad b = \frac{74 \sin 37°}{\sin 100°}$$

$$a = 51.246... \qquad\qquad b = 45.221...$$

$$a + b = 51.246... + 45.221...$$

$$a + b = 96.467...$$

The length of the cable is 96.5 m.

Example 2

From a 10 m lookout tower, the angles of depression to two tents measure 22° and 29°. One tent is on a heading of S35°W. The other tent is on a heading of S68°E. What is the distance, *AC*, between the two tents, to the nearest metre?

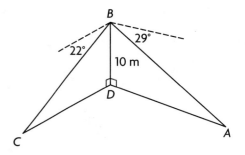

Solution

Step 1. Using parallel lines, I knew the measure of ∠*C* is 22° and the measure of ∠*A* is 29°.

Step 2. I used the tangent ratio to determine *CD* and *DA*.

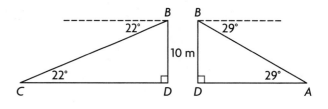

$$\tan 22° = \frac{10}{CD} \qquad\qquad \tan 29° = \frac{10}{DA}$$

$$CD = \frac{10}{\tan 22°} \qquad\qquad DA = \frac{10}{\tan 29°}$$

$$CD = 24.750... \qquad\qquad DA = 18.040...$$

Step 3. I drew a diagram of the situation from above to determine the measure of ∠*D*.

$$\angle D = 35° + 68°$$

$$\angle D = 103°$$

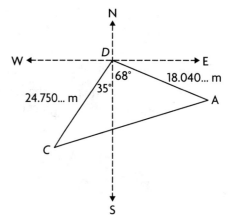

Step 4. I used the cosine law to determine the distance between the tents, *CA*.

$$CA^2 = (24.750...)^2 + (18.040...)^2 - 2(24.750...)(18.040...) \cos 103°$$

$$CA^2 = 1138.953...$$

$$CA = 33.748...$$

The distance between the tents is 34 m.

Practice

1. Two lighthouses, *A* and *B*, are 22.8 km apart. From lighthouse *A*, the compass heading for lighthouse *B* is S72°E. The keeper in each lighthouse sees the same ship. The heading of the ship from lighthouse *A* is N46°E. The heading of the ship from lighthouse *B* is N51°W. How far, to the nearest tenth of a kilometre, is the ship from each lighthouse?

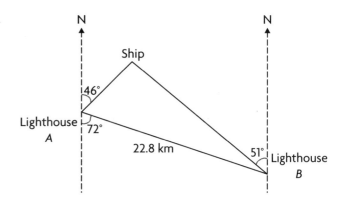

2. Calculate the height, *h*, to the nearest tenth of a metre.

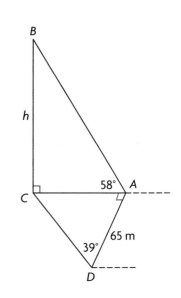

3. An 8.2 m tall telephone pole stands on level ground and leans 3.2° from the vertical. When the pole's shadow is 7 m long, what is the distance, *d*, from the top of the pole to the tip of the shadow, to the nearest tenth of a metre?

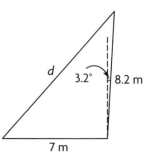

4. Jasleen leaves her campsite at *C* and hikes 4 km in a S70°E direction to *A*. She then turns and hikes 3 km in a N25°E direction to *B*. How far is Jasleen from the campsite? Round your answer to the nearest tenth of a kilometre.

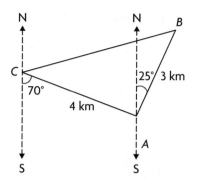

NUMERICAL RESPONSE

5. From the top of a 25 m building, the angle of depression to one parked car is 63° and the angle of depression to another parked car is 52°. The cars are parked in the same line of sight.

The distance between the two cars, to the nearest tenth of a metre,

is _____ m.

6. The diagram shows the measurements Roberta made to determine the height, *CD*, of a skyscraper, using a baseline *AB*.

a) The first thing Roberta needed to know, based on her measurements, was the measure of ∠*ACB*.

∠*ACB* = _____ °

b) Roberta then used this angle measure to determine the length of *AC* from one end of her baseline to the foot of the building.

AC = _____ ... m   (Include three decimal places.)

c) Finally, Roberta was able to determine the height of the skyscraper, using the angle of elevation she had measured.

CD = _____ m   (Round to the nearest metre.)

7. To determine the length of a lake, a surveyor took angle measurements from two positions, *A* and *B*, that are 220 m apart and on opposite sides of the lake. From *B*, the angle between the sight lines to the ends of the lake is 115°, and the angle between the sight lines to *A* and one end of the lake is 96°. From *A*, the angle between the sight lines to the ends of the lake is 53°, and the angle between the sight lines to *B* and the same end of the lake is 10°. Calculate the length of the lake, to the nearest metre. Show your work, including a diagram.

8. Ships *A* and *B* are both somewhere to the southwest of coastal radar station *C*, but on different bearings. Station *C* is experiencing technical problems and can tell the ships only that their bearings are 17° apart. However, ship *B*'s skipper knows she is 8.4 km due south of ship *A* and 14.7 km out from station *C*. What are the bearings of the two ships from station *C*?

Complete the following to summarize the important ideas from this chapter.

Q: How are values of the trigonometric ratios of acute angles related to values of the same ratios for their supplements?

NEED HELP?
• See Lesson 4.1

A: • The sine ratios are related by _____ θ = +_____ (180° − θ).

    • The cosine and tangent ratios are related by

      _____ θ = −_____ (180° − θ) and _____ θ = −_____ (180° − θ).

Q: When should you use the sine law, and when should you use the cosine law?

NEED HELP?
• See Lesson 4.2

A: This table may be helfpul. (The first column has already been completed.)

SSS	SAS	SSA	ASA	AAS
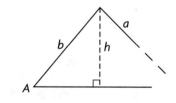				
cosine law				

Q: When is the sine law ambiguous?

NEED HELP?
• See Lesson 4.3

A: • If $\angle A$, the given angle, is obtuse, the unknown $\angle B$ (opposite b) must

     be _____, so at most one _____ is possible.

    • If $\angle A$ is _____ , you can compare the given sides a and b

     with the triangle's _____ , ____ to determine how

     many _____ are possible.

    • The only _____ case, where two triangles are possible, is when

     $\angle A$ is acute and a, b, and h are related by _____.

Q: For solving problems involving triangles, which tools should you use?

NEED HELP?
• See Lesson 4.4

A: • A matching like this between triangle types and tools can be helpful.
(The matching for acute triangles has already been completed.)

     acute triangle   right triangle   obtuse triangle

     sine rule   cosine rule   primary trigonometric ratios

4   Chapter Test

1. Which of the following equations is true?

   A. $\sin 60° = \sin 120°$ **C.** $\sin 45° = -\sin 135°$

   B. $\sin 80° = -\sin 80°$ **D.** all of these

2. Calculate $\tan 78°$ to four decimal places. Predict another expression that equals $\tan 78°$.

   A. -4.7046; $\tan 102°$ **C.** 4.7046; $-\tan 78°$

   B. 4.7046; $-\tan 102°$ **D.** none of these

3. Which law or combination of laws would you use to determine the measure of x in this triangle?

   A. the cosine law, once

   B. the sine law, twice

   C. both the sine law and the cosine law

   D. neither the sine law nor the cosine law

4. Determine the length of x, to the nearest metre.

   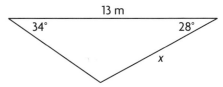

   A. 118 m   **C.** 11 m

   B. 15 m   **D.** 8 m

5. Which set of measurements could result in two possible triangles?

   A. $\angle A = 25°$, $a = 2.5$ m, $b = 6.2$ m   **C.** $\angle A = 96°$, $a = 5.2$ m, $b = 5.0$ m

   B. $\angle A = 135°$, $a = 3.8$ m, $b = 4.0$ m   **D.** $\angle A = 48°$, $a = 7.4$ m, $b = 7.1$ m

6. In $\triangle RST$, $\angle R = 29°$, $s = 5.4$ m, and $t = 5.8$ m.

   Which statement is true for this set of measurements?

   A. This is an *SSA* situation; no triangle is possible.

   B. This is an *SSA* situation; only one triangle is possible.

   C. This is an *SSA* situation; two triangles are possible.

   D. This is not an *SSA* situation; only one triangle is possible.

7. Which would you use to determine the length of x?

    A. the primary trigonometric ratios

    B. the sine law

    C. the cosine law

    D. None of the above; x cannot be determined.

8. Determine the measure of x, to the nearest degree.

    A. $10°$ **C.** $11°$

    B. $19°$ **D.** None of these;
                                         x cannot be determined.

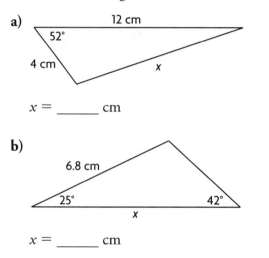

NUMERICAL RESPONSE

9. Determine the length of x, to the nearest tenth of a centimetre.

    a)

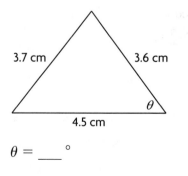

    $x =$ _____ cm

    b)

    $x =$ _____ cm

10. Determine the measure of θ, to the nearest degree.

    $\theta =$ ___ $°$

11. Determine the length of x to the nearest tenth of a centimetre and the measure of θ to the nearest degree.

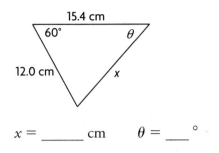

$x = $ _____ cm $\qquad \theta = $ ____ °

WRITTEN RESPONSE

12. In $\triangle ABC$, $\angle A = 47°$, $a = 3.5$ cm, and $b = 5.0$ cm. Determine the number of triangles (zero, one, or two) that are possible. Draw a diagram to support your answer.

13. A mass is suspended on a length of cord. The ends of the cord are attached to the ceiling 1.4 m apart. The angles formed by the ceiling and the cord are 26° and 32°. Determine the length of the cord, to the nearest tenth of a metre.

14. In ΔPQR, $\angle P = 41°$, $p = 35$ mm, and $r = 47$ mm.

    a) Predict, with reasons, how many triangles are possible for this situation.

    b) Determine the area of each possible triangle, to the nearest square millimetre.

15. Two beams support part of a platform.
- At their upper ends, the beams meet the platform at the same point.
- The beams are intended to rest on the ground at different points, but on the same horizontal level.
- The beams will both be in the same vertical plane.
- The main beam is 12.5 m long and is at an angle of 38° to the horizontal.
- The support beam is 7.2 m long.

    a) Using a sketch, describe the problem with this design as it stands.

    b) The design is revised by increasing the support beam's length to 8.4 m long. What is the problem with the revised design? How could it be fixed without changing either of the beam lengths again?

Chapter 5 Statistical Reasoning

Getting Started

1. Reorganize this data set in a way that would help you determine the mean, median, mode, range, and any outliers.

   Masses of baseballs, in grams:

   145.3   144.7   143.9   145.8   144.2   146.3   148.0   144.7   145.5   145.0

2. Match each term with the appropriate statistical value for the data in question 1.

   a) mean   ___
   b) median ___
   c) mode   ___
   d) outlier ___
   e) range   ___

   i)   145.0
   ii) 1.12
   iii) 144.7
   iv) 145.15

   v)   4.1
   vi) 145.34
   vii) 148.0

3. a) Determine the mean, median, and mode of the data.

Heights of Tomato Plants (cm)
45, 48, 42, 43, 43, 47, 49, 37

   b) Which value might be considered an outlier?   ___ cm

   c) Discard this outlier and determine the new mean, median, and mode.

   d) Which measure of central tendency is most affected by an outlier? Which is least affected? Explain your answers.

   > **TIP**
   > The mean, median, and mode are the most commonly used measures of central tendency.

4. Which measure of central tendency would be most useful for analyzing data in each of the following situations?

   a) the annual incomes of college graduates aged 30   _____

   b) the number of runs scored by a professional baseball player   _____

   c) the sizes of running shoes stocked by a sporting goods store   _____

5. This line plot shows the daily numbers of new clients arriving at a tax accounting firm throughout March.

New Clients, Daily

Number per day

a) On how many days did at least 3 new clients arrive? ___

b) What is the mode of this data set? ___

c) What is the range of this data set? ___

d) Identify any outliers in the data. ___

e) What is the median of the data? ___

6. Ravi and Kumiko work together and catch the same bus to work every day from the same stop. Ravi says the mean travel time on the bus is 17.3 min, but Kumiko thinks it is 18.2 min. Suggest a reason for their disagreement.

7. Long jumpers Gary and Jaycee both have the same mean distance of 7.23 m. The range of Gary's jumps is 0.67 m, while Jaycee's range is 1.25 cm.

a) Explain how this is possible.

b) Who likely has the longer personal best and why?

8. Patricia recorded the duration, rounded to the nearest 5 min, that she spent on the phone with her best friend, Kara, each day for a month.

Time (min)	25	30	35	40	45	50	55
Frequency	1	0	0	3	5	7	6

Time (min)	60	65	70	75	80	85	90
Frequency	9	8	10	8	5	3	1

a) Construct a line plot of the data.

b) Comment on the distribution of the data. Identify any outliers in the data.

5.1 Exploring Data

YOU WILL NEED
- ruler
- graph paper OR computer spreadsheet software

Keep in Mind

▸ The mean, median, and mode may not be enough to represent or compare two or more sets of data. Looking at how the data is spread around the mean or median of a set of data can help you draw inferences.

▸ When comparing two or more sets of data, organize the data, and then look at similarities and differences.

Example

Greenhouse gas (GHG) emissions (in tonnes) per person were recorded from 1990 to 2005 for Canada and the United States.

a) Construct a graph to illustrate the GHG emissions for both countries.

b) Determine the range, mean, median, and mode for the average GHG emissions in the two countries.

c) How do the two countries compare in the amount of GHG emissions?

GHG Emissions (t/Person)		
Year	Canada	U.S.
1990	18	22
1991	18	21
1992	16	21
1993	19	21
1994	19	21
1995	27	21
1996	20	21
1997	19	21
1998	26	21
1999	21	21
2000	20	22
2001	20	21
2002	25	21
2003	24	21
2004	26	21
2005	22	21

Solution

a) The data was organized by country and year. I used spreadsheet software to create a line graph of the data so I could compare trends.

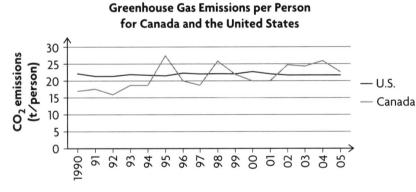

b) To calculate the range, I used this equation:

range = greatest emission value − least emission value

Canada: range = 27 t − 18 t, or 9 t   U.S.: range = 22 t − 21 t, or 1 t

To calculate the mean emission value, I used this equation:

$$\text{mean} = \frac{\text{sum of emission values}}{\text{number of values}}$$

TIP

Spreadsheet software has functions that calculate the mean, median, mode, and range of a set of data.

Canada: mean = $\dfrac{340\ t}{16}$, or 21.25 t   U.S.: mean = $\dfrac{338\ t}{16}$, or 21.125 t

To calculate the median, I ordered the data for each country from least to greatest. Then, I determined the middle value of each data set.

Canada: median = $\dfrac{20\ t + 20\ t}{2}$, or 20 t   U.S.: median = $\dfrac{21\ t + 21\ t}{2}$, or 21 t

To calculate the mode, I looked for the most frequently repeated values.

Canada: mode = 19 t or 20 t   U.S.: mode = 21 t

c) I examined the trends in the graph and the values from part b) to compare the data from the two countries. The graph showed that the United States was more consistent in GHG emissions from 1990 to 2005. Canada started off with lower emissions per person; then emissions increased from 1994 to 1996, 1997 to 1999, and 2001 and beyond. Canada and the United States had approximately the same mean output of emissions. Canada had a lower median output but a greater range of emission levels.

Practice

1. a) Order the lifespan data, in thousands of hours, for each of these two brands of compact fluorescent light bulbs

Brand A (10³ h)		Brand B (10³ h)	
6.0	8.0	6.1	7.5
6.5	7.5	6.0	7.5
7.0	7.8	6.5	7.5
7.3	6.9	7.2	7.5

b) Determine the range, mean, median, and mode of each brand.

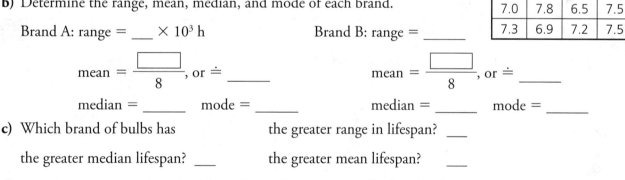

c) Which brand of bulbs has   the greater range in lifespan? ___

the greater median lifespan? ___   the greater mean lifespan?   ___

d) Based on these statistics, which brand would you choose, if either? Explain.

WRITTEN RESPONSE

2. The heights of two groups of female high school students is compared. Which group likely has the lower average age? Which group likely contains the youngest students?

	Group A (cm)	Group B (cm)
mean	163.3	163.2
median	164.5	163.0
mode	163	—
range	29	37

5.2 Frequency Tables, Histograms, and Frequency Polygons

YOU WILL NEED
• ruler

Keep in Mind

▶ To display a large set of data, you can use a histogram or a frequency polygon.

  • To compare two or more data sets in frequency tables, use frequency polygons.

▶ For a histogram:

  • Plot frequency data on the vertical axis and intervals on the horizontal axis.

  • The graph looks like a bar graph with no spaces between the bars.

▶ For a frequency polygon:

  • Plot frequency data on the vertical axis and intervals on the horizontal axis.

  • The graph looks like a line graph with the midpoints of each interval joined.

Example

The table shows the number of earthquakes measuring 7 and greater on the Richter scale that occurred from 1980 to 2009.

a) Determine a suitable interval size for the data.

b) Create a frequency table to organize the data.

c) Display the data using a histogram and a frequency polygon.

d) Compare the two graphs. Describe how the data is distributed.

Year	#	Year	#	Year	#
1980	14	1990	18	2000	15
1981	13	1991	16	2001	16
1982	10	1992	13	2002	13
1983	14	1993	12	2003	15
1984	8	1994	13	2004	16
1985	14	1995	20	2005	11
1986	6	1996	15	2006	11
1987	11	1997	16	2007	18
1988	8	1998	12	2008	12
1989	7	1999	18	2009	17

Solution

a) The data is for 31 years. I decided to organize the data into ten intervals of 4 years.

b) I determined the frequency of earthquakes for each interval. The year data is discrete, not continuous, so it was clear which interval each year falls into.

Interval	#
1980–1982	37
1983–1985	32
1986–1988	25
1989–1991	43
1992–1994	38
1995–1997	51
1998–2000	45
2001–2003	44
2004–2006	38
2007–2009	47

TIP

Create a frequency table for a large set of data:

• Organize the data into a number of equal intervals, and count the number of values that fall within each interval.

• Use between 5 and 12 intervals.

• For continuous data, include an endpoint such as 100 in the interval 50–100, not the interval 100–150.

c) I created a histogram to display the frequency versus the year intervals. I then joined the midpoints of the intervals with a line to create a frequency polygon.

d) The same trend is shown in both graphs. The least number of earthquakes occurred from 1986 to 1988. The greatest number of earthquakes occurred from 1995 to 1997. The trend may indicate that the number of earthquakes measuring 7 and greater on the Richter scale is generally increasing with time, or that this number is simply higher after about 1990.

World Wide Earthquakes (M7 >)

Frequency vs. Year

Practice

1. Jerry uses the Internet to help him complete his homework. He recorded the time he spent online each day for one month. He grouped the data in a frequency table.

   a) On the first day of the month, he was online for 1.45 h. In which interval did he record this time?

   Interval: _____ h

   b) Use the grid provided to create a frequency polygon representing the data. Describe how the data is distributed.

Internet Time (h)	Frequency
0.5–1.0	0
1.0–1.5	4
1.5–2.0	6
2.0–2.5	7
2.5–3.0	8
3.0–3.5	1
3.5–4.0	1
4.0–4.5	1
4.5–5.0	0
5.0–5.5	2
5.5–6.0	1

2. A Macintosh apple orchard has 40 trees with these heights, given in metres.

1.1	1.3	1.4	1.2	1.5	1.7	1.6	1.3
1.5	2.0	2.1	1.8	1.9	2.3	2.2	2.1
1.7	2.0	2.2	2.5	2.3	2.4	1.9	1.8
3.1	3.2	3.3	2.7	2.8	2.6	2.5	2.3
3.0	2.4	2.7	2.4	2.6	2.8	2.2	2.1

   a) Complete this frequency table to organize the heights into eight equal intervals.

Height (m)	Frequency
1.0–1.3	4
1.3–1.6	

b) Use the grid provided to construct a histogram of the data.

c) Which range of heights occurs most frequently? Which occurs least frequently?

3. Farooq is an apprentice at a bakery. The times he spends after school at the bakery, in hours, over one month are shown.

2.5	3.0	3.5	4.0	5.0	5.0
1.5	2.0	3.0	3.0	5.0	6.0
1.0	2.5	2.5	2.5	4.0	4.0
3.0	3.0	3.0	2.0	3.5	7.0
3.0	2.0	2.5	2.5	7.0	8.0

a) Suggest an appropriate interval width to represent how the data is distributed.

b) Complete this frequency distribution table.

c) Use the grid provided to construct a histogram of the data.

Time (h)	Frequency

d) Describe how the data is distributed.

4. Tamiko works after school at her father's convenience store. The hours she worked some days after school and on weekends in February are shown.

2.0	2.5	3.0	4.0	2.0	2.5	3.5	4.0
3.0	2.5	3.0	4.0	1.0	0.5	2.5	3.0
5.0	7.0	4.5	6.0	3.5	4.0	8.0	7.5

a) Suggest an appropriate interval width for this data. Justify your choice.

b) Determine the midpoint of each interval you have chosen to represent the data values in each interval.

c) Use the grid provided to draw a frequency polygon showing the distribution of the time Tamiko worked.

5. a) As of July 1, 2010, the total population of Nunavut was 33 220. On the grid provided, draw frequency polygons to compare the populations of males and females in Nunavut.

b) Examine the graph. Describe any differences you notice in the populations of the two sexes.

Age Group	Male (%)	Female (%)
0–4	5.8	5.2
5–9	5.4	4.9
10–14	5.3	5.0
15–19	5.0	4.8
20–24	4.9	4.5
25–29	4.0	4.3
30–34	4.0	3.7
35–39	3.4	3.2
40–44	3.2	3.6
45–49	3.1	2.7
50–54	2.7	2.2
55–59	2.0	1.7
60–64	1.3	1.1
65+	1.6	1.5

Statistics Canada

MULTIPLE CHOICE

6. What do histograms and frequency polygons have in common?

A. They show frequency data.

B. They connect interval midpoints.

C. They show percents.

D. They have bars.

WRITTEN RESPONSE

7. When and why should histograms and frequency polygons be used to display data?

8. The mathematics test scores for Kara's class were grouped and displayed using this frequency polygon.

a) What interval width was used when grouping the data?

b) Kara says the most frequently occurring test score was 75%. Is she correct? Explain your answer.

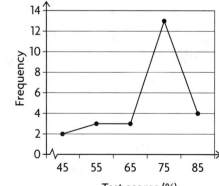

Mathematics Test Results

5.3 Standard Deviation

YOU WILL NEED
- calculator OR computer spreadsheet software

Keep in Mind

▸ Standard deviation, σ, is a measure of how spread out a data set is around the mean.

- A low standard deviation means the data is close to the mean.
- A high standard deviation means the data is scattered farther away from the mean.

▸ To calculate the standard deviation for a data set with n values:

- Square the difference of each data value, x, from the mean, $\bar{x}$; use this expression: $(x - \bar{x})^2$.

- Determine the mean of all values of $(x - \bar{x})^2$; use this expression: $\dfrac{\sum (x - \bar{x})^2}{n}$.

- The square root of the mean of all $(x - \bar{x})^2$ is the standard deviation; use this expression: $\sqrt{\dfrac{\sum (x - \bar{x})^2}{n}}$.

- For grouped data, the midpoints are used as the x values.

Example 1

Rhonda works in human resources at a car plant. She records the number of overtime hours worked in a month by 35 employees.

1.5	2.0	3.0	4.5	5.0	6.0	7.5
2.0	1.0	2.5	3.0	4.0	2.5	3.5
5.0	2.5	1.5	2.0	3.0	5.0	4.0
6.0	3.5	4.0	5.0	4.0	4.5	6.0
8.5	9.0	8.0	7.0	6.0	10.0	12.0

a) Determine the mean and the standard deviation of the number of overtime hours, to the nearest tenth.

b) Group the data into reasonable intervals. Determine the mean and standard deviation of the grouped data, to the nearest tenth.

c) How do the means and standard deviations compare? What do the results mean?

Solution

a) I entered the hours into computer spreadsheet software. I used the software to calculate the mean and standard deviation for the ungrouped data.

mean: $\bar{x} = 4.7$ h   standard deviation: $\sigma = 2.6$ h

b) I grouped the data into intervals of 2 h, starting at 0.0 h for six intervals. I calculated the midpoint of each interval. Then I determined the total number of hours worked for each interval.

Overtime Hours	Frequency, f	Midpoint of Interval, x	$f \cdot x$
0.0–2.0	6	1.0	6.0
2.0–4.0	12	3.0	36.0
4.0–6.0	10	5.0	50.0
6.0–8.0	3	7.0	21.0
8.0–10.0	3	9.0	27.0
10.0–12.0	1	11.0	11.0
	35		**151.0**

mean: $\bar{x} = 4.3$ h   standard deviation: $\sigma = 2.5$ h

c) The mean for the ungrouped data was greater than the mean for the grouped data. The standard deviations for the ungrouped and grouped data were about the same. The mean for the ungrouped data is a more accurate representation of the average number of overtime hours worked. The standard deviations show that the data was scattered from the mean for both types of data.

Example 2

Randall wants to adopt a cat from a local animal shelter. He is looking to adopt a Persian cat or a Burmese cat. He searched 10 different Internet sites for the lifespan of each breed. His results are shown.

Persian Lifespan (in years)

11   13   14   15   15   16   18   14   13   14

Burmese Lifespan (in years)

15   16   10   14   16   15   18   15   11   16

Which breed of cat should Randall adopt and why?

Solution

Step 1. I used computer spreadsheet software to calculate the mean and the standard deviation for the lifespan of each breed of cat. I rounded the values to one decimal place.

> Persian: mean: $\bar{x} = 14.3$ years   Burmese: mean: $\bar{x} = 14.6$ years
> standard deviation: $\sigma = 1.8$ years   standard deviation: $\sigma = 2.9$ years

Step 2. The Persian breed has a mean lifespan of 14.3 years, with a standard deviation of 1.8 years. The Burmese breed has a mean lifespan of 14.6 years, with a standard deviation of 2.9 years. The mean lifespans for the two breeds are similar. However, the standard deviation is less for Persians than for Burmese. So, a Persian cat's lifespan will generally be closer to the mean than a Burmese cat's will. If Randall does not want to risk owning a cat with an unpredictable lifespan, he should probably adopt a Persian cat.

Practice

1. Callie researched the prices of two different brands of jeans at four stores.

   a) Complete the table to determine the standard deviation of jean prices.

Store	Jean A ($)	Jean B ($)
1	45.99	46.59
2	46.49	45.99
3	44.99	45.29
4	45.99	44.99

Store	Jean A ($)	$(x - \bar{x})^2$	Jean B ($)	$(x - \bar{x})^2$
1	45.99		46.59	
2	46.49		45.99	
3	44.99		45.29	
4	45.99		44.99	
Σx				
$\bar{x}$		—		—
$\sqrt{\dfrac{\Sigma (x - \bar{x})^2}{n}}$		—		—

   b) Which brand of jeans had the more consistent prices over the four stores? Explain how you know.

Use technology to determine the mean and standard deviation in questions 2 to 6.

2. Candice is in a video game league. The game scores for her and four other team members are shown.

   a) Determine the mean and standard deviation of the game scores for the players, rounded to the nearest thousand.

   b) Describe the performances of the players.

Scores (100 000's)	Frequency
1–2	1
2–3	4
3–4	7
4–5	12
5–6	20
6–7	25
7–8	21
8–9	2

3. Three groups of students recorded the number of books read for a literacy fundraiser.

   a) Determine the mean and standard deviation of each group, to the nearest tenth.

Group	Number of Books Read
1	10, 12, 10, 9, 8, 10, 12, 14, 15
2	12, 8, 10, 11, 12, 9, 9, 8, 10
3	11, 13, 12, 10, 7, 9, 9, 9, 12

b) Which group performed best? Explain your answer.

4. Brendan and Jordan pick bushels of apples for a local farmer. The farmer records how many bushels each person fills each hour.

Hour	1	2	3	4	5	6	7
Brendan	5	6	6	5	7	6	5
Jordan	6	7	8	4	5	5	6

a) Which person picks more bushels of apples per hour?

b) Who is more consistent? Explain your answer.

5. Jarome Iginla's points for the Calgary Flames from 1997 to 2010 are shown.

a) Determine the mean and standard deviation of the points Jarome Iginla earned from 1997 to 2010, to one decimal place.

b) Determine the effect on the mean and standard deviation when the two lowest data values are removed from the data set.

Season	Points
1997–98	32
1998–99	51
1999–00	63
2000–01	71
2001–02	96
2002–03	67
2003–04	73
2004–05	67
2005–06	94
2006–07	98
2007–08	89
2008–09	69
2009–10	86

6. Mario is a baker. He orders flour from two different companies. He recorded the masses of 88 kg bags he received over the course of a month. His results are shown. Which company should Mario continue buying flour from, and why? Assume that both brands of flour sell for the same price.

Brand A: Masses of 88 kg Bags (kg)

88.1 87.9 88.0 88.2 87.9 87.9 88.1 88.2 88.3 88.4 88.1

Brand B: Masses of 88 kg Bags (kg)

88.0 88.1 88.0 87.9 88.2 87.9 88.0 88.0 88.2 88.2 88.1

7. Two tutoring services monitored the number of hours per month that a random sample of their clients spent studying.

Ever Study	
Hours	**Frequency**
0–4	5
4–8	10
8–12	25
12–16	30
16–20	40

Elite Education	
Hours	**Frequency**
0–2	1
2–4	1
4–6	7
6–8	8
8–10	9
10–12	10
12–14	20
14–16	25
16–18	24
18–20	20

a) Determine the mean and standard deviation of the hours per month for clients of each service, to one decimal place.

b) Which service is more successful at encouraging its clients to study more consistently? How do you know?

8. What is the standard deviation for this set of data, to one decimal place?

| 1.2 | 1.5 | 2.0 | 3.1 | 1.8 | 2.2 | 2.4 | 2.8 |

A. 0.8   **B.** 0.7   **C.** 0.6   **D.** none of the above

WRITTEN RESPONSE

9. The means and standard deviations of math scores on a test of two classes are shown. Which class performed better on the test? Explain your answer.

Class	$\bar{x}$	σ
A	89.5	2.7
B	90.2	7.5

10. Tammy works as a waitress. She records the amount she receives in tips each day she works in a month, rounded to the nearest dollar.

| 25 | 30 | 35 | 45 | 50 | 40 | 34 | 45 | 20 | 30 |

| 40 | 50 | 35 | 50 | 20 | 15 | 30 | 40 | 50 | 60 |

a) Determine the mean and the standard deviation for the amount of tips, to the nearest dollar.

b) Group the data into reasonable intervals. Determine the mean and standard deviation of the grouped data, to the nearest dollar.

Tips ($)	Frequency, f	Midpoint of Interval, x	f · x

c) How do the means and standard deviations compare? Interpret the results.

5.4 The Normal Distribution

YOU WILL NEED
- calculator
- ruler

Keep in Mind

▶ A set of data that is normally distributed has a symmetric bell shape when graphed as a frequency polygon. Generally, measurements of living things (such as mass, height, and lifespan) have this type of distribution.

▶ The properties of a normal distribution are

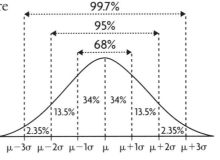

- The mean, median, and mode are close to equal and fall at the vertical line of symmetry.

- The amounts of data within one, two, and three standard deviations of the mean are as shown in the graph.

- The area under the curve can be considered as equal to 1, since it represents 100% of the data.

Example

The ages of the grandparents of Elaine's classmates were collected.

65	70	60	74	71	75	56	68
85	72	82	74	61	75	83	62
72	64	81	71	90	71	78	73
65	74	69	71	70	76	80	69

a) Does the data approximate a normal curve? Sketch a graph to help you explain.

b) Hal is a new student in Elaine's class. What is the likelihood that his grandparent is at least 80 years old?

Solution

a) I checked the "fit" with a normal curve:

Step 1. I calculated the mean and standard deviation for the ages.

mean: $\mu = 72.1$ years

standard deviation: $\sigma = 7.4$ years

Step 2. I created a frequency distribution table so that I could draw a frequency polygon.

Interval (years)	Midpoint (years)	Frequency
55–60	57.5	1
60–65	62.5	4
65–70	67.5	5
70–75	72.5	12
75–80	77.5	4
80–85	82.5	4
85–90	87.5	1
90–95	92.5	1

TIP

For age data, include (e.g.) 55 through 59 in the interval 55–60, since "59" could mean 59 years and 364 days. This gives a midpoint of 57.5.

Step 3. I plotted the midpoint of each interval and joined the points for my frequency polygon. The curve looks like a normal distribution.

Step 4. I checked the percents of data within one and two standard deviations of the mean. Since the percents are close to 68% and 95% for the two intervals around the mean, the data has a normal distribution.

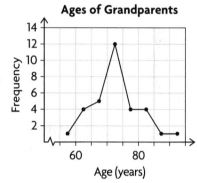

Ages of Grandparents

Range	Age Range	Percent of Data
$\mu - 1\sigma$ to $\mu + 1\sigma$	64.7 to 79.5	$\frac{21}{32} \doteq 66\%$
$\mu - 2\sigma$ to $\mu + 2\sigma$	57.3 to 86.9	$\frac{30}{32} \doteq 94\%$

b) 80 years old or more corresponds exactly to being at least one standard deviation above the mean. Since the data is normal, the probability that Hal's grandparent is at least 80 years old is about $\frac{1}{2}$ (100% − 68%), or 16%.

Practice

1. The ages of members of a seniors' lawn bowling club are normally distributed. The mean is 65 years and the standard deviation is 3 years. What percent of the bowlers is in each of the following age groups?

   a) between 59 and 65 years old, inclusive

   b) between 68 and 74 years old, inclusive

c) older than 74 years

2. A teacher is analyzing these class results for three history tests. The results of all three tests were normally distributed.

   a) Describe and compare the normal curves for tests 1 and 2.

Test	Mean (μ)	Standard Deviation (σ)
1	85	2.5
2	85	4.9
3	75	2.5

   b) Compare the normal curves for tests 1 and 3.

   c) Determine Jasmine's marks on each test, given the information. Round to the nearest percent.

Test	Jasmine's Mark	Jasmine's Mark (%)
1	$\mu + 2\sigma$	
2	$\mu - 1.5\sigma$	
3	$\mu + 3.5\sigma$	

3. Is the data in each set normally distributed? Use a frequency polygon to help you explain.

   a)

Interval	11–15	16–20	21–25	26–30	31–35	36–40
Frequency	4	6	15	18	9	4
Midpoint						

   b)

Interval	20–24	25–29	30–34	35–39	40–44	45–49
Frequency	1	5	5	2	3	4
Midpoint						

c)

Interval	1–6	7–12	13–18	19–24	25–30	31–36
Frequency	1	8	5	8	4	4
Midpoint						

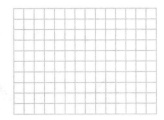

NUMERICAL RESPONSE

4. Reggie recorded the points he scored playing basketball during the year.

22	24	23	10	0	0	3	36	28	15	0	28
32	12	11	10	31	10	32	29	14	22	21	30

a) Determine the mean and standard deviation of the set of data.

b) Complete the frequency table.

Left Boundary (years)	Interval (years)	Midpoint (years)	Frequency
$\mu - 4\sigma = -25.2$	$-25.2 - (-14.4)$	-19.8	0
$\mu - 3\sigma = -14.4$	$-14.4 - (-3.6)$	-9.0	0
$\mu - 2\sigma = -3.6$	$-3.6 - 7.2$		
$\mu - 1\sigma =$			
$\mu =$			
$\mu + 1\sigma =$			
$\mu + 2\sigma =$			
$\mu + 3\sigma =$			

c) Create a frequency polygon, using the grid provided.

d) Are Reggie's basketball scores normally distributed? Explain your answer.

5. A manufacturer offers a warranty on its toasters. The toaster has a mean lifespan of 6.5 years, with a standard deviation of 0.5 years. How long should the toasters be covered by the warranty, if the manufacturer wants to repair no more than 2.5% of the toasters sold?

Length of warranty: _____ years

5.5 Z-Scores

Keep in Mind

▸ A standard normal distribution has a mean of 0 and a standard deviation of 1.

▸ A z-score is a standardized value that indicates the number of standard deviations a data value is above or below the mean.

$z = \dfrac{x - \mu}{\sigma}$, where x is the data value, μ is the mean of the data set, and σ is the standard deviation.

▸ Z-scores can be used to compare different sets of data that do not have the same mean and/or standard deviation.

▸ A positive z-score indicates a data point above the mean. A negative z-score indicates a data point below the mean.

Example 1

The mathematics test scores in Ramone's class are normally distributed. The mean is 80, with a standard deviation of 5. Callie is in Ramone's class. She scored 83 on the test. Compare her score with the rest of the class scores.

Solution

Step 1. I sketched a normal curve. Then I determined the test scores for one, two, and three standard deviations from the mean. I marked these intervals on my sketch. Then I drew a dashed line to indicate a test score of 83.

Step 2. I calculated the z-score for 83:

$$z = \frac{x - \mu}{\sigma}$$

$$z = \frac{83 - 80}{5}$$

$$z = 0.6$$

Step 3. I located the z-score on a standard normal distribution curve.

Step 4. I used a z-score table to determine the percent of people who scored less than 83. This is equivalent to the area under the curve to the left of 0.6 on the standard normal curve. I used the 0.6 row and the 0.00 column of the table. The value is 0.7257. So, 72.57% of the people have a score less than Callie's.

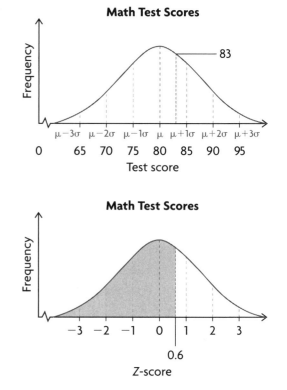

Copyright © 2012 by Nelson Education Ltd.

Example 2

The mean lifespan of a non-stick frying pan is two years, with a standard deviation of 0.5 years. Karnie is an avid cook and wants to replace her frying pan after 65% of its natural life. When should she replace the frying pan? Assume that lifespans of this type of frying pan are normally distributed.

Solution

Step 1. I sketched a standard normal curve. I shaded the area under the curve that represents 65%.

Step 2. I used a *z*-score table to determine an area value close to 0.65. The *z*-score that represents an area of 0.65 is about halfway between 0.38 and 0.39, or 0.385.

Step 3. I substituted the values I knew into the *z*-score formula and solved for *x*.

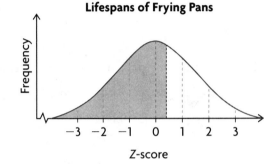

Lifespans of Frying Pans

$$z = \frac{x - \mu}{\sigma}$$

$$0.385 = \frac{x - 2.0}{0.5}$$

$$0.1925 = x - 2.0$$

$$2.1925 = x$$

Karnie should replace her frying pan after 2 years.

Practice

1. Determine the *z*-score for each value of *x*.

a) $\bar{x} = 200, \sigma = 25.4, x = 250$ c) $\bar{x} = 18, \sigma = 2.2, x = 17$

b) $\bar{x} = 260, \sigma = 12.5, x = 289$ d) $\bar{x} = 3.2, \sigma = 0.3, x = 2.7$

2. Using a z-score table, determine the percent of data to the left of each z-score in question 1.

3. Determine the percent of data between each pair of z-scores.

a) $z = -2.12$ and $z = -1.33$ b) $z = 0.85$ and $z = 1.24$

4. What z-score is required for each situation?

a) 15% of the data is to the right of the z-score.

b) 15% of the data is to the left of the z-score.

c) 57% of the data is above the z-score.

5. A vinyl tile manufacturer produces floor tile that has an average thickness of 5 mm, with a standard deviation of 0.2 mm. For premium floor tiles, the flooring must have a thickness between 4.8 mm and 5.4 mm. What percent, to the nearest whole number, of the total production can be sold as premium tiles? Thicknesses of both types of tiles are assumed normally distributed.

6. A sample of males across the country who rode motorcycles were surveyed. Their ages were recorded and the ages assumed to be normally distributed. The mean age was 35 years, with a standard deviation of 6.3 years.

Age (years)	Number of Males (%)
16–20	2.0
21–25	7.7
26–30	9.2
31–35	11.4
36–40	23.4
41–45	24.3
46–50	11.7
51–55	8.1
56–60	2.2
Total	100

a) Determine the percent of males who were younger than 45 years.

b) Determine the percent of males who were younger than 21 years.

MULTIPLE CHOICE

7. Which formula is used to calculate a z-score?

A. $z = \dfrac{x - \sigma}{\mu}$ B. $z = \dfrac{\mu - x}{\sigma}$ C. $z = \dfrac{x}{\sigma}$ D. $z = \dfrac{x - \mu}{\sigma}$

WRITTEN RESPONSE

8. Tyrone is considering a career in business, because he does well in accounting. He also does well in chemistry and has thought of becoming a chemical engineer. The marks for both these subjects in all classes at his school are normally distributed.

Subject	Tests Results (%)		Tyrone's Marks (%)
	μ	σ	
Accounting	75	5.2	90
Chemistry	78	6.1	92

a) Determine the z-score for each of Tyrone's marks.

b) In each subject, what percent of Tyrone's peers have marks less than his?

c) Which subject is Tyrone better in, relative to his peers?

5.6 Confidence Intervals

YOU WILL NEED
- calculator
- z-score tables
(pages 294 to 295)

Keep in Mind

▶ A confidence interval is a range in which a polled or surveyed value, x, is predicted to lie. A confidence interval has the form

$$x \pm \text{margin of error}$$

where the margin of error is expressed as a percent.

▶ A confidence interval is used to make predictions about a population, based on samples from the population.

▶ A confidence interval is affected by the margin of error and sample size.

- If the sample size stays the same, the margin of error increases as the confidence level increases.

- If the confidence level stays the same, the margin of error decreases as the sample size increases.

Example

A telephone survey of 500 randomly selected people was conducted in an urban area. The survey determined that 35% of Canadians from 24 to 45 years of age have an electronic book reader. The results are accurate within plus or minus 5 percent points, 19 times out of 20. The number of people in this age range in Canada in 2011 was approximately 8.7 million. It is assumed that the ages are normally distributed.

a) What range of people own an electronic book reader?

b) Determine the certainty of the results.

c) How many people in Canada between the ages of 24 and 45 years would you expect to own an electronic book reader, based on this survey's results?

Solution

a) The surveyed value was 35%. The margin of error for the data was ±5%.
I inserted this value into the format for a confidence interval.

$$35\% \pm 5\%$$

$$35\% - 5\% = 30\% \qquad 35\% + 5\% = 40\%$$

The confidence interval is 30% to 40%.

b) The survey results are accurate 19 times out of 20. This means the confidence level is $\frac{19}{20}$, or 95%, or there is a 5% probability of error for this result. So, if the survey were conducted 100 times, 95 times out of 100 the percent of people in the population who owned an electronic book reader would be between 30% and 40%.

c) I used the confidence interval 35% ± 5% to determine the number of people who own an electronic book reader.

$$8\ 700\ 000 \times 35\% = 3\ 045\ 000$$

$$8\ 700\ 000 \times 5\% = 435\ 000$$

$$3\ 045\ 000 - 435\ 000 = 2\ 610\ 000$$

$$3\ 045\ 000 + 435\ 000 = 3\ 480\ 000$$

It can be said with 95% confidence that between 2 610 000 and 3 480 000 Canadians from ages 24 to 45 have an electronic book reader.

Practice

For the following questions, assume that the data approximates a normal distribution.

1. A 2010 poll determined that 65% of the people agreed that wind power should be used over hydro power. The results of the survey are accurate within ±2.9 percent points, 19 times out of 20.

a) State the confidence level.

b) Determine the confidence interval.

c) The population of Nunavut was 33 220 in 2010. State the range of the number of Nunavut residents who agreed that wind power should be used over hydro power for generating electricity.

2. A fruit juice company takes a random sample to check the volume of cartons of juice. For a sample of 300 cartons, the mean volume is 1.1 L, with a margin of error of ±0.1 L. The result is accurate 99% of the time.

a) State the confidence interval for the mean volume of the juice cartons.

b) Three other samples were taken using the same confidence level, but the margin of error for each sample was mixed up in the report to the company's quality-control department. Complete the table by matching the correct margin of error with each sample size. Give a reason for your answer.

Sample Size (cartons)	Margin of Error (L) (mixed up)	Margin of Error (L) (correct)
75	±0.15	
150	±0.05	
500	±0.20	

3. An advertisement for a body lotion claims that 80% of its users reported smoother and softer skin after two weeks. The results of the survey are accurate within 3.5 percent points, 4 out of 5 times.

a) State the confidence level.

b) Determine the confidence interval for the survey results.

c) If all 2500 people at a shopping mall used this lotion, determine the range of the mean number of people who could expect smoother and softer skin after two weeks.

4. Compact fluorescent light (CFL) bulbs can save on electricity use and costs, but they contain a small amount of mercury. Disposal of these bulbs in landfill can be hazardous to the environment. In a recent survey, 95% of Canadians surveyed said they would not place spent bulbs in their garbage if there were conveniently located disposal sites. The survey is considered accurate within 3.7 percent points, 9 times out of 10.

a) Determine the confidence level and confidence interval.

b) If 8 500 000 Canadian households use CFL bulbs, what is the range of the number of households who would use the disposal sites?

5. A poll was conducted to asked shoppers the following question: If you had a choice of car A or car B, which would you buy? The results were 55% for car A and 45% for car B. The results are accurate within 4.2 percent points, 17 times out of 20. Which car will be sold the most?

6. SportzGoodz produces tennis balls. The tennis balls have a mean diameter of 6.7 cm, with a standard deviation of 0.05 cm. For quality control, tennis balls with a diameter in the range of 6.65 cm to 6.75 cm are acceptable.

a) What is the confidence interval?

b) What is the margin of error?

7. Which is the correct expression for the confidence interval "sixty percent with a three point five percent-point margin of error"?

    A. $60\% \pm 3.5$ **B.** $60\% \pm 3.5\%$ **C.** 60 ± 3.5 **D.** $60 \pm 3.5\%$

NUMERICAL RESPONSE

8. In a recent poll, 34% of Canadians said they would vote for the Conservative Party in the next federal election. The results are considered accurate within 3.2 percent points.

The confidence interval for these results is _____ $\pm$ _____

or _____ to _____.

WRITTEN RESPONSE

9. In a recent poll, 28% of Canadians said they would vote for the New Democratic Party in the next federal election. The results are considered accurate within 3.2 percent points. The results are accurate 19 times out of 20.

    a) State the confidence level.

    b) Determine the confidence interval.

    c) In 2011, the population of Canada was approximately 33 740 000. Determine the range for the number of people whom you would expect to vote for the New Democratic Party.

Complete the following to summarize the important ideas from this chapter.

Q: How can you compare two data sets in terms of their dispersion?

NEED HELP?
• See Lessons 5.2, 5.3

A1: Graph the frequency _____ for both data sets on the same graph and visually compare their distributions.

A2: Calculate the _____ _____ of each data set.

A high (or low) _____ _____ indicates a _____

(or _____) dispersed set.

Q: Why is it useful to determine whether a set of grouped data is well approximated by a normal curve? What properties does this curve have? What is the significance of a z-score?

NEED HELP?
• See Lessons 5.4, 5.5

A: • If the data set is well approximated, you can make _____

based on properties of _____ curves.

• A normal distribution is _____ about its mean, which

also equals the _____ and the mode. About ___%

of the data is within one _____ _____ of

the mean, and about ___% is within two _____

_____ of the mean.

• A z-score indicates how many _____ _____ a data

value is above or below the _____. The z-score for a data

value x is $z = \dfrac{x - \boxed{}}{\boxed{}}$.

Q: "In a poll of 1023 respondents, support for the Conservative Party stood at 33.1%. The result is considered accurate to within 3.2%, 19 times out of 20." What does this statement tell you?

NEED HELP?
• See Lesson 5.6

A: • The sample size is $n =$ _____ . The margin of error is _____ .

• The _____ level, based on the phrase "19 times out of 20,"

is ___%.

• The ___% confidence interval for support for the Conservative Party is 29.9% to ___%.

MULTIPLE CHOICE

1. Which measure would be best for comparing marks on several math tests?

   A. range   **B.** mean   **C.** median   **D.** mode

2. For this set of data, what are the mean, median, and mode, respectively, to one decimal place?

   2, 4, 6, 6, 7, 8, 10, 12, 15

   A. 70, 7.8, 6   **B.** 7.8, 7, 6   **C.** 6, 7, 7.8   **D.** 7.1, 7, 6

3. Which of these is a feature of a histogram but not of a frequency polygon?

   A. Data is organized into 5 to 12 equal-sized intervals.

   B. The frequencies of values that fall within each interval are recorded.

   C. The frequency data is plotted on the vertical axis.

   D. The data is represented by bars.

4. What is the expression for calculating the standard deviation of a set of data?

   A. $\sqrt{\dfrac{\sum(x-\bar{x})^2}{n}}$ **B.** $\sqrt{\dfrac{\sum(\bar{x}-x)^2}{n}}$ **C.** $\dfrac{\sum(x-\bar{x})^2}{n}$ **D.** $(x-\bar{x})^2$

5. Which set of percents correctly describes the distribution of data one, two, and three standard deviations about the mean in a normal distribution?

   A. 34%, 50%, 52.35%   **C.** 68%, 95%, 99.7%

   B. 68%, 95%, 100%   **D.** 95%, 99.7%, 100%

6. Which is the correct formula for calculating a *z*-score?

   A. $z = \dfrac{x-\mu}{\sigma}$ **B.** $z = \dfrac{\mu-x}{\sigma}$ **C.** $z = \dfrac{x}{\sigma}$ **D.** $z = \dfrac{x-\sigma}{\mu}$

7. The mean of a set of data is 4.5, with a standard deviation of 0.6. What is the *z*-score for a value of 10.9?

   A. -10.7 **B.** -0.4 **C.** 10.7   **D.** 2.3

8. Which is the correct expression for the confidence interval "twenty-one percent with a two point four percent point margin of error"?

   A. 21% ± 2.4   **B.** 21 ± 2.4%   **C.** 21 ± 2.4   **D.** 21% ± 2.4%

9. What is the range for the confidence interval 47.8% ± 3.7%?

   A. 47.8%   **C.** 44.1% to 47.8%

   B. 44.1% to 51.5%   **D.** 47.8% to 51.5%

10. The results of a poll are accurate 19 out of 20 times. What is the confidence level for these results?

    A. 19%   **B.** 90%   **C.** 95%   **D.** 100%

NUMERICAL RESPONSE

11. The durability of two brands of performance cycling tires was tested. The distances covered, in thousands of kilometres, before the tires became bald were recorded in the table. What is the mean distance covered by each brand of tire?

Brand A: _____ km   Brand B: _____ km

Brand A (10^3 km)		Brand B (10^3 km)	
2.0	2.0	2.1	1.5
2.5	2.5	2.0	1.5
1.0	1.8	1.5	1.5
1.3	1.9	2.2	1.6

12. The widths of the trunks of 30 redwood trees in a forest were measured. The data was organized into intervals.

Which range of trunk widths occurs most frequently? _____ m

Which ranges of trunk widths occur least frequently?

_____ m and _____ m

Width (m)	Frequency
4.5–5.0	2
5.0–5.5	4
5.5–6.0	8
6.0–6.5	9
6.5–7.0	5
7.0–7.5	2

13. Nancy grooms cats and dogs. The time she spends grooming animals, in hours, over one month are shown.

2.5	3.0	3.5	2.0	3.0	1.5	4.0	5.0
8.0	4.0	5.0	6.0	3.0	3.5	4.5	2.5
4.0	5.0	4.0	3.5	4.0	3.0	3.5	7.0

Suggest an interval width that will give a good representation of how the data is distributed, and determine how many intervals this interval width creates.

___ intervals of width _____

14. Using a *z*-score table, determine the percent of data to the right of a *z*-score of 0.98.

_____ % of the data is to the right of 0.98.

15. A poll determined that 76% of the people buying gasoline felt that $1.09/L was a fair price. The results of the survey are accurate within 3.4% percent points.

The confidence interval is ___% ± ___%, or from ___% to ___%.

16. Tom researched the price of two different brands of 100 pack of DVDs at four different stores.

a) What is the mean price and standard deviation for each brand?

Store	DVD A ($)	$(x - \bar{x})^2$	DVD B ($)	$(x - \bar{x})^2$
1	32.94	5.06	34.59	9.30
2	31.97	10.37	38.99	1.82
3	35.92	0.53	36.99	0.42
4	39.93	22.47	39.99	5.52
Σ	140.76	38.43	150.56	17.06
$\bar{x}$		—		—
$\sqrt{\dfrac{\Sigma(x - \bar{x})^2}{n}}$	—		—	

b) Compare the pricing of the two brands.

17. Gretchen plays the guitar. The numbers of hours in a day she spends practising over one month are shown.

2.5	3.0	3.5	2.0	3.0	1.5
4.0	5.0	8.0	4.0	5.0	6.0
3.0	3.5	4.5	2.5	4.0	5.0
4.0	3.5	4.0	3.0	3.5	7.0

Time (h)	Frequency
1.0–	

a) Complete the frequency distribution table.

b) Construct a frequency polygon of the data, using the grid provided.

c) What is the mean number of hours?

d) What is the standard deviation?

e) Is the data normally distributed? Explain your answer.

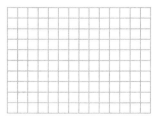

18. The ages of members of a cycling club are normally distributed. The mean is 35 years, and the standard deviation is 5 years.

   a) What percent of members are between 25 and 40 years old?

   b) John is a member of the club and is 20 years old. What percent of members are less than 20 years old?

19. A manufacturer offers a warranty on its CD burners. The burner has a mean lifespan of 7 years, with a standard deviation of 0.5 years. For how long should the burners be covered by the warranty if the manufacturer wants to repair no more than 2.5% of the burners sold?

20. A survey of 200 shoppers at a grocery store indicated that 75% preferred smooth over chunky peanut butter. The results were accurate within 3.3 percent points, 9 times out of 10.

   a) State the confidence level.

   b) Determine the confidence interval.

   c) If there were 1000 shoppers that day, how many would prefer chunky peanut butter?

MULTIPLE CHOICE

Determine the measure of the indicated angle, to the nearest degree.

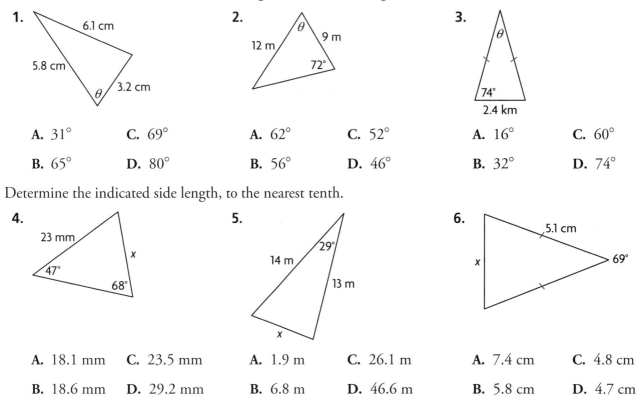

1.

A. $31°$ **C.** $69°$

B. $65°$ **D.** $80°$

2.

A. $62°$ **C.** $52°$

B. $56°$ **D.** $46°$

3.

A. $16°$ **C.** $60°$

B. $32°$ **D.** $74°$

Determine the indicated side length, to the nearest tenth.

4.

A. 18.1 mm   **C.** 23.5 mm

B. 18.6 mm   **D.** 29.2 mm

5.

A. 1.9 m   **C.** 26.1 m

B. 6.8 m   **D.** 46.6 m

6.

A. 7.4 cm   **C.** 4.8 cm

B. 5.8 cm   **D.** 4.7 cm

7. Simon knows lengths *a* and *c* in $\triangle ABC$. He also knows one of the angles, and this gives him enough information to use the cosine law to determine *b*. Which angle could be the one Simon knows?

A. $\angle A$ **B.** $\angle B$ **C.** $\angle C$ **D.** any of these

8. Which of the following ratios is the same for each side–angle pair in a triangle?

A. $\dfrac{\sin A}{a}$ **B.** $\dfrac{a}{\sin A}$ **C.** both   **D.** neither

9. You are given three pieces of information about the measures of the angles and sides in a triangle. In which of the following situations can the sine law NOT be used to solve the triangle?

A. *SSA*   **B.** *SAS*   **C.** *ASA*   **D.** *AAS*

10. In $\triangle XYZ$, $x = 4.3$ cm, $y = 3.1$ cm, and $z = 5.9$ cm. Which is the largest angle, and is it obtuse?

A. $\angle Y$; yes   **B.** $\angle Z$; yes   **C.** $\angle Z$; no   **D.** $\angle Y$; no

11. Given the information shown, in which situation are two triangles possible?

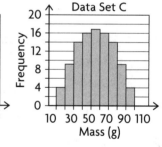

A. $\angle A$ obtuse, $h < b < a$

C. $\angle A$ acute, $h < a < b$

B. $\angle A$ acute, $a < h < b$

D. $\angle A$ obtuse, $a > b$

12. Which set of measurements results in no possible triangles?

A. $\angle P = 25°$, $p = 3.5$ m, $q = 6.2$ m

C. $\angle P = 135°$, $p = 3.8$ m, $q = 4.0$ m

B. $\angle P = 96°$, $p = 5.2$ m, $q = 5.0$ m

D. $\angle P = 48°$, $p = 7.4$ m, $q = 7.1$ m

13. The cosine law does not have an ambiguous case. Why not?

A. The cosine law does not apply to obtuse triangles.

B. The cosine of an obtuse angle is always negative.

C. The principal value of a square root is always positive.

D. The cosine law cannot be used if the unknown angle is obtuse.

14. For which of these data sets are the mean, median, and mode equal?

A. 5.5 cm, 6.0 cm, 7.5 cm, 9.0 cm, 9.5 cm

B. 1.0 m, 4.0 m, 4.0 m, 4.5 m, 5.0 m, 5.5 m

C. 8 g, 11 g, 13 g, 13 g, 16 g, 17 g

D. sizes: 21, 22, 24, 24, 25, 29

15. Predict which data set has the smallest standard deviation.

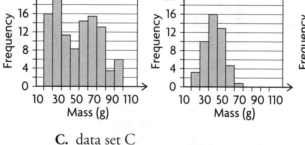

A. data set A

C. data set C

B. data set B

D. not enough information to decide

16. The lengths of a sample of fully grown monarch butterfly caterpillars are normally distributed, with a mean of 4.9 cm and a standard deviation of 0.3 cm. What percent of caterpillars would you expect to be longer than 5.5 cm?

A. 5%   **B.** 95%   **C.** 2% to 3%   **D.** 17%

17. Which of the following increases the width of a confidence interval and the margin of error?

A. an increased confidence level

C. an increased sample size

B. a reduced confidence level

D. none of these choices

18. Solve △*PQR*. Round lengths to the nearest tenth of a centimetre and angles to the nearest degree.

$q =$ _____ cm $r =$ _____ cm $\angle R =$ ___°

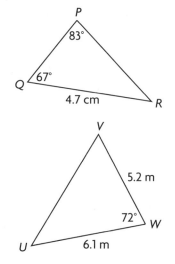

19. Solve △*UVW*. Round angles to the nearest degree and lengths to the nearest tenth of a metre.

$\angle U =$ ___° $\angle V =$ ___° $w =$ _____ m

20. Ricardo is landscaping part of a garden in the shape of an acute triangle. He wants the sides of the triangle to be 13 m, 17 m, and 19 m long. Determine, to the nearest degree,

a) the measure of the smallest angle in Ricardo's triangle: ___°

b) the measure of the largest angle in Ricardo's triangle: ___°

21. Richard has copied down a question about △*XYZ*. He knows that $\angle X$ measures 50° and that two of the side lengths are 11 cm and 15 cm, but he does not know which given side length is *x* and which is *y*. However, Richard's friend Pam assures him that there is a possible solution for △*XYZ*.

a) What are the given side lengths? $x =$ ___ cm $y =$ ___ cm

b) Solve △*XYZ*. Round to the nearest degree or the nearest tenth of a centimetre.

△*Y* = ___°   △*Z* = ___° $z =$ _____ cm

22. A parallelogram has side lengths of 13 mm and 24 mm. Two of the internal angles measure 74°. What are the lengths of the two diagonals, to the nearest millimetre?

Shorter diagonal = ___ mm   Longer diagonal = ___ mm

23. Twin brothers Eric and Basil are arguing about who did better overall in recent math tests. Eric scored 83 in Algebra and 92 in Geometry, while Basil scored 87 in Algebra and 90 in Geometry. Suppose the scores in Algebra were approximately normally distributed with mean 67 and standard deviation 15, and the scores in Geometry were approximately normally distributed with mean 69 and standard deviation 18.

a) What are Eric's *z*-scores on the tests?

Algebra: _____   Geometry: _____

b) What are Basil's *z*-scores?

Algebra: _____   Geometry: _____

c) Based on each brother's average *z*-score, who did better overall? _____

24. The table shows reported sales by shoe size from two shoe stores on the same day in June 2011. To the nearest tenth,

a) what was the mean shoe size sold, μ, at store A? _____

at store B? _____

b) what was the standard deviation, σ, for store A? _____

for store B? _____

c) for which store was the value of $\mu - \sigma$ lower? Store ___

d) which store sold the greater proportion of sizes 39 or smaller? Store ___

Shoe Size	Store A	Store B
34–36	3	3
37–39	12	12
40–42	33	27
43–45	43	32
46–48	38	33
49–51	35	29
52–54	5	9
55–57	1	2

WRITTEN RESPONSE

25. A tree standing on the side of a hill casts a shadow uphill. The hill slopes at an angle of 12°. When the angle of elevation of the Sun is 37°, the shadow is 48 m long. How tall is the tree, to the nearest metre?

26. The base of a cliff, *A*, is surveyed from two different points, *C* and *D*, at the same horizontal level. The elevation of the top of the cliff, *B*, is taken from *C*.

a) What is the height of the cliff, to the nearest metre?

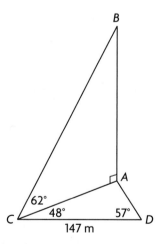

b) To the nearest degree, what is the elevation of the cliff taken from *D*?

27. a) Determine the diagonal length *AC* of the rectangle, to the nearest millimetre.

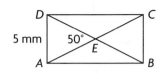

b) Determine the longer side length of the rectangle, to the nearest millimetre.

28. Marina's tiger kite has the measurements shown.

a) What is the length of the spar, *AC*, from tip to tail of the kite, to the nearest tenth?

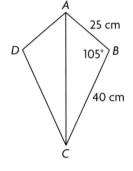

b) Take *BC* as the base of △*ABC*. Determine the height of △*ABC* relative to this base, to the nearest tenth.

c) What is the area of Marina's kite, to the nearest square centimetre?

d) For a math project, Marina decides to investigate further and discovers a general formula for the area of a kite with short side length *a*, long side length *b*, and angle *θ* between the long and short sides. What is Marina's formula?

29. a) Using the tally chart and grid, create a histogram for the following data:

Heights of Bean Plants (cm)
23, 72, 35, 32, 70, 40, 28, 61, 55, 63,
59, 25, 32, 36, 53, 64, 68, 71, 39, 28,
60, 44, 47, 31, 63, 30, 73, 35, 42, 68

Height (cm)	Tally	Frequency

b) State a hypothesis about the heights of bean plants.

30. a) Consider the height data in question 29 that are 45 cm or greater. How well does this part of the data set approximate a normal distribution?

b) Repeat part a) for the height data that are 44 cm or less.

31. Cartons of a brand of breakfast cereal have a mean net mass of 300.5 g, with a standard deviation of 3.3 g. The quality control officer wants to ensure that regularly taken samples of cartons have a mean mass between 299.9 g and 301.1 g. The table guides the sampling process.

Confidence Level	Sample Size Needed
90%	50
95%	82
99%	164

a) What confidence interval and margin of error are being used?

b) Approximately how many cartons should be sampled to ensure the mean mass is within the acceptable range 99% of the time? 19 times out of 20?

c) What happens to the sample size as the confidence level increases? Why?

Chapter 6 **Systems of Linear Inequalities**

Getting Started

1. Match each term with the best example or description.

   a) dependent variable _____   i) describes a solution set from the set of integers

   b) continuous _____   ii) the value -2 in the equation $y = -2x + 3$

   c) x- and y-intercepts _____   iii) the variable graphed on the horizontal axis

   d) discrete _____   iv) describes a solution set from the set of real numbers

   e) independent variable _____   v) $(-2, 0)$ and $(0, 6)$ for the graph of $y = 3x + 6$

   f) quadrant I _____   vi) the part of the coordinate plane where $x > 0$ and $y > 0$

   g) slope _____   vii) the variable graphed on the vertical axis

2. State an ordered pair that belongs in each solution set.

   a) $\{(x, y) \mid x \in R, y \in R\}$ b) $\{(b, p) \mid b \in W, p \in W\}$ c) $\{(m, n) \mid m \in I, n \in I\}$

3. Isolate the variable in each equation or inequality.

   a) $2x + 3 = 15$ b) $2(w + 4) = w - 3$ c) $3b < 4 - b$

4. Rearrange each equation or inequality to isolate y.

   a) $2x - 3y - 9 = 0$ b) $2y - x \geq 8$ c) $6x - 3y + 14 < 2$

5. Simplify and evaluate each expression for $x = 4$ and $y = -3$.

   a) $2x - 3 + 4(5 - x)$ b) $7 - \dfrac{3}{4}y + \dfrac{y}{6} - 5$ c) $\dfrac{1}{2}x + \dfrac{1}{3}(y - 2x)$

6. Verify that point $(2, -3)$ is a solution to each equation or system.

a) $2x - 3y = 13$

	LS	RS

b) $5x + 2 = 9 - y$

c) $y = \dfrac{1}{2}x - 4$ and $2y - x + 8 = 0$

7. Use the method indicated to graph each given equation on the grid.

a) table of values: $y = -2x + 7$

x									
y									

b) y-intercept and slope: $2y - 5x + 8 = 0$

c) x- and y-intercepts: $3y - 4x = 6$

8. Solve this system of linear equalities graphically, using the grid.

$\{(x, y) \mid x = y + 3, x \in R, y \in R\}$ Solution: $(x, y) = (\_\_, \_\_)$

$\{(x, y) \mid x + y = 8, x \in R, y \in R\}$

9. Represent the following problem algebraically, and then solve it.
A jar holds mints and toffees. There are twice as many toffees as mints.
If the jar contains 16 candies, how many mints and toffees could be in the jar?

10. For the problem in question 9,

a) State the number set the domain and range belong to: ___

b) State whether the solution is discrete or continuous: _____

6.1 Graphing Linear Inequalities in Two Variables

Keep in Mind

▶ The boundary of an inequality in two variables is a straight line that creates two half planes. One of these half planes includes the solution set of the inequality. The boundary may or may not be part of the solution set.

▶ A continuous solution set contains all of the points in the solution region.

▶ A discrete solution set contains some, but not all, of the points in the solution region: the points with whole-number or integer coordinates.

▶ When no domain, range, or context is given, assume the domain and range are the set of real numbers: $\{(x, y) \mid x \in \mathrm{R}, y \in \mathrm{R}\}$ (continuous solution set).

▶ In real-world situations, solution sets may be restricted to specific quadrants.

▶ To graph the solution set of a linear inequality, first graph the boundary:
  • For < or > inequalities, draw a dashed line.
  • For ≤ or ≥ inequalities with a continuous solution set, draw a solid line.
  • For ≤ or ≥ inequalities with a discrete solution set, stipple the boundary line at points with whole-number or integer coordinates as indicated.

▶ To complete the graph of the solution set:
  • Test a point not on the boundary to see whether it is in the solution region.
  • If it is, shade the half plane containing it. If not, shade the other half plane.
  • If the solution set is discrete, stipple points with whole-number or integer coordinates.

Example 1

Graph the solution set for $-3x + 4y \leq 12$.

Solution

Step 1. I replaced the inequality sign (≤) with an equal sign to determine the equation of the boundary: $-3x + 4y = 12$.

Step 2. The domain and range are not stated, and no context is given, so I assumed the domain and range are the set of real numbers. This means the solution set is continuous.

Step 3. I determined the boundary's y-intercept and x-intercept:

For $x = 0$, $\quad -3(0) + 4y = 12$ $\qquad\qquad$ For $y = 0$, $\quad -3x + 4(0) = 12$

$\qquad\qquad\qquad\qquad y = 3$ $\qquad\qquad\qquad\qquad\qquad\qquad\qquad x = -4$

The intercepts are $(0, 3)$ and $(-4, 0)$. Since there is the possibility of equality ($\leq$), the boundary must be a solid line.

Step 4. I tested whether point $(0, 0)$ was in the solution region.

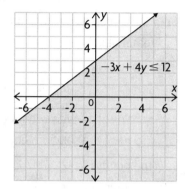

LS	RS
$-3(0) + 4(0)$	12
0	

Since it is true that $0 \leq 12$, then $(0, 0)$ is in the solution region.

Step 5. I drew the boundary and shaded the half plane containing $(0, 0)$. Since the solution set is continuous, the solution region contains all of the points in the shaded area and on the solid boundary.

Example 2

Sanjit and Mary are competing in a spelling quiz. Mary gets a point for every word she spells correctly. Sanjit is younger than Mary, so he gets 3 points for every word he spells correctly, plus 1 bonus point. What combinations of correctly spelled words for Sanjit and for Mary result in Mary scoring more points than Sanjit? Choose two combinations that make sense, and explain your choices.

Solution

Step 1. I represented the relationship between the number of correctly spelled words for Sanjit, x, and the number for Mary, y, by a linear inequality:

$y > 3x + 1$

I knew that the variables represented whole numbers:

$x \in W, y \in W$

> **TIP**
> Discrete contexts often have domain and range $x \in W, y \in W$ (first quadrant) or $x \in I, y \in I$ (whole plane).

Step 2. I noticed that the inequality already had y isolated.

Step 3. I entered the inequality into my graphing calculator. I adjusted the window to show only the first quadrant. The boundary was a dashed line, meaning that the solution set did not include values on the line.

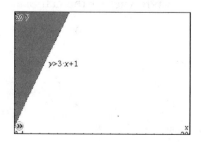

Step 4. I used the test point (0, 0) to verify that the correct half plane was shaded:

LS	RS
0	3(0) + 1
	1

Since 0 is not greater than 1, (0, 0) is not in the solution set.

Step 5. I picked two points in the solution region. I chose numbers that seemed reasonable in the context of the problem. I knew that

- Only points with whole-number coordinates in the solution region made sense.

- Points along the dashed boundary were not part of the solution region.

- Points with whole-number coordinates along the x- or y-axis boundaries were part of the solution region.

The points (2, 12) and (4, 19) are possible solutions to the problem. I verified that each point is a solution to the linear equality:

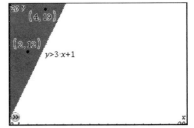

LS	RS
12	3(2) + 1
	7

LS	RS
19	3(4) + 1
	13

Since 12 > 7, (2, 12) is a solution.   Since 19 > 13, (4, 19) is a solution.

Sanjit spelling 2 words correctly and Mary spelling 12 words correctly, or Sanjit spelling 4 words correctly and Mary spelling 19 words correctly, result in Mary scoring more points than Sanjit.

Practice

1. Determine the following for each linear inequality:

i) the equation of the boundary line

ii) whether the boundary line is solid or dashed

iii) if (0, 0) is a solution

iv) whether the half plane is shaded above or below the boundary line

a) $y - x \geq 10$ **b)** $y < x + 3$ **c)** $y > -3$

2. Graph each inequality in question 1.

a)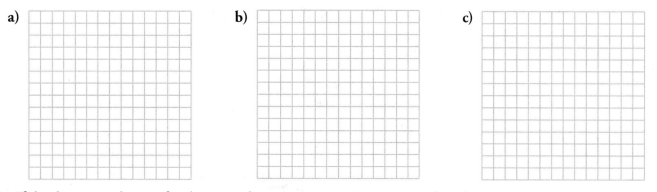

b)

c)

3. If the domain and range for the inequalities in question 1 are restricted to the set of integers, describe how each graph in question 2 changes.

a)

b)

c)

4. If the domain and range for the inequalities in question 1 are restricted to the set of whole numbers, describe what happens to each graph.

5. Consider the graph of the inequality $x - 2y < 7$.
Determine whether each point is in its solution region.

a) $(-1, 0)$ b) $(2, 4)$ c) $(-3, -10)$

6. Graph each inequality.

   a) $\{(x, y) \mid x - y + 1 \le 2, x \in W, y \in W\}$

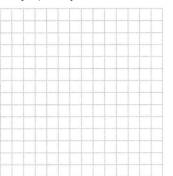

   b) $\{(x, y) \mid -3x + 1 > 4, x \in I, y \in I\}$

   TIP
   Use Question 1 as a guide
   or a checklist.

7. The specifications for a new school hall state that the width of the hall should be at most 10 m more than 3 times its height. (All dimensions are in metres.)

   a) State the variables you would use in this situation.

   b) Write the inequality that models the situation.

   c) Will the solution region be stippled or not? Explain.

   d) Will the boundary be solid, dashed, or stippled? Explain.

8. Frank and Roger sell ice cream cones on the boardwalk during summer. They each work the same number of hours per day. On an average day, they will sell 110 cones. Frank is very sociable, so he can sell two cones while Roger sells one during the same time period.

   a) Define variables and write a linear inequality to represent this situation.

   b) What are the restrictions on the variables? How do you know?

c) Graph the linear inequality on the grid provided. Use your graph to determine a combination of sales where

   i) Frank and Roger sell fewer than 110 ice cream cones in a day.

   ii) Frank and Roger sell exactly 110 ice cream cones in a day.

MULTIPLE CHOICE

9. For which inequality is $(0, -2)$ a solution?

   A. $y - 0.5x \geq 5$ **B.** $y \leq 3 - 2x$ **C.** $y < -x - 3$ **D.** $y > -1$

WRITTEN RESPONSE

10. Hailey and Caitlin make and sell bracelets to raise money for their school social committee. Beaded bracelets sell for $10 each, and rubber band bracelets sell for $2 each. In one day, they raised $278.

   a) Define variables for this situation and state any restrictions, with reasons. Write a linear inequality to represent the situation.

   b) Graph the linear inequality on the grid provided. Use your graph to determine

   i) if Hailey and Caitlin could have sold 25 of each type of bracelet

   ii) if 15 of one type and 25 of the other type could have been sold

▶ Graph all the inequalities in a system of linear inequalities on the same coordinate plane. The area in which all the solution regions overlap represents the solution set to the system. For example, this graph shows the solution region to this system:

$$\{(x, y) \mid y \geq x, x \in R, y \in R\} \quad \{(x, y) \mid y \leq 4, x \in R, y \in R\}$$

▶ The solution region for a system of linear inequalities can be discrete or continuous. It may be restricted to certain quadrants.

▶ If the solution regions do not overlap, then the system has no solution.

Example

Graph this system of linear inequalities. Justify your representation of the solution set.

$$\{(x, y) \mid x + y \leq 5, x \in I, y \in I\}$$

$$\{(x, y) \mid x + 3y > 0, x \in I, y \in I\}$$

Solution

Step 1. I knew that the equations of the boundaries were $x + y = 5$ and $x + 3y = 0$.

$x + y = 5$ must be a stippled line, and $x + 3y = 0$ must be dashed.

Step 2. I determined two points on each boundary.

For $x = 0$,	For $y = 0$,	For $x = 0$,	For $y = 1$,
$0 + y = 5$	$x + 0 = 5$	$0 + 3y = 0$	$x + 3 = 0$
$y = 5$	$x = 5$	$3y = 0$	$x = -3$
		$y = 0$	

$x + y = 5$ passes through $(0, 5)$ and $(5, 0)$.

$x + 3y = 0$ passes through $(0, 0)$ and $(-3, 1)$.

Step 3. I tested points $(0, 1)$ and $(1, 0)$.

$1 \leq 5$ and $3 \geq 0$, so $(0, 1)$ is a solution for both inequalities.

$1 \leq 5$ and $3 \geq 1$, so $(1, 0)$ is a solution for both inequalities.

Step 4. I graphed both inequalities on the same coordinate plane. The domain and range are the set of integers, so the solution set is discrete. Therefore, I stippled the area of the solution set.

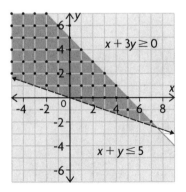

Practice

1. Match each graph with the correct system of linear inequalities.

a) ___

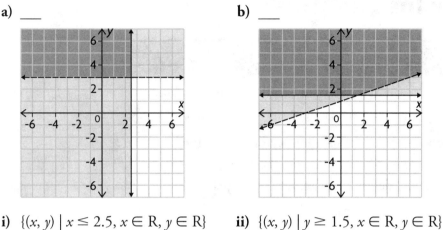

b) ___

i) $\{(x, y) \mid x \le 2.5, x \in R, y \in R\}$

$\{(x, y) \mid y > 3, x \in R, y \in R\}$

ii) $\{(x, y) \mid y \ge 1.5, x \in R, y \in R\}$

$\{(x, y) \mid 3y - x > 3, x \in R, y \in R\}$

2. State three sets of coordinates that lie in the solution region shown in the graph at the right.

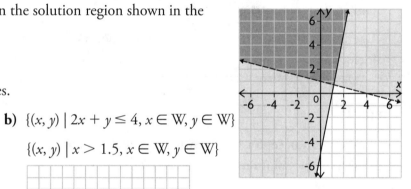

3. Graph each system of linear inequalities.

a) $\{(x, y) \mid x > -3, x \in R, y \in R\}$

$\{(x, y) \mid x + y \le 2, x \in R, y \in R\}$

b) $\{(x, y) \mid 2x + y \le 4, x \in W, y \in W\}$

$\{(x, y) \mid x > 1.5, x \in W, y \in W\}$

4. Suppose you graph this system of linear inequalities:

$\{(x, y) \mid 2x + y \le 4, x \in W, y \in W\}$

$\{(x, y) \mid y \ge 2, x \in W, y \in W\}$

Would the solution region be shaded or shaded and stippled?

5. Graph the system of linear inequalities in question 4 on the grid provided.

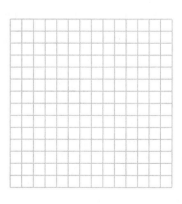

6.3 Graphing to Solve Systems of Linear Inequalities

Keep in Mind

▶ The boundaries of the solution region of a system of inequalities may or may not be included, depending on which inequality signs the system contains.

▶ You can validate a possible solution from the solution region by checking that it satisfies each inequality in the system. Substitute the coordinates of the solution into the inequality, and determine whether the inequality is true for these coordinates.

▶ Use an open dot to show that an intersection point of a system's boundaries is excluded from the solution set. An intersection point is excluded when a dashed line intersects either a dashed or a solid line.

▶ Use a solid dot to show that an intersection point of a system's boundaries is included in the solution set. This occurs when both boundary lines are solid.

Example 1

Graph the solution set for the following system of inequalities.
State two possible solutions from the set. Check your work.

$$\{(x, y) \mid 2x + y > 6, x \in W, y \in W\}$$

$$\{(x, y) \mid y \leq 3, x \in W, y \in W\}$$

Solution

Step 1. From the domain and range, I knew the graph would have a discrete solution region and would be restricted to the first quadrant.

Step 2. I knew the boundary line $2x + y = 6$ would be dashed, because the inequality sign is $>$. The boundary line $y = 3$ would be stippled, because the inequality sign is $\leq$ and the solution set is discrete.

Step 3. To graph the boundary line $2x + y = 6$, I determined the x- and y-intercepts:

x-intercept:	y-intercept:
$2x + 0 = 6$	$2(0) + y = 6$
$2x = 6$	$y = 6$
$x = 3$	

The boundary line $2x + y = 6$ passes through $(3, 0)$ and $(0, 6)$.

Then, I tested (0, 0) to determine which region to shade:

LS	RS
2(0) + (0)	6
0	

0 is not greater than 6, so (0, 0) is not in the solution region of $2x + y > 6$.

Step 4. For the inequality $y \leq 3$, I shaded the half plane below the boundary line $y = 3$, since all the points in this region have y-coordinates less than 3.

Step 5. I stippled the overlapping solution region. I drew an open dot where the two boundaries intersect, to show that this point is not part of the solution region.

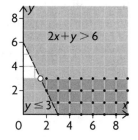

Step 6. For the two possible solutions, I needed stippled points in the overlapping solution region, including points along its stippled boundary. Two possible solutions are (2, 3) and (5, 1). I validated both solutions:

(2, 3):

LS	RS
$2x + y$	6
2(2) + (3)	
7	

LS	RS
y	3
3	

This solution is valid, since 7 is greater than 6 and 3 is less than or equal to 3.

(5, 1):

LS	RS
$2x + y$	6
2(5) + (1)	
11	

LS	RS
y	3
1	

This solution is valid, since 11 is greater than 6 and 1 is less than or equal to 3.

Example 2

To raise funds to buy new instruments, the band committee has 500 T-shirts to sell. The T-shirts come in red or blue. Based on sales of the same T-shirts at a fundraiser five years ago, the committee expects to sell at least twice as many blue T-shirts as red T-shirts.

a) Define the variables and restrictions. Write a system of linear inequalities that models the situation.

b) Graph the system of inequalities.

c) Suggest a combination of T-shirt sales that could be made.

Solution

a) I let x represent the number of blue T-shirts that could be sold. I let y represent the number of red T-shirts that could be sold. Since the number of T-shirts is discrete, and 0 to 500 T-shirts of any colour can be sold, the domain and range of this system belong to the set of whole numbers. I wrote one inequality to represent the total number of T-shirts to be sold, and a second inequality to represent the rate of sale of blue T-shirts compared to red.

$\{(x, y) \mid x + y \leq 500, x \in W, y \in W\}$

$\{(x, y) \mid x \geq 2y, x \in W, y \in W\}$

b) I rearranged the inequalities by isolating y:

$x + y \leq 500$

$\quad y \leq 500 - x$

and

$\quad x \geq 2y$

$\dfrac{1}{2}x \geq y$

$\quad y \leq 0.5x$

I entered $y \leq 500 - x$ and $y \leq 0.5x$ into my graphing calculator and graphed the inequalities. I adjusted the calculator window to show only the first quadrant.

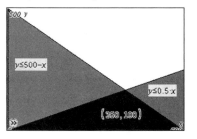

c) I selected the point (350, 100) in the solution region.

This means that the sale of 350 blue T-shirts and 100 red T-shirts satisfies the system of inequalities and is therefore possible.

Practice

1. For each system of linear inequalities:

   i) Determine the point of intersection of the boundaries.

   ii) Will the point be a solid or an open dot on a graph of the system? Explain.

   a) $\{(x, y) \mid y - x < 2, x \in R, y \in R\}$ **b)** $\{(x, y) \mid y - 2x \geq 7, x \in I, y \in I\}$

   $\{(x, y) \mid x + y \geq 0, x \in R, y \in R\}$ $\{(x, y) \mid x + y \leq 4, x \in I, y \in I\}$

2. Graph each system of linear inequalities in question 1. Then, determine a solution, and check its validity.

   a)

   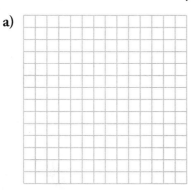

   b)

   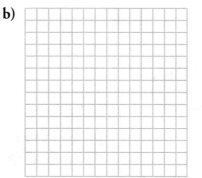

3. For each system of linear inequalities:

  i) Explain whether the boundaries and their point of intersection are part of the solution region.

  ii) Graph the system of linear inequalities. Determine a solution.

  a) $\{(x, y) \mid -2y - x \geq 1, x \in I, y \in I\}$

     $\{(x, y) \mid x - 1 \leq y, x \in I, y \in I\}$

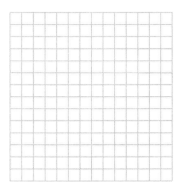

  b) $\{(x, y) \mid x - 2y < 12, x \in R, y \in R\}$

     $\{(x, y) \mid 2y + 5x \geq 10, x \in R, y \in R\}$

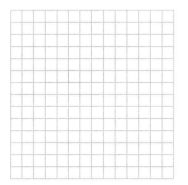

4. A banner is being created for a bake sale.

  • The length of the banner must be less than 200 cm.

  • The perimeter must be 500 cm or less.

  a) Write a system of linear inequalities to model the situation. Define the variables and describe the restrictions.

  b) Graph the system of linear inequalities on the grid provided.

  c) Determine a possible solution for the system.

5. Which is a solution to the system of linear inequalities?

$\{(x, y) \mid 3x - y > 4, x \in R, y \in R\}$

$\{(x, y) \mid 2x + y \leq 6, x \in R, y \in R\}$

A. $(-2, 3)$ **B.** $(2, 0)$ **C.** $(2, 5)$ **D.** $(5, 2)$

WRITTEN RESPONSE

6. For the system of linear inequalities in question 5, are the boundary lines and point of intersection included in the solution region? Explain.

7. Becca likes to collect sea shells on beach vacations.

- She has decided to limit her collection to 300 shells altogether.
- She collects only white shells and mottled shells, and wants to have no more than four white shells for every mottled one.

a) Define the variables and write a system of inequalities that models this situation. Include the restrictions on the domain and range of the variables.

b) Graph the solution set on the grid provided. Determine two possible combinations of shells Becca could have.

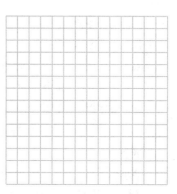

6.4 Optimization Problems I: Creating the Model

Keep in Mind

▸ To solve an optimization problem, determine which combination of values of two variables results in a maximum or minimum value of a related quantity.

▸ When creating a model, first represent the situation algebraically. Include

  • a defining statement of the variables in your model

  • a statement describing the restrictions on the variables

  • a system of inequalities that describes the constraints

  • an objective function that expresses the quantity to be maximized or minimized in terms of the variables

▸ Next, create a graphical model by representing the system of inequalities graphically. This helps you identify the feasible region for solutions.

Example

Four teams are travelling to a baseball tournament in cars and minivans. Each team has no more than 3 coaches and 10 athletes. Each car can take 5 team members, and each minivan can take 8 team members. No more than 5 minivans and 11 cars are available. The school wants to know what combination of cars and minivans will require the maximum or minimum number of vehicles. Create and verify a model to represent this situation.

TIP

When you read an optimization problem, identify which quantity is to be optimized. Look for key words, such as *maximize, minimize, largest, smallest, greatest,* or *least.*

Solution

Step 1. I represented the different vehicles with variables.

　Let c represent the number of cars.

　Let m represent the number of minivans.

Step 2. I wrote the restrictions and constraints.

　The variables must represent whole numbers.

　Restrictions: $c \in W$ and $m \in W$

　Constraints: number of cars: $c \geq 0$ (from restriction) and $c \leq 11$

　Number of minivans: $m \geq 0$ (from restriction) and $m \leq 5$

　There can be 4(3 coaches) + 4(10 players) = 52 players and coaches at most.

　$5c + 8m \leq 52$

　Objective function to maximize: let V represent the number of vehicles.

　$V = c + m$

TIP

Restrictions on the variables, such as $x \geq 0$ and $y \geq 0$ if you are working with positive real numbers, are also constraints and should be included in the system of linear inequalities.

Step 3. I graphed the inequalities on my calculator. (For the inequalities for c, I used the Window function to set a range for x from 0 to 11.) Then, I determined intersection points of the boundary lines for the feasible region. The intersection points are (0, 0), (0, 11), (1, 11), (5, 3), and (5, 0).

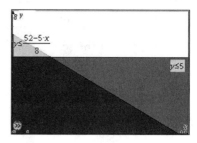

Practice

1. Using these terms: *defining statement*, *restrictions*, *constraints*, and *objective function*, identify each part of the algebraic model.

Statements	Part of Model
Let V represent the total volume. $V = 500b + 250t$	
Let b represent the number of bottles. Let t represent the number of drink cartons.	
$b \geq 0$ (from restriction) and $b \leq 6$ $t \geq 0$ (from restriction) and $t \leq 8$	
$b \in W$ and $t \in W$	

2. A vending machine sells juice and water.

   • The machine holds, at most, 100 bottles of drinks.

   • At most 3 bottles of water are sold for each bottle of juice.

   • Each bottle of water sells for $1.00, and each bottle of juice sells for $1.25.

   a) What are the two variables in this situation? Describe any restrictions.

   Let w represent the number of _____ and j the number

   of _____.

   b) Write a system of linear inequalities to represent each constraint.

   i) the number of _____: $\{(w, j) \mid w \leq$ ___, $w \in$ ___, $j \in$ ___$\}$

   ii) the number of _____: $\{(w, j) \mid j \leq$ ___, $w \in$ ___, $j \in$ ___$\}$

   iii) the number of bottles of each type of drink sold:

   $\{(w, j) \mid$ _____, $w \in$ ___, $j \in$ ___$\}$

   $\{(w, j) \mid$ _____, $w \in$ ___, $j \in$ ___$\}$

   c) Graph the system on the grid.

   d) The intersection points of the solution region are

   _____, _____, and _____.

   e) Let R represent the revenue from drink sales from the vending machine.

   The objective function is $R =$ _____.

3. A football stadium has 60 000 seats.

- 75% of the seats are in the lower deck.
- 25% of the seats are in the upper deck.
- At least 40 000 tickets are sold per game.
- A lower-deck ticket costs $100, and an upper-deck ticket costs $60.

Create an algebraic and graphical model that could be used to determine a combination of tickets that should be sold to maximize revenue. Use the grid provided.

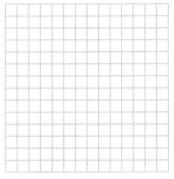

4. Kathy and Ravi volunteer at the local food bank each weekend.

- Kathy can work no more than 10 h per weekend.
- Ravi can work no more than 12 h per weekend.
- The food bank can assign both of them for 18 h or less per weekend.
- Kathy can fill 10 boxes with food in 1 h, while Ravi can fill 12 boxes.

The food bank wants to maximize the number of boxes filled in one weekend by these two volunteers.

Create an algebraic model and a graphical model to represent this situation. Use the grid provided.

5. A British Columbia farmer wants to plant a combination of apple and pear trees that will maximize revenue.

- She wants to plant no more than 500 trees altogether.
- She wants at least four times as many apple as pear trees.
- The yield per apple tree is 4 bushels, and the yield per pear tree is 3 bushels.
- Apples pay the farmer $8.75 per bushel, and pears pay $9.50 per bushel.

a) Create an algebraic model and a graphical model to represent this situation. Use the grid provided.

b) What are the intersection points of the feasible region?

c) How would the objective function change if apples paid $9.00 per bushel?

MULTIPLE CHOICE

6. A local animal shelter is preparing pamphlets and letters to raise awareness of the shelter and to solicit donations.

- No more than 250 of each type of correspondence are needed.
- No more than 500 pamphlets and letters in total will be printed.
- Pamphlets cost 45¢ each to print, and letters cost 20¢ each to print.

Let p represent the number of pamphlets to be printed and l represent the number of letters. Which system of linear inequalities models the situation?

A. $\{(p, l) \mid p \leq 250, l \leq 250, p + l \leq 500, p \in I, l \in I\}$

B. $\{(p, l) \mid p \leq 250, l \leq 250, p + l \leq 500, p \in R, l \in R\}$

C. $\{(p, l) \mid p \leq 250, l \leq 250, p + l \leq 500, p \in W, l \in W\}$

D. none of the above

NUMERICAL RESPONSE

7. Write the objective function to minimize the cost, C, of printing the pamphlets and letters from question 6. $C =$ _____

6.5 Optimization Problems II: Exploring Solutions

Keep in Mind

▸ The value of the objective function for a system of linear inequalities varies throughout the feasible region, but in a predictable way.

▸ The boundary intersection points are the vertices of the feasible region.

• These vertices represent the optimal solutions for the objective function.

• If a vertex is not part of the solution set, then the optimal solution may be found nearby.

▸ To verify an optimal solution, substitute its coordinates into each inequality in the system and evaluate.

Example

Consider the model shown:
Restrictions: $x \in R, y \in R$
Constraints: $x + 3y \leq 9, x - y \leq 3, x \geq -3$
Objective function: $P = 2x + y$

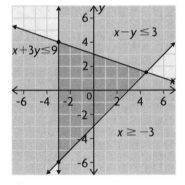

a) What point in the feasible region would result in the maximum value of the objective function? How could you have predicted this graphically?

b) What point in the feasible region would result in the minimum value of the objective function? How could you have predicted this graphically?

Solution

Step 1. Since the solution set is continuous, I knew the maximum value had to occur at one of the vertices of the feasible region, so I looked for these.

There were three vertices: $(-3, -6), (-3, 4)$, and $(4.5, 1.5)$.

Step 2. I evaluated the objective function for each vertex.

$(-3, -6)$: $P = 2(-3) + (-6)$, or -12 $(-3, 4)$: $P = 2(-3) + 4$, or -2 $(4.5, 1.5)$: $P = 2(4.5) + 1.5$, or 10.5

Step 3. $P = 2x + y$, so $y = -2x + P$. I thought about parallel lines with slope -2 passing through the feasible region. The value of P for each line is its y-intercept, so the lines meeting the feasible region with the greatest and least y-intercepts should give the maximum and minimum values of P.

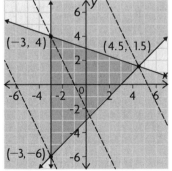

a) The line with slope -2 passing through the vertex $(4.5, 1.5)$ has the greatest y-intercept, so it is reasonable that $(4.5, 1.5)$ gives the maximum value.

b) The line with slope -2 passing through the vertex $(-3, -6)$ has the least y-intercept, so it is reasonable that $(-3, -6)$ gives the minimum value.

Practice

1. a) What are the vertices of the feasible region of the graph?

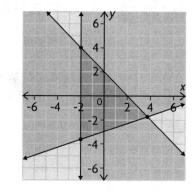

b) Which point in the model would result in the maximum value of the objective function $W = y + 4x$? Explain.

c) Which point in the model would result in the minimum value?

2. Hans and Mei make MP3 player covers to sell, using beads or stickers.

- At most, 45 covers with stickers and 55 bead covers can be made per day.
- Hans and Mei can make 85 or more covers, in total, each day.
- It costs $0.75 to make a cover with stickers, $1.00 to make one with beads.

Let s represent the number of covers with stickers, and let b represent the number of bead covers. Let C represent the cost of making the covers.

Restrictions: $s \in W$, $b \in W$

Constraints: $s \geq 0$, $b \geq 0$, $s \leq 45$, $b \leq 55$, $s + b \geq 85$

Objective function: $C = 0.75s + 1.00b$

a) What are the vertices of the feasible region?

b) Which point would result in the maximum value of the objective function?

c) Which point would result in the minimum value of the objective function?

WRITTEN RESPONSE

3. The vertices of the feasible region of a graph of a system of linear inequalities are $(-4, -8)$, $(5, 0)$, and $(1, -6)$. Which point would result in the minimum value of the objective function $C = 0.50x + 0.60y$?

6.6 Optimization Problems III: Linear Programming

Keep in Mind

▸ To solve an optimization problem using linear programming, begin by creating algebraic and graphical models of the problem (as shown in Section 6.4). Then use the objective function to determine which vertex of the feasible region results in the optimal solution.

▸ The solution to an optimization problem is usually located at one vertex of the feasible region.

Example 1

The following model represents an optimization problem. Determine the maximum solution.

Optimization Model

Restrictions: $x \in R$ and $y \in R$

Constraints: $y \leq 1, 2y \geq -3x + 2, y \geq 3x - 8$

Objective function: $D = -4x + 3y$

Solution

Step 1. Using technology, I graphed the system of inequalities and determined the vertices of the feasible region formed by the boundary lines.

The vertices of the feasible region are (0, 1), (2, −2), and (3, 1).

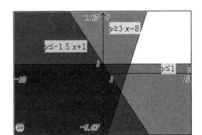

Step 2. I substituted the coordinates of each vertex into the objective function, $D = -4x + 3y$.

For (0, 1): $-4(0) + 3(1) = 3$

For (2, −2): $-4(2) + 3(-2) = -14$

For (3, 1): $-4(3) + 3(1) = -9$

The maximum solution is (0, 1).

TIP

To determine the optimal solution, use linear programming:

A. Create an algebraic model that includes

- a defining statement of the variables used in your model
- the restrictions on the variables
- a system of linear inequalities that describes the constraints
- an objective function that shows how the variables are related to the quantity to be optimized

B. Graph the system of inequalities to determine the coordinates of the vertices of its feasible region.

C. Evaluate the objective function by substituting the values of the coordinates of each vertex.

D. Compare the results and choose the desired solution.

E. Verify that the solution(s) satisfies the constraints of the problem situation.

Step 3. I verified the solution.

(x, y) is $(0, 1)$

$y \leq 1$

LS	RS
1	1

$1 \leq 1$ valid

(x, y) is $(0, 1)$

$2y \geq -3x + 2$

LS	RS
2	2

$2 \geq 2$ valid

(x, y) is $(0, 1)$

$y \geq 3x - 8$

LS	RS
1	-8

$1 \geq -8$ valid

Each inequality statement was valid for this optimal solution.

Example 2

Larry and Tony are baking cupcakes and banana mini-loaves to sell at a school fundraiser.

- No more than 60 cupcakes and 35 mini-loaves can be made each day.
- Larry and Tony can make more than 80 baked goods, in total, each day.
- It costs $0.50 to make a cupcake and $0.75 to make a mini-loaf.

They want to know the minimum costs to produce the baked goods.

Solution

Step 1. I wrote an algebraic model to represent the situation.

Let c represent the number of cupcakes that can be made.

Let m represent the number of mini-loaves that can be made.

Let C represent the cost of making the baked goods.

Restrictions: $c \in W$, $m \in W$

Constraints: $c \geq 0$, $m \geq 0$, $c \leq 60$, $m \leq 35$, $c + m \geq 80$

Objective function: $C = 0.50c + 0.75m$

Step 2. I graphed the system of linear inequalities.

Step 3. I determined the vertices of the feasible region. These points represent the solutions that will optimize the objective function. The points are (60, 20), (45, 35), and (60, 35).

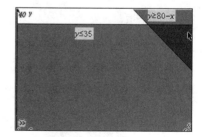

Step 4. To determine which vertex results in a minimum cost of production, I substituted the values into the objective function and evaluated.

For (60, 20): $0.50(60) + 0.75(20) = 45$

For (45, 35): $0.50(45) + 0.75(35) = 48.75$

For (60, 35): $0.50(60) + 0.75(35) = 56.25$

Step 5. The minimum solution is (60, 20). So to minimize costs, Larry and Tony should bake 60 cupcakes and 20 mini-loaves.

Practice

1. The graph of a system of linear inequalities is shown. The system represents the constraints of an algebraic model.

   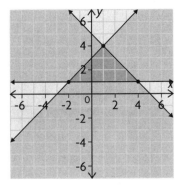

   a) Determine the vertices of the feasible region.

   b) What is the minimum solution for the system, if the objective function is $R = 2.5x + 3y$?

   c) What is the maximum solution for the system and objective function?

2. Determine the vertices of the feasible region for the system of linear inequalities shown, where the objective function is $R = 2x - 2y$. What values do they represent?

   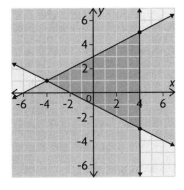

3. The following model represents an optimization problem. Determine the maximum solution.

   Restrictions: $x \in W, y \in W$
   Constraints: $y \leq 1, x \leq y + 2, x + 2y \leq 5$
   Objective function: $T = y - 2x$

4. The following model represents an optimization problem. Determine the maximum solution.

Restrictions: $x \in W$, $y \in W$
Constraints: $x \geq 0$, $y \geq 0$, $4x \geq y + 5$, $x + y \leq 4$, $y \leq 2$
Objective function: $A = x + 2y$

5. Yanni collects stamps and baseball cards.

- He has at most 100 stamps and at most 75 cards, but at least one of each.
- There were no more than 150 items, in total.
- Each stamp cost him 10¢, and each card cost him 50¢.

a) Create an algebraic model to represent the situation.

b) What is the minimum solution to this system, and what does it mean?

6. Four teams are travelling to a badminton tournament in cars and minivans.

- Each team has no more than 2 coaches and 9 athletes.
- Each car can take 4 team members. Each minivan can take 6 team members.
- No more than 6 cars are available, but more than 3 minivans are available. The school wants to know the combination of cars and minivans that will require the maximum number of vehicles.

a) Create and verify an algebraic model to represent this situation.

b) Use the optimization model to determine the combination of cars and minivans that will use the maximum number of vehicles.

c) How many team members can travel in the maximum number of vehicles?

7. The vertices of the feasible region for a system of linear inequalities are $(-1, 2)$, $(2, 4)$, $(-3, -5)$, and $(0, 0)$. The objective function for the system is $P = 3x - y$. What is the maximum solution?

A. $(-1, 2)$ **B.** $(2, 4)$ **C.** $(-3, -5)$ **D.** $(0, 0)$

8. Adir makes wallets and belts from recycled tires.

- He can make no more than 4 wallets and at least 10 belts in a day.
- On an average day, he makes no more than 20 items.
- Each belt costs $1.50 to make, and each wallet costs $2.25.

a) Create an algebraic model to represent the situation, if w represents the number of wallets Adir can make and b represents the number of belts he can make.

b) The vertices of the feasible region are $(0, 10)$, $(0, 20)$, $(4, 10)$, and $(4, 16)$. What is the minimum cost of production for the day? Explain your answer.

Complete the following to summarize the important ideas from this chapter.

Q: When you graph a linear inequality in two variables, how do you decide which points are in the solution set?

NEED HELP?
• See Lesson 6.1

A: • First, determine the _____ by turning the inequality _____ into an ___ sign.

• To determine which half _____ is included in the solution set, use the inequality to test a _____ on either side of the _____.

• If the inequality type is < or >, the boundary is/is not included. Use a _____ line for the boundary.

• If the inequality type is ≤ or ≥, the boundary is/is not included. Use a _____ line for the boundary with a continuous _____ set, and a stippled line with a _____ _____ set.

Q: How can you locate the points representing an optimal solution?

NEED HELP?
• See Lesson 6.5

A: • In the _____ case, the optimal solutions will be at the _____ of the _____ region.

• In the _____ case, the optimal solutions may not be at the _____ of the _____ region. However, they will be near to the _____.

Q: What are the key steps in linear programming?

NEED HELP?
• See Lesson 6.6

A: • Create an _____ model with a _____ statement, _____, constraints, and an _____ function.

• Create a _____ model of the system of _____; locate the _____ of the _____ region.

• Evaluate the _____ function at (or near) the _____.

• Choose the desired _____(s). Verify that each _____ satisfies the _____ for the problem.

MULTIPLE CHOICE

1. Suppose you graph the linear inequality $2x + y < 4$. Which set of statements describes the graph of the linear inequality?

   A. The boundary line is a solid line. The plane is shaded above the line.

   B. The boundary line is a dashed line. The plane is shaded above the line.

   C. The boundary line is a dashed line. The plane is shaded below the line.

   D. The boundary line is a solid line. The plane is shaded below the line.

2. Which linear inequality is shown in the graph?

   A. $\{(x, y) \mid y - x \geq -2, x \in W, y \in W\}$ **C.** $\{(x, y) \mid y - x \geq -2, x \in R, y \in R\}$

   B. $\{(x, y) \mid y - x > -2, x \in W, y \in W\}$ **D.** $\{(x, y) \mid y - x > -2, x \in I, y \in I\}$

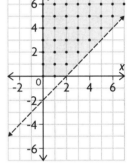

3. Which is a solution to the system of linear inequalities?

   $\{(x, y) \mid 2x + y > 5, x \in I, y \in I\}$

   $\{(x, y) \mid y - x < 4, x \in I, y \in I\}$

   A. $(3, 1)$ **B.** $(4.5, 0)$ **C.** $(-2, 1)$ **D.** $(-3, -1)$

4. Consider this system:

   $\{(x, y) \mid 3y + x \geq 3, x \in R, y \in R\}$

   $\{(x, y) \mid x - y < 4, x \in R, y \in R\}$

   The boundaries for the two inequalities intersect at the point $(3.75, -0.25)$. Which statement about this point is most accurate?

   A. The point is not in the solution set, because its coordinates are not whole numbers.

   B. The point is in the solution set, because it lies on both boundaries.

   C. The point is not in the solution set, because one of the inequality signs is $<$ or $>$.

   D. The point is in the solution set, because one of the inequality signs is $\leq$ or $\geq$.

5. A sports equipment manufacturer produces snowboards and skis. It takes 4 h to cut and mould each board and 1 h to put on the finishes. It takes 4 h to cut and mould and 2 h to put on the finishes for a pair of skis. The total number of snowboards and pairs of skis produced per day is at most 15.

   Let a represent the number of snowboards and b represent the number of pairs of skis made in one day or less. What are the restrictions on a and b?

   A. no restrictions   **B.** $a \in N, b \in N$ **C.** $a \in I, b \in I$ **D.** $a \in W, b \in W$

6. Which algebraic model represents the situation in question 5?

   A. $\{(a, b) \mid a \geq 0, b \geq 0, a + b \leq 15, a \in R, b \in R\}$

   $\{(a, b) \mid a \geq 0, b \geq 0, 5a + 6b \leq 24, a \in R, b \in R\}$

   B. $\{(a, b) \mid a \geq 0, b \geq 0, a + b \leq 15, a \in I, b \in I\}$

   $\{(a, b) \mid a \geq 0, b \geq 0, 5a + 6b \leq 24, a \in I, b \in I\}$

   C. $\{(a, b) \mid a \geq 0, b \geq 0, a + b \leq 15, a \in W, b \in W\}$

   $\{(a, b) \mid a \geq 0, b \geq 0, 5a + 6b \leq 24, a \in W, b \in W\}$

   D. $\{(a, b) \mid a \geq 0, b \geq 0, a + b \leq 4, a \in N, b \in N\}$

   $\{(a, b) \mid a \geq 0, b \geq 0, 5a + 6b \leq 24, a \in N, b \in N\}$

NUMERICAL RESPONSE

7. Consider the inequality $-3x - y \geq -1$.

   a) State a point that is a solution to the inequality: _____

   b) State a point that is not a solution to the inequality: _____

8. Consider this system of linear inequalities:

   $y + 3x \geq 9$

   $y < 2x - 3$

   a) Determine the point of intersection for the system of linear inequalities.

   Point of intersection: _____

   b) Will the point be a solid dot or an open dot on a graph of the system?

   A(n) _____ dot

9. Graph each system. Determine a solution for each.

   a) $\{(x, y) \mid y \geq 0.5x, x \in R, y \in R\}$

   $\{(x, y) \mid x + y < 7, x \in R, y \in R\}$

   b) $\{(x, y) \mid y - 2x > 2, x \in W, y \in W\}$

   $\{(x, y) \mid x + 2y < 12, x \in W, y \in W\}$

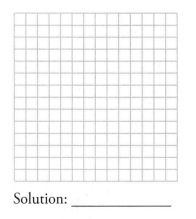

Solution: _____

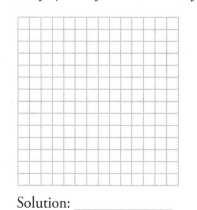

Solution: _____

10. The graph of a system of linear inequalities is shown, where the objective function is $P = 1.5x + 4y$.

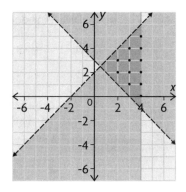

a) Determine the vertices of the feasible region.

_____ , _____ , _____

b) What is the minimum solution for the system? _____

c) If P represents the amount of profit, in thousands of dollars, what is the minimum profit that can be made? $ _____

d) What is the maximum solution for the system? _____

e) If P represents the amount of profit, in thousands of dollars, what is the maximum profit that can be made? $ _____

11. A snack machine sells granola bars and bags of trail mix.

- The machine holds, at most, 200 units of snacks.

- At least 4 granola bars are sold for each bag of trail mix.

- Each granola bar sells for $1.00, and each bag of trail mix sells for $1.25.

Let g represent the number of granola bars and t represent the number of bags of trail mix.

a) Write a linear inequality to represent the number of units of snacks the machine holds.

$\{(g, t) \mid$ ___ $+$ ___ $\leq$ _____ $, g \in$ ___ $, t \in$ ___ $\}$

b) Write a linear inequality to represent the number of granola bars sold compared to bags of trail mix.

$\{(g, t) \mid$ _____ $, g \in$ ___ $, t \in$ ___ $\}$

c) Write an objective function for the revenue, R, from snack sales.

$R =$ _____

WRITTEN RESPONSE

12. Lite Lights manufactures two types of book light: type A is a solar-powered light; type B requires batteries. In one day, the company can make at most 55 of type A and 65 of type B. Type A requires 4 h to produce, and type B requires 2 h to produce. The production team can work a total of 240 hours each day.

a) Define the variables for this situation. State any restrictions.

b) Write a system of linear inequalities to model this situation.

c) Graph the system of linear inequalities on the grid provided.

d) Determine the vertices of the feasible region.

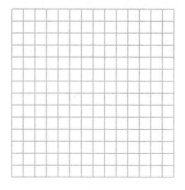

e) Which of the following are solutions to the system?

(55, 65), (25, 25), (45, 50)

What does each solution mean?

13. Jenna and Rhiana sell tacos and burritos from a food cart.

- No more than 50 tacos and 75 burritos can be made each day.
- Jenna and Rhiana can make no more than 110 items, in total, each day.
- It costs $0.75 to make a taco and $1.25 to make a burrito.

Create an optimization model and use it to determine the maximum and minimum costs to produce the food items.

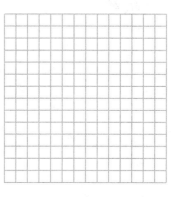

Chapter 7 · Quadratic Functions and Equations

Getting Started

1. Match each term with an image or example.

   a) *x*-intercept ___

   b) linear factors ___

   c) slope–*y*-intercept form ___

   d) evaluating a function ___

   i) $x - 6, 2x + 3$

   ii) $f(2) = 5 + 3(2)$, or 11

   iii) $y = -3x + 7$

   iv)

2. Determine whether each relation is a function, and explain why or why not.

   a) $x = \dfrac{1}{2}y - 2$ **b)** $y = 14$ **c)** $\{(0, -1), (1, -2), (1, 3), (3, -1)\}$

3. Use the vertical-line test to determine whether each relation is a function.

   a)

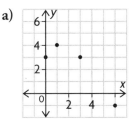

   b)

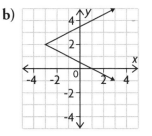

> **TIP**
>
> Apply the vertical-line test by moving a vertical line over the graph of the relation from left to right. If the vertical line never crosses the graph at more than one point at a time, the relation is a function.

4. Solve each equation.

   a) $2x - 5 = 11$ **b)** $9 = 24 - 5x$ **c)** $9x^2 = 144$

5. Graph each linear relation.

a) $y = -x + 3$

b) $y - 1 = \dfrac{1}{2}(x + 3)$

c) $y + 3 = 2x$

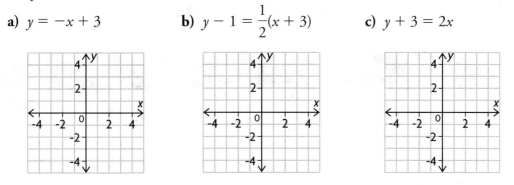

6. Factor each quadratic expression, if possible.

a) $x^2 + 2x - 24$

b) $x^2 - 4x + 8$

c) $3x^2 - 15x - 42$

7. Solve each equation.

a) $50 - 2x^2 = 0$

b) $4(x - 3) = 22$

c) $x(4x - 3) = (2x - 1)^2$

8. Solve these equations by determining the value of the variable that makes each factor equal to 0.

a) $2x(x - 3) = 0$

c) $(b + 4)(2b - 5) = 0$

b) $p(3p + 2) = 0$

d) $(3x + 1)(5x - 7) = 0$

7.1 Exploring Quadratic Relations

Keep in Mind

▸ The degree of all quadratic functions is 2.

▸ The standard form of a quadratic function is
$$y = ax^2 + bx + c, \text{ where } a \neq 0$$

▸ The graph of any quadratic function is a parabola with these properties:

- The parabola has a single vertical line of symmetry.
- The highest or lowest point of the parabola lies on its line of symmetry.
- If $a > 0$, the parabola opens up. If $a < 0$, it opens down.
- The y-intercept of the parabola is c.

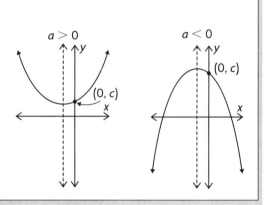

Example

A quadratic function is defined by $y = -x^2 + bx + 3$. Make a prediction about the effect on the corresponding parabola when the value of b is varied. Test your prediction by trying several values of b.

Solution

Step 1. I knew that $a = -1$ defines the shape of the parabola and the direction it opens (down in this case), so that wouldn't change. I also knew that the y-intercept of 3 wouldn't change. So I predicted that the line of symmetry and the highest point would move as b varied.

Step 2. I began by trying $b = 0$. This gave me a parabola with the y-axis as the line of symmetry.

Step 3. Trying $b = 1$ and $b = 2$, I saw that the line of symmetry shifted to the right. Also, the highest point shifted upward as well as to the right.

Step 4. Trying $b = -1$ and $b = -3$, I saw that the line of symmetry shifted to the left. Also, the highest point shifted upward as well as to the left.

Practice

1. Rewrite these relations in standard form. Then, state whether each is quadratic (circle yes or no).

a) $y = 4 - x^2 + 2x$

$y = \underline{\ \ } + \underline{\ \ } + 4$

Quadratic: yes/no

b) $y = 2(5x - 3)$

$y = \underline{\hspace{2cm}}$

yes/no

c) $y = (2x - 1)(x + 3)$

$y = \underline{\hspace{2cm}}$

yes/no

2. For the relations in question 1 that are quadratic, state the direction of opening of the parabola and its y-intercept.

3. A quadratic function is defined by $y = 2x^2 - 4x + c$. As the value of c varies, predict what happens to the line of symmetry and the lowest point on the parabola. Check your predictions by graphing several functions on the grid provided.

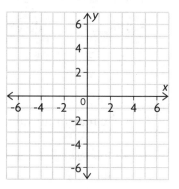

4. Identify the value of c for each parabola.

a)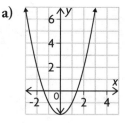

b)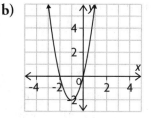

c)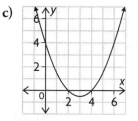

5. This table of values lists points in a quadratic relation.

a) What is the y-intercept of the parabola? _____

Is this the highest or lowest point on the parabola? _____

b) Without graphing, predict the direction in which the parabola opens. Explain how you know.

x	y
−3	1
−2	−2
−1	−3
0	−2
1	1
2	6

7.2 Properties of Graphs of Quadratic Functions

Keep in Mind

▸ A parabola that is the graph of a quadratic function is symmetric about a vertical line, the axis of symmetry, through its vertex.

▸ If the function $f(x) = ax^2 + bx + c$ has an axis of symmetry that is defined by the equation $x = d$, then $(d, f(d))$ are the coordinates of the vertex of the parabola.

▸ For a quadratic function $y = ax^2 + bx + c$:

- The domain is all real numbers: $\{x \mid x \in R\}$.
- When $a > 0$, the parabola opens up, and the y-coordinate of the vertex is the minimum value m of the function; the range is $\{y \mid y \geq m, y \in R\}$.
- When $a < 0$, the parabola opens down, and the y-coordinate of the vertex is the maximum value M of the function; the range is $\{y \mid y \leq M, y \in R\}$.

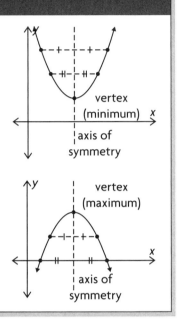

Example

Determine the y-intercept, any x-intercepts, the equation of the axis of symmetry, the coordinates of the vertex, and the domain and range of the function $f(x) = -x^2 + 2x + 8$. Sketch its graph.

Solution

Step 1. I determined the y-intercept. In this case $c = 8$ and $f(0) = 8$. The y-intercept is 8.

Step 2. To determine points on the parabola, I completed a table of values for $f(x)$. I chose numbers for x and substituted into $f(x)$.

x	-2	-1	0	1	2	3	4	5
$f(x)$	0	5	8	9	8	5	0	-7

Step 3. The x-intercepts occur when $f(x)$ or $y = 0$. From my table I could see that the x-intercepts are -2 and 4.

Step 4. The vertex of $f(x)$ lies on the axis of symmetry, which passes midway between $(-1, 5)$ and $(3, 5)$. I used the x-coordinates of these points to determine the equation of the axis of symmetry:

$$x = \frac{-1 + 3}{2} \quad \text{or} \quad x = 1$$

From the table, $f(1) = 9$. So, the vertex is $(1, 9)$.

> **TIP**
>
> The axis of symmetry of a parabola is defined by the average of the x-coordinates of any pair of points that have the same y-coordinate.

Step 5. I sketched the graph of $f(x)$ on a grid.

The domain of $f(x)$ is $\{x \mid x \in \mathbb{R}\}$.

The range of $f(x)$ is $\{y \mid y \leq 9, y \in \mathbb{R}\}$.

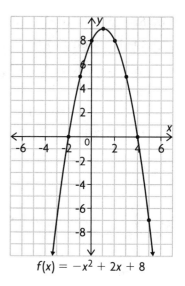

$f(x) = -x^2 + 2x + 8$

Practice

1. State the coordinates of the y-intercept and one additional ordered pair for each function.

    a) $f(x) = -x^2 + 7x + 2$ **b)** $f(x) = 2x^2 - 5x$

2. State whether each parabola has a maximum or minimum value, and then determine this value.

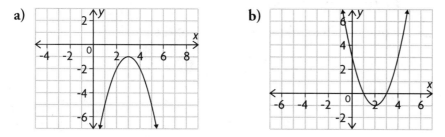

3. Does the function in the example on page 182 have a minimum or maximum value? Explain how you know and state its value.

4. State whether each quadratic function has a maximum or minimum value. State briefly how you know.

    a) $f(x) = 0.5x^2 + 3x - 99$ **b)** $f(x) = -2x^2 + 8x + 11$

5. A quadratic function is given by $f(x) = 4x^2 - 28x + 13$.

    a) Complete the table of values for $f(x)$.

x	0	1	2	3	4	5	6	7
$f(x)$	13							

    b) Determine the axis of symmetry of $f(x)$.

    c) Determine the vertex of $f(x)$. Does $f(x)$ have a maximum or a minimum?

    d) Sketch a graph of the function, using the grid provided.

    e) State the domain and range of $f(x)$.

6. Sid knows that the points $(-1, 41)$ and $(5, 41)$ lie on a parabola defined by the function $f(x) = 4x^2 - 16x + 21$.

a) Does $f(x)$ have a maximum value or a minimum value? Explain.

b) Determine the coordinates of the vertex of the parabola.

7. a) Use graphing technology to graph each function. Choose appropriate axis scales.

i) $f(x) = x^2 - 6x + 9$ **ii)** $f(x) = -\dfrac{1}{2}x^2 - 4x + 3$

b) Determine the equation of the axis of symmetry and the coordinates of the vertex for each parabola.

8. A cliff has been eroded into an arch in the shape of a parabola. The height y of the arch, in metres, above the water at high tide can be modelled by the function $y = -2.5x^2 - 30x - 67.5$, where x is the horizontal distance in metres from the cliff's edge.

a) Create an appropriate table of values.

x							
y							

b) Determine the maximum height of the arch.

c) Determine the width of the arch where it meets the water.

d) State the domain and range of the function, including restrictions.

9. The parabola shown corresponds to a quadratic function $y = ax^2 + bx + c$. Which is a possible value for a?

   A. -3　　　　B. 5　　　　C. $\dfrac{1}{2}$　　　　D. $-\dfrac{1}{3}$

10. What is the range of the parabola shown in question 9?

    A. $\{y \mid y \in R\}$　　　　　　C. $\{y \mid y \le 7, y \in R\}$

    B. $\{y \mid 0 \le y \le 7, y \in R\}$　　D. $\{y \mid y \ge 7, y \in R\}$

11. The points $(-1, 12)$ and $(7, 12)$ lie on a parabola. What is the equation of its axis of symmetry?

    A. $x = 12$　　　B. $x = 4$　　　C. $x = 3$　　　D. $x = 6$

NUMERICAL RESPONSE

12. For each function, identify the x- and y-intercepts, the equation of the axis of symmetry, the vertex, and the domain and range.

    a)
    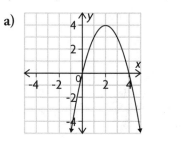

    b)
    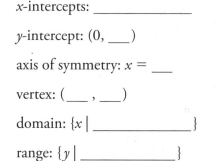

    a)　　　　　　　　　　　　　　b)

    x-intercepts: _____　　　x-intercepts: _____

    y-intercept: $(0, \_\_\_)$　　　　　　y-intercept: $(0, \_\_\_)$

    axis of symmetry: $x = \_\_\_$　　　　　axis of symmetry: $x = \_\_\_$

    vertex: $(\_\_\_, \_\_\_)$　　　　　　　vertex: $(\_\_\_, \_\_\_)$

    domain: $\{x \mid _____\}$　　　domain: $\{x \mid _____\}$

    range: $\{y \mid _____\}$　　　range: $\{y \mid _____\}$

13. The graph of $y = x^2 - 5x$ passes through the point $(0, 0)$.

    a) What is the other x-intercept of this parabola? $(0, \_\_\_)$

    b) Determine the equation of the axis of symmetry: $x = \_\_\_$

    c) Determine the vertex of the parabola: $(\_\_\_, \_\_\_)$

    d) The graph of $y = -3x^2 + kx$ has the same axis of symmetry as the graph of $y = x^2 - 5x$. What is the value of k? $k = \_\_\_$

    e) Determine the vertex of the parabola defined by $y = -3x^2 + kx$: $(\_\_\_, \_\_\_)$

7.3 Solving Quadratic Equations by Graphing

YOU WILL NEED
• graphing technology

Keep in Mind

▸ A second-degree equation in one variable is quadratic.

   • These equations are quadratic: $4x^2 + 3x + 3 = 0$; $-2x^2 + 2x = 4x + 6$.

   • These equations are not quadratic: $5x + 3 = 2x$; $-5x^3 + 4x + 3 = 0$.

▸ The number of real roots or solutions a quadratic equation has in standard form $ax^2 + bx + c = 0$ (zero, one, or two) is the number of times the corresponding parabola $y = ax^2 + bx + c$ intersects the x-axis.

▸ You can always use a graph to determine how many roots a quadratic equation has.

▸ A graph will give an approximate value of a solution.

Example 1

Solve this quadratic equation by graphing. Verify your solutions.

$$-4.9x^2 + 19.2x - 5.2 = 0$$

Solution

Step 1. This equation was in standard form, so I graphed the related function, $h(x) = -4.9x^2 + 19.2x - 5.2$, on my calculator.

Step 2. I adjusted the window to show the vertex and the intercepts.

Step 3. I used the calculator to determine the x-intercepts. To the nearest thousandth, the x-intercepts are 0.293 and 3.626.

Step 4. I verified by substituting the values into the original equation.

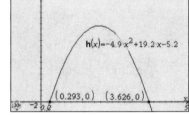

LS	RS
$-4.9(0.293)^2 + 19.2(0.293) - 5.2$ $-0.420\ldots + 5.625\ldots - 5.2$ $0.00493\ldots$	0

LS	RS
$-4.9(3.626\ldots)^2 + 19.2(3.626) - 5.2$ $-64.424\ldots + 69.619\ldots - 5.2$ $-0.005\ 39\ldots$	0

TIP

When the equation is in standard form, $ax^2 + bx + c = 0$, graph the related function $y = ax^2 + bx + c$ and determine where the graph intersects the x-axis.

Step 5. In each case, there is a slight difference because I rounded the solutions, but I could see that the solutions are correct.

Example 2

Solve this quadratic equation by graphing. Verify your solutions.

$$2x^2 - 5x + 3 = 3x(2 - x)$$

Solution

Step 1. This equation was not in standard form, so I graphed the corresponding functions on each side of the equal sign.

$$f(x) = 2x^2 - 5x + 3;\ g(x) = 3x(2 - x)$$

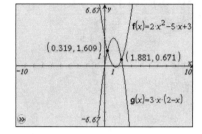

Step 2. I adjusted the window to show where the two graphs intersected.

Step 3. I used the calculator to determine the x-coordinate of each point of intersection. To the nearest thousandth, the solutions are 0.319 and 1.881.

Step 4. I verified my solutions by substituting the values into the original equations.

LS	RS
$2(0.319)^2 - 5(0.319) + 3$ $0.203... - 1.595 + 3$ $1.608...$	$3(0.319)(2 - 0.319)$ $1.608...$

LS	RS
$2(1.881)^2 - 5(1.881) + 3$ $7.076... - 9.405 + 3$ $0.671...$	$3(1.881)(2 - 1.881)$ $0.671...$

Step 5. I knew my solutions were correct because in each case, the left side equalled the right side.

Practice

1. State whether each equation is quadratic or not.

   a) $6x^2 - 2x + 1 = 0$ ___

   b) $3x^3 + 2x^2 - 3x - 1 = 0$ ___

   c) $-x^2 + 2 = 0$ ___

   d) $3x^2 + 2y^2 + 3x + 1 = 0$ ___

   e) $x^2 + 1 = 0$ ___

   f) $4x + 3 = 0$ ___

2. State whether each quadratic equation is in standard form or not. If it is not, then rewrite it in standard form.

   a) $12x^2 + 3x + 17 = 0$

   b) $1 + 3x + 0.6x^2 = 3$

   c) $4x^2 + 3 = 0$

   d) $-6x + 2x^2 = 2 - 2x$

3. This is the graph of $f(x) = -8x^2 + 22x + 21$.

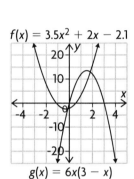

$f(x) = -8x^2 + 22x + 21$

a) Estimate the roots of $-8x^2 + 22x + 21 = 0$ based on this graph.

b) Verify your solutions.

	LS	RS		LS	RS

4. These are the graphs of $f(x) = 3.5x^2 + 2x - 2.1$ and $g(x) = 6x(3 - x)$.

$f(x) = 3.5x^2 + 2x - 2.1$

$g(x) = 6x(3 - x)$

a) Estimate the roots of $3.5x^2 + 2x - 2.1 = 6x(3 - x)$ based on these graphs.

b) Verify your solutions.

	LS	RS		LS	RS

5. a) Solve the quadratic equation $3x^2 + 2x - 4 = 4x(3 - x)$ by graphing.

b) Verify your solution.

	LS	RS		LS	RS

6. Jenna was asked to solve $x(6 - 3x) = 2x^2 - 1$. She graphed both expressions and estimated the solutions as $x = 0$ and $x = 2$. When she verified her solutions, the left side did not equal the right side.

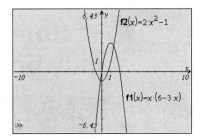

LS	RS		LS	RS
$x(6 - 3x)$	$2x^2 - 1$		$x(6 - 3x)$	$2x^2 - 1$
$0(6 - 3(0))$	$2(0)^2 - 1$		$2(6 - 3(2))$	$2(2)^2 - 1$
0	-1		0	7

a) Identify Jenna's error.

b) Determine the correct solution.

MULTIPLE CHOICE

7. Why are solutions obtained by graphing sometimes inexact?

A. A graph may not always intersect at precise grid lines.

B. A graph drawn by hand may be inaccurate.

C. A graph drawn by a calculator may not be precise.

D. All of the above.

8. Why can you always use a graph to determine whether an equation has a solution?

A. Every equation has at least one real root.

B. You can look at the graph to see whether it intersects the x-axis.

C. Every equation that can be graphed must have a solution.

D. None of the above.

WRITTEN RESPONSE

9. Fred slammed on his car's brakes to avoid an accident, creating skid marks 100 m long. For Fred's car on a dry road, the equation for stopping distance is $d = 0.0059s^2 + 0.187s$, where d is Fred's stopping distance in metres and s is his speed in kilometres per hour. Fred said he was driving at 90 km/h. Was he? Explain.

7.4 Factored Form of a Quadratic Function

Keep in Mind

▶ When a quadratic function is written in factored form, $y = a(x - r)(x - s)$:

- The zeros of the function are $x = r$ and $x = s$, because when $x = r$, the factor $(x - r)$ equals 0, and similarly when $x = s$, the factor $(x - s)$ equals 0.
- $x = r$ and $x = s$ are the x-intercepts of the corresponding parabola.
- The axis of symmetry is given by $x = \dfrac{r + s}{2}$.
- The y-intercept is $c = a \cdot r \cdot s$.

▶ If a parabola has one or two x-intercepts, its equation can be written in factored form using the x-intercepts and one other point.

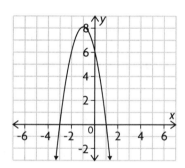

Example 1

Determine the quadratic function that defines this parabola. Write the equation of the function in standard form.

Solution

Step 1. I used the x-intercepts from the graph, $x = -3$ and $x = 1$,

to start writing the factored form of the function:

$$y = a(x - r)(x - s)$$
$$y = a(x - (-3))(x - (1))$$
$$y = a(x + 3)(x - 1)$$

Step 2. I knew from the graph that the y-intercept was at $(0, 6)$.

I substituted these coordinates, then solved for a:

$$6 = a(0 + 3)(0 - 1)$$
$$6 = a(3)(-1)$$
$$6 = -3a$$
$$-2 = a$$

Step 3. I substituted the value of a into my equation for the function

in factored form:

$$y = -2(x + 3)(x - 1)$$

Step 4. I rewrote the equation in standard form:

$$y = -2(x^2 + 2x - 3)$$
$$y = -2x^2 - 4x + 6$$

The equation seemed reasonable, because it defines a parabola with a y-intercept of 6, opening down.

Example 2

Sketch the graph of the quadratic function $f(x) = x^2 - 3x - 5$. State the maximum or minimum value of the function.

Solution

Step 1. I couldn't identify two integers with product -5 and sum 3, so I knew I could not write the function in factored form. I removed a partial factor of x from the first two terms to find two points with the same y-coordinate.

$$f(x) = x(x - 3) - 5$$

Step 2. This gave me two points with y-coordinate -5:

$$x = 0 \quad \text{or} \quad x - 3 = 0$$
$$x = 3$$

I now knew the points $(0, -5)$ and $(3, -5)$ would be on the graph.

Step 3. The axis of symmetry must be midway between these two points.

$$x = \frac{0 + 3}{2}$$
$$x = 1.5$$

Step 4. I knew $f(x)$ has a minimum value at $x = 1.5$ because the coefficient of x^2 is positive, so this parabola opens up.

$$f(1.5) = (1.5)^2 - 3(1.5) - 5$$
$$f(1.5) = 2.25 - 4.5 - 5, \text{ or } -7.25$$

This gave me another point, the vertex: $(1.5, -7.25)$. I could now choose my axis scales and sketch the graph.

> **TIP**
>
> Determine the points you need to sketch the graph, and then choose your axes based on these points.

$f(x) = x^2 - 3x - 5$

Practice

1. Each quadratic function defines one of the parabolas shown at right. Label each parabola with the letter for the correct function.

   a) $y = (x - 3)(x + 1)$ **b)** $y = (2x + 3)(x - 2)$ **c)** $y = -3x(x + 3)$

2. Write these quadratic functions in factored form.

   a) $f(x) = -x^2 + 7x - 12$ 　　　　　**b)** $g(x) = 2x^2 - x - 3$

   　$f(x) = $ _____   　　　　　$g(x) = $ _____

   _____   　　　　　_____

3. Determine the x-intercepts and axes of symmetry of the parabolas defined by the functions in question 2.

   x-intercept(s):   　　**a)** _____   　　　　**b)** _____

   axis of symmetry: 　　　_____   　　　　_____

4. Determine the *y*-intercepts of the parabolas in question 2, and sketch these parabolas on the grid provided.

y-intercept: **a)** _____   **b)** _____

5. Sketch the graph of the function $f(x) = 5x^2 - 30x + 55$ on the grid provided.

6. A quadratic function $f(x)$ defines a parabola with *x*-intercepts $x = 2$ and $x = 6$ and a *y*-intercept at $(0, 6)$. Write the function

a) in factored form

$f(x) = a(x - r)(x - s)$

$f(x) =$

b) in standard form

$f(x) =$

7. Determine the quadratic function that defines this parabola.

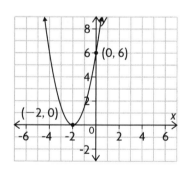

MULTIPLE CHOICE

8. Which pair of points are symmetric points for the parabola defined by $y = x^2 - 5x + 7$?

A. $(0, 7)$ and $(-5, 7)$

C. $(0, -7)$ and $(5, -7)$

B. $(0, 5)$ and $(-7, 5)$

D. $(0, 7)$ and $(5, 7)$

9. A quadratic function has vertex $(2, -8)$, and one of its x-intercepts is -2. Which of these could be the factored form of the function?

A. $f(x) = -3(x - 2)(x + 2)$ **C.** $f(x) = 2(x - 2)(x + 6)$

B. $f(x) = 0.5(x - 6)(x + 2)$ **D.** $f(x) = -(x - 18)(x - 2)$

WRITTEN RESPONSE

10. A quadratic function defines a parabola with the vertex at $(1, 18)$.

a) One zero of the function is $x = 4$. Determine the other zero.

> **TIP**
>
> How are the zeros related to the axis of symmetry?

b) Write the equation of the function in factored form.

c) Sketch the graph of the function on the grid provided.

7.5 Solving Quadratic Equations by Factoring

YOU WILL NEED
• graphing technology

Keep in Mind

▶ You can solve some quadratic equations by

- • factoring them into a product of two factors
- • setting the factors equal to zero and
- • solving the resultant linear equations

▶ An equation with two equal real roots is said to have one solution.

Example 1

Solve this quadratic equation by factoring. Verify your solutions.

$$0.125x^2 - 0.875x = -1.5$$

Solution

Step 1. I rewrote the equation in standard form, and then divided by 0.125 to simplify it.

$$0.125x^2 - 0.875x + 1.5 = 0$$

$$\frac{0.125\,x^2}{0.125} - \frac{0.875x}{0.125} + \frac{1.5}{0.125} = \frac{0}{0.125}$$

$$x^2 - 7x + 12 = 0$$

Step 2. I factored the equation.

$$(x - 3)(x - 4) = 0$$

Step 3. The product of the two factors is 0. I knew that this occurs when either factor is equal to 0.

$$x - 3 = 0 \quad \text{or} \quad x - 4 = 0$$
$$x = 3 \qquad\qquad x = 4$$

Step 4. I verified my solutions by substituting the values into the original equation. For both solutions, the left side is equal to the right side. Therefore, the solutions are correct.

LS	RS		LS	RS
$0.125(3)^2 - 0.875(3) + 1.5$ $1.125 - 2.625 + 1.5$ 0	0		$0.125(4)^2 - 0.875(4) + 1.5$ $2 - 3.5 + 1.5$ 0	0

Example 2

Solve the following equation. Verify your solutions.

$$9x^2 + 42x = -49$$

Solution

Step 1. I put the equation into standard form:

$$9x^2 + 42x = -49$$
$$9x^2 + 42x + 49 = 0$$

Step 2. I factored the trinomial.

$$9x^2 + 42x + 49 = 0$$
$$(3x + 7)(3x + 7) = 0$$

Step 3. Both factors are the same, so I knew the equation has only one root.

$$3x + 7 = 0$$
$$3x = -7$$
$$x = -\frac{7}{3} \text{ or } -2\frac{1}{3}$$

Step 4. I verified my solutions by graphing. The vertex of the function is on the x-axis at $-2\frac{1}{3}$, so the solution makes sense.

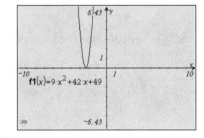

Practice

1. Solve by factoring.

   a) $x^2 + 3x - 18 = 0$ b) $x^2 + 12x + 20 = 0$ c) $81x^2 - 36 = 0$

2. Solve by factoring.

   a) $x^2 - 10x + 25 = 0$ b) $x^2 + 36 = -12x$

3. Solve by factoring. Verify your solutions by graphing.

   a) $x^2 - 4x + 3 = 0$ b) $8x = 48 - x^2$

4. Solve by factoring. Verify your solutions by substituting.

   a) $9x^2 - 36 = 0$ **b)** $49x^2 = 4$

5. Solve each of the following equations by factoring, if possible. If it is not possible, explain why.

   a) $x^2 + 6x - 3 = 0$ **b)** $x^2 - 4x + 4 = 0$

6. Determine the roots of this equation by factoring.

$$0.0625x^2 = 0.125x + 1.5$$

7. What quadratic equation could have the roots -6 and 8?

8. Govinda solved this equation: $15x^2 + x - 2 = 0$.

   His solutions were $x = -\dfrac{1}{3}$ and $x = \dfrac{2}{5}$.

   a) Factor and solve the equation.

   b) What error do you think Govinda made?

9. A bus company charges $2 per ticket but wants to raise the price. The daily revenue is modelled by $R(x) = -30(x - 6)^2 + 34\,320$, where x is the number of 15¢ price increases and $R(x)$ is the revenue in dollars. What should the price per ticket be if the bus company wants to collect daily revenue of $30\,000?

MULTIPLE CHOICE

10. Matilda solved an equation and said that the roots were -7 and -8. Which one of the following equations could NOT be the one that Matilda solved?

A. $x^2 - 15x = -56$ **C.** $2x^2 - 16x + 56 = 0$

B. $0.5x^2 - 7.5x + 28 = 0$ **D.** $0.5x^2 = 7.5x - 28$

WRITTEN RESPONSE

11. a) Solve the quadratic equation $-3x = 28 - x^2$ by graphing.

b) Put the equation into standard form. Use your solutions from part a) to predict the factors of the left side of the standard-form equation, and justify your prediction.

c) Check your prediction from part b).

7.6 Vertex Form of a Quadratic Function

YOU WILL NEED
• graphing technology

Keep in Mind

▸ The vertex form of the equation of a quadratic function is

$$y = a(x - h)^2 + k$$

▸ To sketch the graph of a quadratic function in vertex form:

- Plot the vertex at (h, k). The line of symmetry is $x = h$.
- If $a > 0$, sketch the parabola opening up.
- If $a < 0$, sketch the parabola opening down.

▸ You can use the values of a and k to determine the number of x-intercepts of a parabola whose equation is in vertex form.

Example 1

Sketch the graph of the quadratic function $y = -2(x + 4)^2 + 10$. State the domain and range of the function.

Solution

Step 1. The function is in vertex form, so I knew the vertex is at $(-4, 10)$. Since $a < 0$, I knew that the parabola opens downward.

Step 2. I substituted 0 for x to determine another point on the parabola (the y-intercept):

$$y = -2(x + 4)^2 + 10$$
$$y = -2[(0) + 4]^2 + 10$$
$$y = -32 + 10, \text{ or } -22$$

Point $(0, -22)$ is on the parabola. The equation of the axis of symmetry is $x = 4$. I knew there was another symmetric point equally far from the axis of symmetry with y-coordinate -22. That point is $(-8, -22)$. This point is also on the parabola. I chose my axis scales and sketched the graph.

Step 3. The value 10 is a maximum value, so the domain and range are

$$\{(x, y) \mid x \in \mathbb{R}, y \leq 10, y \in \mathbb{R}\}$$

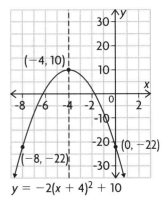

$y = -2(x + 4)^2 + 10$

Example 2

Determine the quadratic function corresponding to this parabola.

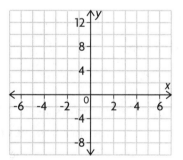

Solution

Step 1. The point (7, 8) on the parabola is the vertex, so I could start writing the equation of the function in vertex form:

$$f(x) = a(x - h)^2 + k$$
$$f(x) = a(x - 7)^2 + 8$$

Step 2. I decided to use the coordinates of the other known point on the parabola, $(4, -1)$, to determine the value of a:

$$f(x) = a(x - 7)^2 + 8$$
$$-1 = a[(4) - 7]^2 + 8$$
$$-1 = a(-3)^2 + 8$$
$$-1 = 9a + 8$$
$$-9 = 9a$$
$$-1 = a$$

Step 3. The equation of the quadratic function is

$$f(x) = -(x - 7)^2 + 8$$

Practice

1. For each quadratic function, identify the information listed.

   a) $f(x) = -(x - 1)^2 + 4$

      i) direction of opening: _____

      ii) coordinates of vertex: _____

   b) $m(x) = \dfrac{1}{2}(x + 2)^2 + 7$

      i) direction of opening: _____

      ii) coordinates of vertex: _____

2. The quadratic function $f(x) = -2(x + 3)^2 + 12$ is in vertex form.

   a) What are the coordinates of the vertex? _____

      Plot the vertex using the set of axes on the grid provided.

   b) What is the axis of symmetry? _____

      Draw in the axis of symmetry on the grid.

   c) Identify the y-intercept.

      $f(0) =$

      y-intercept: ___

      Plot point (0, ___) on the grid.

   d) Identify one other point: (___, ___) is the same horizontal distance from the axis of symmetry as (0, ___). Plot this point and complete your sketch of the graph of $f(x)$.

3. Which of these functions is shown by the graph? Explain.

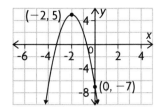

   A. $f(x) = 3(x + 2)^2 + 5$ **B.** $f(x) = 3(x - 2)^2 + 5$ **C.** $f(x) = -3(x + 2)^2 + 5$

4. Use graphing technology to create a family of three parabolas with each property. Provide the equation that defines each parabola.

   • The shape, direction of opening, and axis of symmetry are all the same.

   • The vertex is always the same.

5. The parabola shown is the graph of the function $g(x)$.

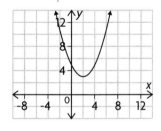

   a) What are the coordinates of the vertex and y-intercept?

   b) Write $g(x)$ in vertex form. Substitute values you know for h and k, and then determine a.

> **TIP**
> What information can you use to determine a?

6. Jasmine throws a softball to Lauren. The height of the ball $h(t)$, in metres, t seconds after Jasmine's throw can be modelled as $h(t) = -4.9(t - 0.8)^2 + 4.5$. Lauren then misses the catch.

   a) Use technology to graph the function and determine its zeros.

   b) Do either of the zeros have meaning in this situation? Explain.

7. A plan for an arch in the shape of a parabola is drawn on a grid with a scale of 1 m per square. The base of the arch is located at the points $(0, 0)$ and $(15, 0)$. The maximum height of the arch is 18 m.

a) Determine the quadratic function that models the arch.

b) State the domain and range of the function.

MULTIPLE CHOICE

8. Which information can you use to write a quadratic function in vertex form?

A. vertex and y-intercept   **C.** y-intercept and axis of symmetry

B. vertex and axis of symmetry   **D.** vertex and direction of opening

9. How many zeros does the function $y = 2(x - h)^2 + 5$ have?

A. none   **C.** two

B. one   **D.** depends on the value of h

NUMERICAL RESPONSE

10. Determine the vertex and y-intercept of the parabola corresponding to the quadratic function $f(x) = -0.25(x - 6)^2 - 1$.

vertex: (___, ___) y-intercept: ___

11. Determine the vertex form of the equation for this parabola.

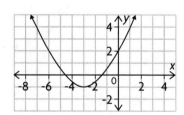

7.7 Solving Quadratic Equations Using the Quadratic Formula

YOU WILL NEED
• graphing technology

Keep in Mind

▸ The roots of a quadratic equation in the form $ax^2 + bx + c = 0$, where $a \neq 0$, can be determined using the quadratic formula:

$$x = \frac{-b \pm \sqrt{b^2 - 4ac}}{2a}$$

▸ You can use this formula to determine the roots, if they exist, of any quadratic equation, even if it is not factorable.

▸ The quadratic formula will give you an exact value for the solution.

▸ If the radicand, $b^2 - 4ac$, simplifies to a perfect square, then the equation can be solved by factoring.

▸ If the value of the radicand is negative, then the equation has no real solution.

Example 1

Solve the quadratic equation $4x^2 - 3 = 7x$. Give an exact answer and an approximate answer to three decimal places.

Solution

Step 1. I put the equation in standard form to determine a, b, and c.

$$4x^2 - 7x - 3 = 0 \qquad a = 4, b = -7, \text{ and } c = -3$$

Step 2. I entered a, b, and c in the quadratic formula and simplified.

$$x = \frac{-b \pm \sqrt{b^2 - 4ac}}{2a}$$

$$x = \frac{-(-7) \pm \sqrt{(-7)^2 - 4(4)(-3)}}{2(4)}$$

$$x = \frac{7 \pm \sqrt{49 + 48}}{8}$$

$$x = \frac{7 \pm \sqrt{97}}{8}$$

Step 3. I separated the expression into two solutions.

$$x = \frac{7 + \sqrt{97}}{8} \quad \text{or} \quad x = \frac{7 - \sqrt{97}}{8}$$

$$x = 2.106... \quad \text{or} \quad x = -0.356...$$

The exact solutions are $x = \dfrac{7 + \sqrt{97}}{8}$ or $x = \dfrac{7 - \sqrt{97}}{8}$.

The approximate solutions are $x = 2.106$ or $x = -0.356$.

Example 2

Solve the quadratic equation $x^2 + 9x + 23 = 0$. If there is no real solution, explain why.

Solution

Step 1. Since the equation was already in standard form, I knew the values of a, b, and c:

$a = 1$, $b = 9$, and $c = 23$.

Step 2. I entered the values of a, b, and c in the quadratic formula. Then I simplified.

$$x = \frac{-b \pm \sqrt{b^2 - 4ac}}{2a}$$

$$x = \frac{-9 \pm \sqrt{9^2 - 4(1)(23)}}{2(1)}$$

$$x = \frac{-9 \pm \sqrt{81 - 92}}{2}$$

$$x = \frac{-9 \pm \sqrt{-11}}{2}$$

Step 3. The radicand of the quadratic formula was -11, which is negative. This means that the equation has no real solution.

Practice

1. Jamilla and Ryan solved $3x^2 - 5x = 6$ using the quadratic formula. Who entered the values in the formula incorrectly? Explain.

Jamilla: $x = \dfrac{-(-5) \pm \sqrt{(-5)^2 - 4(3)(-6)}}{2(3)}$

Ryan: $x = \dfrac{-5 \pm \sqrt{5^2 - 4(3)(-6)}}{2(3)}$

2. Suppose you were to solve these equations using the quadratic formula. What values of a, b, and c would you use in each case?

a) $3x^2 - 2x + 1 = 0$

b) $-2(x - 1)^2 - 1 = 0$

3. State whether each quadratic equation can be solved by factoring or not. Give your reasoning.

a) $2x^2 + 4x + 1 = 0$

c) $x^2 + x - 6 = 0$

b) $x^2 - 8x - 24 = 0$

d) $2x^2 + x - 15 = 0$

4. Solve each quadratic equation. Identify any equations that do not have real roots. Otherwise, give an exact answer.

a) $2x^2 - x - 3 = 0$

c) $16x^2 + 8x + 3 = 0$

b) $5x^2 = 6x + 2$

d) $-2x^2 + 8x = 3$

5. A landscaper is designing a rectangular garden, as shown. She has enough crushed rock to cover an area of 10.0 m² and wants to make a uniform border around the garden. How wide should the border be, if she wants to use all the crushed rock?

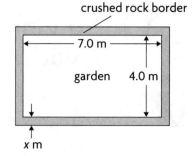

crushed rock border

7.0 m

garden   4.0 m

x m

NUMERICAL RESPONSE

6. On Mars, a ball thrown from the top of a spacecraft 6.5 m high could be modelled by $h(t) = -1.89t^2 + 5t + 7.5$. On Neptune, a ball thrown from the top of the same spacecraft could be modelled by $h(t) = -7.0t^2 + 5t + 7.5$. In these equations, h is the height in metres and t is the time in seconds. How much earlier would a ball fall to the base of the spacecraft on Neptune than on Mars? Give your answer to the nearest hundredth of a second.

on Mars: $t =$ _____ (Choose the positive root.)

on Neptune: $t =$ _____

The ball would fall to the base of the spacecraft _____ earlier on Neptune.

WRITTEN RESPONSE

7. Suppose a pebble were to fall from a 200 m cliff to the water below. The height of the stone, $h(t)$, in metres, after t seconds can be represented by the function $h(t) = -4.9t^2 + 3t + 200$. How long would the stone take to reach the water, to the nearest tenth of a second? Show your work.

7.8 Solving Problems Using Quadratic Models

Keep in Mind

▸ An equation, a graph, or a table of values can represent a relation. Use the form that is most helpful for the context of the problem.

▸ You can use vertex form, factored form, or standard form to create an algebraic model of the situation. Use the form that is most helpful for the context of the problem.

▸ When you solve a quadratic equation, check that your solutions are admissible: that they make sense in the problem's context.

Example 1

You are an astronaut on the Moon. You hit a golf ball with your golf club. The height of the ball, $h(t)$, in metres, over time, t, in seconds, could be modelled by this function:

$$h(t) = -0.81t^2 + 5t$$

What is the maximum height of the ball?

Solution

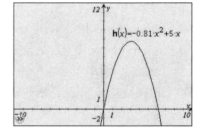

Step 1. Since the function is quadratic, I knew the coordinates for the maximum height would be (t, h), where t is halfway between the t-intercepts of the parabola.

Step 2. I wrote an equation to determine the t-coordinates of the points at which the ball leaves the ground and lands again. The height at each point is 0.

$$h(t) = -0.81t^2 + 5t$$

$$0 = -0.81t^2 + 5t$$

Step 3. I factored the equation and solved for t.

$$0 = t(-0.81t + 5)$$

$$0 = t(-0.81t + 5)$$

$$t = 0 \quad \text{or} \quad -0.81t + 5 = 0$$

$$-0.81t = -5$$

$$t = 6.172...$$

One point is at 0 s, and the other is at 6.172... s.

Step 4. Therefore, the equation of the axis of symmetry is

$$t = \frac{0 + 6.172\ldots}{2}$$

$$t = 3.086\ldots$$

The t-coordinate of the vertex is 3.086….

Step 5. I used this value of t to determine the h-coordinate of the vertex.

$$h(3.086\ldots) = -0.81(3.086\ldots)^2 + 5(3.086\ldots)$$

$$h(3.086\ldots) = -2.5 + 15.432\ldots$$

$$h(3.086\ldots) = 12.932\ldots \text{ m}$$

The ball reaches a maximum height of about 12.9 m.

Example 2

Patricia dives from a platform that is 10 m high. She reaches her maximum height of 0.5 m above the platform after 0.32 s. How long will Patricia take to reach the water?

Solution

Step 1. I sketched a graph of the diver's height over time. I knew the vertex was (0.32, 10.5) because the maximum height of 10.5 m was reached after 0.32 s.

Step 2. I wrote a quadratic function in vertex form and solved for a.

$$h(t) = a(t - 0.32)^2 + 10.5$$

$$10 = a(0 - 0.32)^2 + 10.5$$

$$10 = a(-0.32)^2 + 10.5$$

$$10 = 0.1024a + 10.5$$

$$-0.5 = 0.1024a$$

$$-4.882\ldots = a$$

The function that models her dive is $h(t) = -4.882(t - 0.32)^2 + 10.5$.

Step 3. I graphed my function and determined the t-intercepts.

The zeros of my function are $-1.147\ldots$ and $1.787\ldots$.

The solution $-1.147\ldots$ s is inadmissible. Patricia will reach the water after about 1.8 s.

Practice

1. The sum of two numbers is 2. Their product is -195. What are the numbers?

2. A company manufactures aluminum cans. One customer places an order for cans that must be 15 cm high, with a volume of 1200 cm³.

   a) Use the formula $V = \pi r^2 h$ to determine the radius that the company should use to manufacture these cans.

   b) Graph the function that corresponds to $0 = \pi r^2 h - V$ to determine the radius.

3. Hali is about to eat a bagel. The outer radius of the bagel is 5.5 cm. She notices that the area of the bagel hole is the same as the area of the bagel. Determine the radius of the hole to one decimal place.

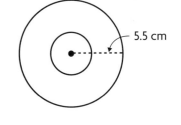

5.5 cm

4. Christopher dives with a junior swim club. In a dive off a 6.5 m platform, he reaches a maximum height of 7.04 m after 0.25 s. How long does Christopher take to reach the water?

5. Two consecutive integers are squared. The sum of these squares is 481. What are the integers?

6. A right triangle has a perimeter of 130 cm. One side of the triangle is 43 cm long. Determine the length of the other sides, to the nearest centimetre.

MULTIPLE CHOICE

7. Mai-Lin says there are three consecutive positive integers for which the sum of the squares of the first two integers is 12 less than the square of the third integer. Choose the best response.

A. The integers exist and could be odd or even.

B. The integers exist and must be odd.

C. The integers exist and must be even.

D. There are no such integers.

WRITTEN RESPONSE

8. Torin is painting a portrait. He wants it to be square, with the mat around it to be 7 cm wide. The area of the mat should be equal to the area of the portrait itself. What should the dimensions of the portrait be, to the nearest tenth of a centimetre?

Complete the following to summarize the important ideas from this chapter.

NEED HELP?
- See Lessons 7.1, 7.4

$a < 0$

Q: What are the characteristics of all quadratic functions and their graphs?

A: • The degree is ___ .

- The graph is a _____ with a single vertical _____ .

- The _____ of a parabola is its highest or lowest point and lies on its _____ .

- A parabola can have ___ , ___ , or ___ x-intercepts.

Q: What are the different forms of a quadratic function and their features?

NEED HELP?
- See Lessons 7.1, 7.4, 7.6

A: • standard form: _____ , where $a \neq 0$

     a ___ 0, parabola opens _____ ; a ___ 0, parabola opens _____

     c is the _____ .

- factored form: $y = $ _____ , where $a \neq 0$

     r and s are the _____ .

- vertex form: $y = $ _____ , where $a \neq 0$

     (h, k) is the _____ .

Q: Given the equation of a quadratic function, how can you sketch its graph?

NEED HELP?
- See Lessons 7.2, 74, 7.6

A: • standard form: use a _____ of values to determine the

     _____ and axis of _____ ; or use _____

     factoring; plot the ___ -intercept

- factored form: plot the ___ -intercepts; also determine the

     _____ of symmetry and _____

- vertex form: plot the _____ , determine the ___ -intercept,

     and use the axis of _____ to determine the other symmetric point

Q: What are the characteristics of a quadratic equation?

NEED HELP?
- See Lesson 7.3

A: • It is a _____ -degree equation with _____ variable(s).

Q: What determines the number of roots a quadratic equation has?

A: • The number of roots is determined by the _____ of times the corresponding parabola intersects the _____.

• There can be ___, ___, or ___ roots.

NEED HELP?
• See Lesson 7.3

Q: One way to solve a quadratic equation is by graphing. What are some of the characteristics of a graphing solution?

A: • Solution values are _____. The number of _____ is obvious.

• The solution process is relatively _____.

NEED HELP?
• See Lesson 7.3

Q: What are some of the characteristics of a factoring solution?

A: • Solution values are _____. The number of _____ is not always obvious.

• The solution process involves solving _____ equations.

NEED HELP?
• See Lesson 7.5

Q: What is the quadratic formula?

A: • The quadratic formula is $x = \dfrac{\boxed{}}{\boxed{}}$.

• It applies to the quadratic equation _____, where _____.

NEED HELP?
• See Lesson 7.7

Q: List some of the characteristics of a solution using the quadratic formula.

A: • Solution values are _____.

• If the radicand, _____, simplifies to a perfect square, then the equation can be solved by _____.

• If the _____ is negative, then the equation has no real solution.

NEED HELP?
• See Lesson 7.7

Q: Why is the context of a problem important for the number of solutions?

A: • A problem may have only one _____ solution, even though the quadratic equation that represents it has two _____ solutions. Solutions that do not make sense for the problem are _____.

NEED HELP?
• See Lesson 7.8

MULTIPLE CHOICE

1. Which parabola corresponds to the greatest value of c, the constant coefficient in the function $y = ax^2 + bx + c$?

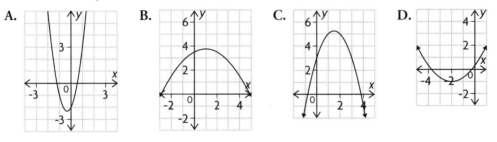

2. Which of these equations represents the parabola shown?

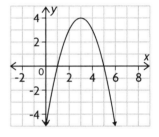

   A. $y = -x(x - 5) + 1$ **C.** $y = -x^2 + 6x - 5$

   B. $y = -x^2 - 6x + 5$ **D.** $y = -(x - 5)^2 + 1$

3. What is the vertex of $f(x) = -0.5(x + 4)^2 - 2$?

   A. $(4, -2)$ **B.** $(-2, -4)$ **C.** $(2, -4)$ **D.** $(-4, -2)$

4. What is the equation of the axis of symmetry of $f(x) = -5x(x - 7) + 21$?

   A. $x = 7$ **B.** $x = 0$ **C.** $x = 3.5$ **D.** $x = -7$

5. Which equation is a quadratic equation in standard form?

   A. $-3x^3 + 2x - 5 = 0$ **B.** $2x^2 - 5x = 15$ **C.** $f(x) = 2x^2 + 3x - 5$ **D.** $4x^2 - 6x + 5 = 0$

6. Select the one correct statement about the quadratic equations corresponding to these graphs.

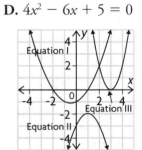

   A. Equation I has no solution.

   B. Equations I and III each have at least one real solution.

   C. Each equation has at least one real solution.

   D. Equation II has two solutions.

7. The graphs of $f(x) = 5.5x^2 + x - 1.1$ and $g(x) = 4x(3 - x)$ are shown. Estimate the roots of $5.5x^2 + x - 1.1 = 4x(3 - x)$.

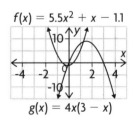

$f(x) = 5.5x^2 + x - 1.1$

$g(x) = 4x(3 - x)$

   A. $x = -0.1$ and $x = -1.2$ **C.** $x = -0.1$ and $x = 1.3$

   B. $x = 1.3$ and $x = 8.8$ **D.** $x = -1.2$ and $x = 8.8$

8. Which of the following are roots of $x^2 - 9x - 52 = 0$?

   A. $x = -4$ and $x = -13$ **C.** $x = -4$ and $x = 13$

   B. $x = 4$ and $x = -13$ **D.** $x = 4$ and $x = 13$

9. A quadratic function has the vertex $(-2, 9)$. Which of the following is a possible equation for this function?

A. $y = -x(x - 5) + 1$ **C.** $y = -x^2 + 4x - 5$

B. $y = -x^2 - 4x + 5$ **D.** $y = -(x - 5)^2 + 1$

10. Which parabola corresponds to the quadratic function $y = 2x^2 + 4x - 16$?

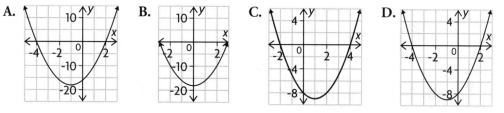

11. Can you solve $x^2 + 14x - 19 = 0$ by factoring? How do you know?

A. No; $14^2 - 4(1)(-19) = 272$, which is not a perfect square.

B. Yes; $14^2 - 4(1)(-19) = 272 > 0$.

C. Yes; because $14^2 - 4(1)(-19) = 272$, which is a perfect square.

D. It is not possible to answer this question.

12. Use the quadratic formula to determine which of the following are roots of the equation $4.4x^2 + 4.3x - 5 = 0$.

A. $x = 0.68$ and $x = 1.66$ **C.** $x = 0.68$ and $x = -1.66$

B. $x = -0.68$ and $x = 1.66$ **D.** $x = -0.68$ and $x = -1.66$

NUMERICAL RESPONSE

13. **a)** Identify the following information for the parabola shown.

x-intercepts: (___, 0), (___, 0)   y-intercept: (0, ___)

axis of symmetry: $x =$ ___   vertex: _____

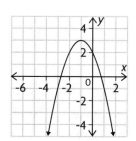

b) What is the range of the function corresponding to this parabola?

range: $\{y \mid y \leq$ ___ $, y \in R\}$

14. The roots of $x^2 + 17x - 38 = 0$ are $x =$ _____ and $x =$ _____.

15. The roots of $x^2 - 2x = 323$ are $x =$ _____ and $x =$ _____.

16. The quadratic function $y = -5x(x + 4) + 7$ has been partially factored.

a) Determine the equation of the axis of symmetry of the function: $x =$ ___

b) Locate the vertex of the function: (___, ___)

c) Write the function in vertex form: $y =$ ___$(x +$ ___$)^2 +$ _____

17. Suppose you were to use the quadratic formula to solve these equations. What values of a, b, and c would you use in each case?

a) $3x^2 - 2x + 1 = 0$

$a =$ ___, $b =$ ___, $c =$ ___

b) $-2(x-1)^2 - 1 = 0$

$a =$ ___, $b =$ ___, $c =$ ___

18. Use the quadratic formula to determine the exact roots of each quadratic equation.

a) $7x^2 + 3x - 2 = 0$

roots: _____

b) $-4x^2 - 2x + 3 = 0$

roots: _____

19. Two consecutive integers are squared. The sum of these squares is 365. What are the integers?

___ and ___   or   ___ and ___

20. A right triangle has a perimeter of 93 cm. One side of the triangle is 36 cm long.

To the nearest whole centimetre, the hypotenuse is _____ long.

The other side is _____ long.

WRITTEN RESPONSE

21. Sketch the graph of the quadratic function $f(x) = -x^2 + 10x - 9$.

State its domain and range.

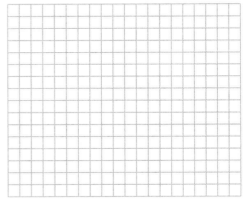

22. Jill braked to avoid an accident, creating skid marks 60 m long. For Jill's car on a dry road, the equation for stopping distance is $d = 0.0081s^2 + 0.137s$, where d is Jill's stopping distance in metres and s is her speed in kilometres per hour. How fast was Jill driving?

23. Write the equation in vertex form of the parabola shown.

24. Determine the real roots of each quadratic equation, if possible. Give an exact answer and an answer to two decimal places. If it is not possible, explain why.

a) $2.6x^2 - 3.1x - 2 = 0$ b) $4.1x^2 - 2.7x + 3 = 0$

25. A midway ride launches passengers into free fall as they rise into the air, then fall until the brakes engage to bring them to a safe stop. The free-fall part of the ride starts at a height of 45 m, reaches a maximum height of 76.25 m after 2.5 s, and ends after 5.5 s.

a) Determine a quadratic model for the height of the ride after t seconds.

b) Determine the height above ground where the brakes engage.

Chapter 8 · Proportional Reasoning

Getting Started

1. Match each term with the example that most closely represents it.

   a) rate ____   e) reciprocals ____   i) $3 - 2x$ v) $\sqrt[3]{64}$

   b) equation ____   f) expression ____   ii) $V(t) = 200 - 20t$ vi) $\dfrac{13}{5}, \dfrac{5}{13}$

   c) linear function ____ g) cube root ____   iii) 20 mL/s   vii) $8 : 27$

   d) square root ____   h) ratio ____   iv) $3 - 2x = 7$ viii) $\sqrt{64}$

2. Determine the slope of the line that passes through each pair of points.

   a) $A(2, 15)$, $B(5, 27)$ b) $E(3, -2)$, $F(7, 9)$ c) $P(25, 8)$, $Q(-15, 24)$

3. Determine the surface area and volume of each 3-D object.

   a) a rectangular prism with side lengths of 4 m, 7 m, and 5 m

   b) a cylinder 14.0 cm tall with a radius of 2.5 cm

   c) a cube with side lengths of 12 mm

4. Identify the greatest common factor for each set of numbers.

   a) 5, 20, 395   b) 45, 225, 540   c) 105, 147, 189

5. Express each percent or ratio as a decimal.

   a) 37.5% **b)** 5:16 **c)** 17:4 **d)** 320%

6. Express each measurement in the unit indicated.

   a) 245 cm, in metres **b)** 7 min 30 s, in seconds **c)** 3.8 m², in square centimetres

7. Expand each expression.

   a) $2(4x + 3)$ **b)** $5(k^2 - 2k)$ **c)** $-4(7 - t + 2t^2)$

8. Write the reciprocal of each fraction or expression.

   a) $\dfrac{3}{25}$ **b)** 11 **c)** $-\dfrac{2}{17}$ **d)** $\dfrac{48}{x}$

9. Simplify each expression.

   a) $(x^4)(x)$ **b)** $\dfrac{x^7}{x^3}$ **c)** $(x^4)^3$ **d)** $\dfrac{x^2}{x^5}$

10. Evaluate each square root or cube root. Round to the nearest tenth, as appropriate.

    a) $\sqrt{625}$ **b)** $\sqrt{180}$ **c)** $\sqrt{0.09}$ **d)** $\sqrt[3]{16}$

11. Solve each equation. Round to the nearest hundredth, as appropriate.

    a) $\dfrac{32}{5} = \dfrac{x}{7}$ **b)** $\dfrac{54}{8} = \dfrac{13}{t}$ **c)** $\dfrac{16}{w} = \dfrac{5}{21}$

12. These 2-D shapes are similar. Identify the corresponding sides.

    $\angle A = \angle B = 135°$ $\angle K = \angle L = 135°$

    $\angle D = 120°$ $\angle H = 120°$

    $\angle E = 150°$ $\angle I = 150°$

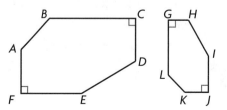

8.1 Comparing and Interpreting Rates

Keep in Mind

▸ You can represent rates in several ways. Try to choose the way that suits your purpose best.

▸ To compare rates:

- Write them with the same units, so the second terms have the same value. OR
- Write them as unit rates, in which the second terms are equal to 1.

▸ In a graph of the relationship between two quantities, the slope of a line segment represents the average rate of change for these quantities.

▸ The slope of a line segment that represents a rate of change is a unit rate.

Example 1

Orange juice is sold in 1.5 L cartons and 250 mL boxes. A 1.5 L carton sells for $3.75, and ten 250 mL boxes sell for $7.39. Which size costs less per millilitre?

Solution

Step 1. I determined the unit rate of each item.

For a carton: 1.5 L = 1500 mL

$$\text{Unit rate} = \frac{\$3.75}{1500 \text{ mL}}$$

Unit rate = $0.0025/mL

The unit rate for cartons is $0.0025/mL.

For ten boxes: 10(250) = 2500 mL

$$\text{Unit rate} = \frac{\$7.39}{2500 \text{ mL}}$$

Unit rate = $0.0029... mL

The unit rate for boxes is about $0.003/mL.

The carton costs less per millilitre.

Step 2. I estimated and used mental math to check my answer.

A 1.5 L carton costs $3.75, so 3 L will cost double that, or $7.50.

Ten boxes have 2500 mL, or 2.5 L, and they cost about $7.50. I get more juice for the same price in the carton, so the carton costs less per millilitre. This confirms my answer.

> **TIP**
> Round values so you can compare rates using mental math.

Example 2

Describe a scenario that can be represented by this graph. Compare the rates that correspond to each line segment, and discuss why the rates may have changed.

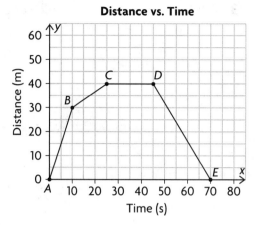

Distance vs. Time

Solution

Step 1. To determine a reasonable scenario, I calculated the slope of each segment. This meant dividing the change in distance by the change in time.

$$\text{Slope} = \frac{\Delta y}{\Delta x}$$

$$\text{Slope} = \frac{y_2 - y_1}{x_2 - x_1}$$

$$\text{Slope}_{AB} = \frac{30 - 0}{10 - 0} \qquad \text{Slope}_{BC} = \frac{40 - 30}{25 - 10} \qquad \text{Slope}_{CD} = \frac{40 - 40}{45 - 25} \qquad \text{Slope}_{DE} = \frac{0 - 40}{70 - 45}$$

$$\text{Slope}_{AB} = 3 \text{ m/s} \qquad \text{Slope}_{BC} = 0.666... \text{ m/s} \qquad \text{Slope}_{CD} = 0 \text{ m/s} \qquad \text{Slope}_{DE} = -1.6 \text{ m/s}$$

Step 2. I thought about what these rates mean, and why they might change. They could be the rates of a person running, walking, and resting. First the person runs quickly, then slows down, then stops, and then returns to the starting point. This could be the graph of a sprinter training. At first, the sprinter goes very fast, at 3 m/s. When the sprinter gets to the 30 m marker, she slows down but keeps running forward. Then, she stops to catch her breath. Lastly, she jogs at a brisk pace back to the starting position to try again.

Practice

1. Jasmine drove for 510 km and used 46.7 L of gas. What is her car's fuel efficiency? Answer to the nearest hundredth.

2. Ian is training to run a half-marathon, which is about 21.1 km. He can run this distance in 2.2 h. What is his speed in kilometres per hour? Answer to the nearest tenth.

3. A 2 L carton of chocolate milk costs $4.26. What is the unit rate?

4. A dozen eggs cost $3.29. What is the unit rate?

5. A 5 kg bag of potatoes costs $8.15. A 10 lb bag of potatoes costs $7.10. Which is the better buy for the consumer? Explain why.

6. The butcher shop sells a 4 lb package of chicken legs for $12.57. The supermarket sells chicken legs for $8.68/kg. Which store has the lower price per kilogram? Justify your answer briefly.

> **TIP**
> 1 kg ≐ 2.2 lb

7. The grocery store sells peaches for $0.89/lb. The farmers' market sells a 10 kg basket of peaches for $15.50. Determine the price per kilogram at each location. Who has the lower price? Justify your answer briefly.

8. A peregrine falcon can fly at a top speed of 16 km in 3 min. A cheetah can run at a top speed of 112 km/h. Which animal can travel faster?

9. A 5.0 L can of Coloura paint will cover 55 m². A 3.5 L can of Brights paint will cover 30 m². Determine the area that 1 L of each type of paint will cover. Which brand of paint will cover a greater surface area?

10. On Wednesday a crew paved 10 km of road in 6 h. On Thursday, the crew paved 11 km in 7 h. On which day did they pave the road at the faster rate? Explain how you know.

11. Giselle is deciding between two long-distance telephone plans:

- Plan A charges $20 per month plus 1¢/min.
- Plan B charges $15 per month plus 3¢/min.

Giselle usually makes about 100 min of long-distance calls each month. Which plan will cost Giselle less? Show your calculations.

12. This graph shows how a cyclist travels over time.

a) Over which interval is the cyclist travelling the slowest?

b) Does the cyclist travel at the same speed over any two intervals? If so, which two?

c) At what speed, in kilometres per hour, is the cyclist travelling in interval *AB*?

d) Is the cyclist travelling the fastest in interval *EF* or *FG*? Explain.

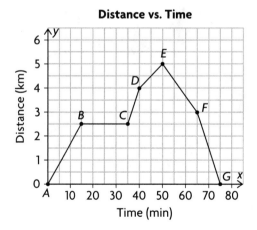

Distance vs. Time

13. Describe a scenario that can be represented by this graph. Compare the rates that correspond to each line segment, and discuss why the rates may have changed.

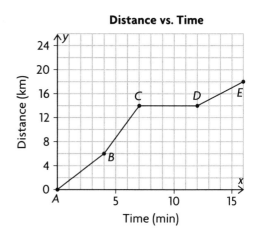

Distance vs. Time

MULTIPLE CHOICE

14. Suppose that tap water, flowing from a faucet at a constant rate, is used to fill a container. This graph shows the depth of the water in the container over time. Into which container is the water flowing?

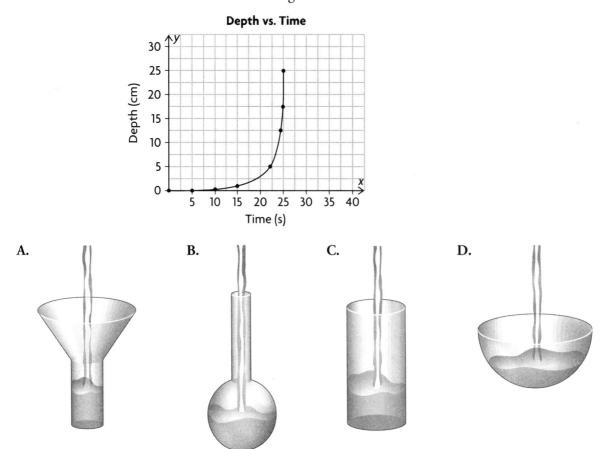

Depth vs. Time

A.   B.   C.   D.

15. A children's story features a jackrabbit and a leatherback turtle. If the jackrabbit could hop at its top speed for 1.5 h, it would travel 67.5 km. If the leatherback turtle could swim at its top speed for 10 min, it would travel 6 km. The forest by the lake is on fire. The fire station is 18 km away by water and 25 km by land. Which animal should go to get the fire brigade?

A. The jackrabbit travels at 45 km/h and the turtle travels at 34 km/h, so the rabbit should go because it is faster.

B. The turtle can swim 18 km in 30 min. The rabbit would take longer than 30 min to hop 25 km, so the turtle should go.

C. The jackrabbit travels at 34 km/h and the turtle travels at 45 km/h, so the rabbit should go because it is faster.

D. none of these

WRITTEN RESPONSE

16. The table shows the attendance, to the nearest ten thousand, for the Pacific National Exhibition. Calculate the rate of change in attendance for each period. During which period did attendance decrease at the greatest rate? During which period did it increase at the greatest rate?

Year	Attendance	Rate of Change (visitors/year)
1950	600 000	—
1960	930 000	
1975	1 290 000	
1980	1 290 000	
1995	1 010 000	
1997	900 000	
2001	952 000	
2002	902 000	
2006	959 000	
2009	855 000	

8.2 Solving Problems That Involve Rates

Keep in Mind

▸ You can solve rate problems in many ways.

▸ You can write an equation with equivalent ratios. Equivalent ratios have the same units in their numerators and the same units in their denominators.

▸ You can multiply, especially to convert from one unit to another. Include the units with each term in the product. Then, eliminate the units to help you verify your product.

▸ Try representing a constant rate of change with a linear function.

Example 1

Michael must order snacks for an office meeting of 170 people. He decides to order tarts, which come in boxes of 12. He estimates that he will need 1.5 tarts per person. How many boxes should Michael buy?

Solution

Step 1. I decided to use unit analysis to help me write a formula.

$$\text{Number of boxes} = \left(\frac{1 \text{ box}}{\text{Number of tarts}}\right)\left(\frac{\text{Number of tarts eaten}}{1 \text{ person}}\right)(\text{Number of people})$$

Step 2. I calculated the number of boxes.

$$\text{Number of boxes} = \left(\frac{1 \text{ box}}{12 \text{ tarts}}\right)\left(\frac{1.5 \text{ tarts}}{1 \text{ person}}\right)(170 \text{ people}), \text{ or } 21.25 \text{ boxes}$$

Michael should buy 22 boxes.

Step 3. I estimated, using proportional reasoning, to check my answer.

Each box holds 12 tarts. If each person eats 1.5 tarts, then Michael needs one box for 8 people. 170 is close to 160, and there are 20 groups of 8 in 160. If there were 160 people, he would need to order 20 boxes. Since there are 170 people, Michael needs to order 2 more boxes, or 22 in all.

Example 2

Jenna wants to defrost a frozen turkey in her microwave. The turkey has a mass of 4.23 kg. A cookbook says it takes 21 min to defrost 3 lb of meat. How long, to the nearest minute, should Jenna set the timer on defrost for?

Solution

Step 1. I converted kilograms to pounds:

$$1 \text{ kg} = 2.2 \text{ lb}$$

$$4.23 \text{ kg} = 4.23 \text{ kg}\left(\frac{2.2 \text{ lb}}{1 \text{ kg}}\right)$$

$$4.23 \text{ kg} = 9.306 \text{ lb}$$

Step 2. I set up equivalent ratios, with x representing the unknown time, and solved for x.

$$\frac{21 \text{ min}}{3 \text{ lb}} = \frac{x}{9.306 \text{ lb}}$$

$$9.306 \text{ lb}\left(\frac{21 \text{ min}}{3 \text{ lb}}\right) = 9.306 \text{ lb}\left(\frac{x}{9.306 \text{ lb}}\right)$$

$$9.306 \cancel{\text{ lb}}\left(\frac{21 \text{ min}}{3 \cancel{\text{ lb}}}\right) = x$$

$$65.142 \text{ min} = x \qquad \text{Jenna should defrost the turkey for 65 min.}$$

> **TIP**
>
> Converting units allows you to compare quantities given in different units.

Example 3

Bob burns 620 Cal in a cardio-kick-box class lasting 2 h, and 120 Cal in a body-sculpt class lasting 30 min. If he does cardio-kick-box for 3 h, how much longer would he have to do body-sculpt to burn the same number of Calories?

Solution

Step 1. I set up a function for Calories burned in one hour of cardio-kick-box.

$$C = \frac{620 \text{ Cal}}{2 \text{ h}}$$

$$C = 310 \text{ Cal/h}$$

If $C(t)$ represents the number of Calories Bob burns and t represents time, in hours, then $C(t) = 310t$.

For 3 h, $C(3) = 310(3)$

$$C(3) = 930 \text{ Cal}$$

Step 2. I set up a function for Calories burned in one hour of body-sculpt.

$$B = \frac{120 \text{ Cal}}{0.5 \text{ h}}$$

$$B = 240 \text{ Cal/h}$$

If $B(t)$ represents the number of Calories burned in body-sculpt and t represents time, in hours, then $B(t) = 240t$.

Step 3. I determined how long Bob would take to burn 930 Cal in body-sculpt.

$$B(t) = 930 \text{ Cal}$$

$$(240 \text{ Cal/h})t = 930 \text{ Cal}$$

$$t = \frac{930 \text{ Cal}}{240 \text{ Cal/h}}$$

$$t = 3.875 \text{ h}$$

Bob would burn the same number of Calories in about 3.9 h of body-sculpt as in 3 h of cardio-kick-box. He would need to do body-sculpt for an additional 0.9 h, or about 54 min.

Practice

1. It takes 3 h 26 min to fill a 3200 L water tank. Determine the time, in hours and minutes, it will take to fill a 2600 L tank. Round your answer to the nearest minute.

2. 17 kg of Yukon Gold potatoes costs $26.80. Determine the cost of 5 lb of potatoes. Round your answer to the nearest cent.

3. A screw has 64 turns over a distance of 50 mm of thread. Determine the number of turns in a screw with the same pattern over 40 mm of thread. Round your answer to the nearest turn.

4. Suppose it costs $3.25/lb, plus a loading fee of $40, to send freight by airplane around Yukon and the Northwest Territories.

a) What is the price to send 20 lb of clothing to Whitehorse from Vancouver?

b) How many pounds of clothing could you ship to Whitehorse for $154?

5. The map shows Wood Buffalo National Park in Alberta and the Northwest Territories. The scale of the map is 1 cm to 50 km.

a) Estimate the area of the park in hectares. One hectare (1 ha) is equivalent to 10 000 m².

b) Suppose the annual cost to monitor and fight forest fires in this region is about $48/ha. Estimate the annual fire management expenditure for the park.

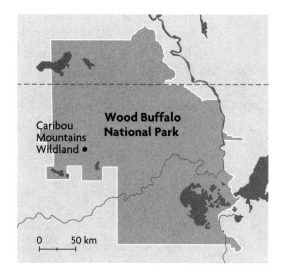

6. The dosage of an antibiotic medicine for a person with a mass of 85 kg is 15 mL. Which equation determines the amount of medicine, *P*, in millilitres, needed for a person with a mass of 65 kg?

A. $\dfrac{P}{85 \text{ kg}} = \dfrac{15 \text{ mL}}{65 \text{ kg}}$

C. $\dfrac{P}{65 \text{ kg}} = \dfrac{15 \text{ mL}}{85 \text{ kg}}$

B. $\dfrac{P}{15 \text{ mL}} = \dfrac{85 \text{ kg}}{65 \text{ kg}}$

D. $\dfrac{P}{65 \text{ kg}} = \dfrac{85 \text{ kg}}{15 \text{ mL}}$

7. A computer can transfer 19 MB (megabytes) of data in 3.5 s. Which equation determines the length of time, *t*, in seconds, the computer will take to transfer 2.4 GB (gigabytes) of data? (1 GB is equivalent to 1024 MB.)

A. $\dfrac{t}{3.5 \text{ s}} = \dfrac{2.4 \cdot 1024 \text{ MB}}{19 \text{ MB}}$

C. $\dfrac{t}{3.5 \text{ s}} = \dfrac{2.4 \cdot 19 \text{ MB}}{1024 \text{ MB}}$

B. $\dfrac{t}{3.5 \text{ s}} = (2.4)(1024 \text{ MB})(19 \text{ MB})$

D. $\dfrac{t}{3.5 \text{ s}} = \dfrac{19 \text{ MB}}{2.4 \cdot 1024 \text{ MB}}$

WRITTEN RESPONSE

8. It costs $0.3172/lb to ship freight by barge along the Pacific coast. Determine the cost, in dollars, to ship 5360 kg of building supplies from Vancouver to Stewart, B.C. Show your work.

9. Jason wants to ship 40 lb of tinned goods and 50 lb of supplies along the Pacific coast. It costs $5.60/lb, plus a loading fee of $30, to send freight by air and $0.3172/lb to ship freight by water. How much will Jason save by shipping by water instead of by air? Show your work.

Scale Diagrams

Example 1

Create a scale diagram of this building footprint using a scale of 1 m : 1000 m.

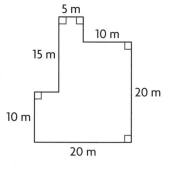

Solution

Step 1. I determined the scale factor and considered whether the diagram would be a reduction or an enlargement.

The scale factor is $k = \dfrac{1\ \cancel{m}}{1000\ \cancel{m}}$, or $\dfrac{1}{1000}$. Since this value is less than 1 ($k < 1$), the diagram will be a reduction.

Step 2. I multiplied each measurement by the scale factor.

$(20\ \text{m})\left(\dfrac{1}{1000}\right) = 0.02\ \text{m}$ or 2.0 cm $(15\ \text{m})\left(\dfrac{1}{1000}\right) = 0.015\ \text{m}$ or 1.5 cm

$(10\ \text{m})\left(\dfrac{1}{1000}\right) = 0.01\ \text{m}$ or 1.0 cm $(5\ \text{m})\left(\dfrac{1}{1000}\right) = 0.005\ \text{m}$ or 0.5 cm

Step 3. I drew the scale diagram.

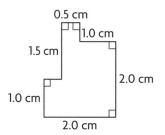

Example 2

A cross-section of an animal cell is shown in a scale diagram. In the diagram, the diameter of the cell is 4.5 cm. In fact, the cell's diameter is 0.15 mm. What scale factor was used to draw the diagram?

Solution

Step 1. I expressed all the measurements in millimetres so they would be in the same unit.

4.5 cm = 45 mm

Step 2. I used the ratio for calculating a scale factor.

$$k = \frac{\text{Diagram measurement}}{\text{Actual measurement}}$$

Step 3. I solved for k.

$$k = \frac{45 \cancel{mm}}{0.15 \cancel{mm}}$$

$$k = \frac{4500}{15}$$

$$k = \frac{300}{1}$$

The scale factor used to draw the diagram was 300.

Practice

1. The original eraser for these scale diagrams was 6.0 cm long. Which diagram was drawn using a scale factor of 0.8?

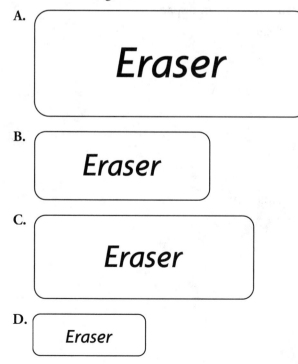

A.

Eraser

B.

Eraser

C.

Eraser

D.

Eraser

2. The original stapler for these scale diagrams was 20 cm long. Which diagram was drawn using a scale factor of 30%?

A.
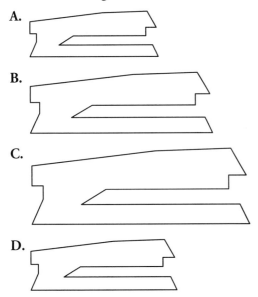
B.

C.

D.

3. A billboard is 4.0 m by 2.5 m. A scale diagram of the billboard must fit in a space that is 15 cm by 12 cm. Write a reasonable scale for the scale diagram.

4. A picture is 42 cm by 36 cm. A scale diagram of the picture must fit in a space that is 3 m by 2 m. Write a reasonable scale for the scale diagram.

5. A computer chip is 14 mm by 26 mm. A scale diagram of the computer chip must fit in a space that is 40 cm by 70 cm. Write a reasonable scale for the scale diagram.

6. A photograph is 6 cm by 11 cm. A copy is made using a scale factor of 150%. What are the dimensions of the copy?

7. An illustration is 14 cm by 20 cm. A copy is made using a scale factor of 75%. What are the dimensions of the copy?

8. A builder plans to construct a house on a rectangular lot, as shown in this sketch.

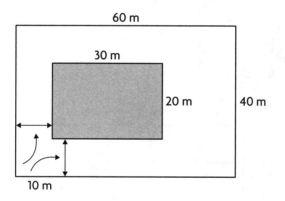

Elizabeth intends to draw a scale diagram of the lot and house, using a scale of 1 m : 400 m. In the diagram, what will be the length and width of the lot, the length and width of the house, and the distance of the house from the left end of the lot?

9. Torry drew this pattern for his Ultimate team. He wants to enlarge it for the team's T-shirts. The manager has suggested that the pattern be no more than 20 cm wide. What is the greatest diameter that the inner circle can have? Answer to the nearest centimetre.

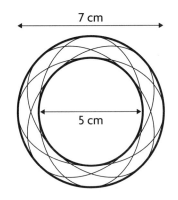

10. Create a scale diagram of this floor plan of a bachelor apartment, using a scale of 1 m : 50 m and the grid provided. Label the lengths of each wall, including the slanted wall.

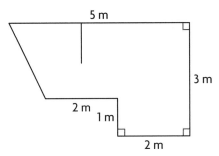

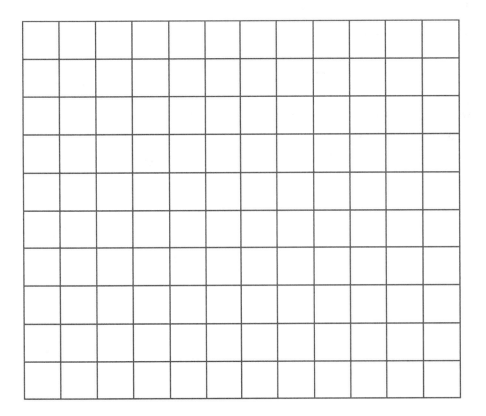

11. Lorenz wants to make a scale diagram of the floor plan of the first floor of his apartment building. He wants his diagram to fit on an 8.5 in. by 11 in. sheet of paper. The rectangular building is 140 ft long and 50 ft wide. What would be a reasonable scale for Lorenz to use so that his diagram will fit on the sheet of paper? What would the length and width of the diagram be with this scale?

WRITTEN RESPONSE

12. The floor plan for a theatre company is drawn as shown, using a scale factor of 0.004.

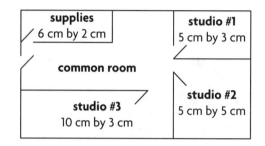

a) What are the actual areas, in square metres, of each studio and the supplies closet?

b) What is the actual area, in square metres, of the common room?

8.4 Scale Factors and Areas of 2-D Shapes

Keep in Mind

▸ When two similar 2-D shapes are related by a scale factor, k, then

Area of similar 2-D shape $= k^2$(Area of original shape)

▸ You can determine the scale factor by which two similar shapes are related if you know their areas:

$$k^2 = \frac{\text{Area of similar 2-D shape}}{\text{Area of original shape}}$$

Example 1

Determine the area of this quadrilateral, to the nearest tenth of a square unit, after it is reduced by a scale factor of $\frac{1}{4}$.

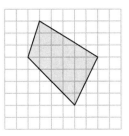

Solution

Step 1. I determined the area of the quadrilateral.

I divided it into two triangles, one with a base of 6 units and a height of 3 units, and one with a base of 6 units and a height of 4 units.

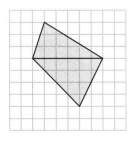

Area of quadrilateral $= \frac{1}{2}(6)(3) + \frac{1}{2}(6)(4)$

Area of quadrilateral $= 21$ unit^2

Step 2. I calculated the area of the reduced quadrilateral.

Area of similar 2-D shape $= \left(\frac{1}{4}\right)^2 (21 \text{ unit}^2)$

Area of similar 2-D shape $= \left(\frac{1}{16}\right)(21 \text{ unit}^2)$

Area of similar 2-D shape $= 1.312\ldots$ unit^2

The area is approximately 1.3 unit^2.

Example 2

A computer screen measures 35 cm by 55 cm. An image on the computer is projected onto a whiteboard with a screen area of 7238 cm^2. Determine the length and width of the whiteboard.

Solution

Step 1. I determined the area of the computer screen.

Area of screen = lw

Area of screen = (35 cm)(55 cm)

Area of screen = 1925 cm^2

Step 2. I determined the scale factor.

$$k^2 = \frac{\text{Area of screen}}{\text{Area of whiteboard}}$$

$$k^2 = \frac{7238 \text{ cm}^2}{1925 \text{ cm}^2}$$

$$k^2 = 3.76$$

$$k = 1.939\ldots$$

The scale factor is about 1.9.

Step 3. I multiplied the computer screen's dimensions by the scale factor to determine the whiteboard's dimensions.

Length of whiteboard = (35 cm)(1.939…)

Length of whiteboard = 67.867… cm

Width of whiteboard = (55 cm)(1.939…)

Width of whiteboard = 106.648… cm

The whiteboard is about 68 cm by 107 cm.

Practice

1. The base and height of a trapezoid with an area of 50 cm^2 will be enlarged by a scale factor of 4. Determine the area of the enlarged trapezoid.

2. The radius of a circle with an area of 10 cm^2 will be enlarged by a scale factor of 5. Determine the area of the enlarged circle.

3. The base and height of a triangle with an area of 76 cm² will be reduced by a scale factor of $\frac{5}{8}$. Determine the area of the reduced triangle, to the nearest square centimetre.

4. The sides of a square with an area of 49 cm² will be reduced by a scale factor of $\frac{3}{8}$. Determine the area of the reduced square, to the nearest square centimetre.

5. Jaidan enlarges this figure, by a scale factor of 2. Determine the area of the enlarged figure, in square units.

6. Misha reduces this figure by a scale factor of $\frac{1}{2}$. Determine the area of the reduced figure, in square units. Round your answer to the nearest whole unit.

7. Triangle *A* is 24 cm wide and 20 cm high.

Triangle *B* is 14.4 cm wide and similar to triangle *A*.

a) Determine the scale factor needed to reduce triangle *A* to form triangle *B*.

b) Determine the areas of triangle *A* and triangle *B*.

c) How many triangles congruent to triangle *B* would fit inside triangle *A*?

8. Travis enlarges this figure by a scale factor of 3.5. Determine the area of the enlarged figure, in square units. Round your answer to the nearest tenth.

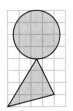

9. Data for triangle *ABC* is shown on the first line of the table. Triangle *ABC* is reduced by a scale factor of 40%. Which triangle is the reduction of triangle *ABC*?

	Triangle	Length of Base (cm)	Height of Triangle (cm)	Area (cm²)	Area of Scaled Triangle / Area of Original Triangle
	ABC	5.00	3.00	7.50	1.00
A.	DEF	2.00	1.00	1.00	0.13
B.	GHI	1.50	1.20	1.25	0.16
C.	JKL	1.20	2.00	1.20	0.15
D.	MNO	2.00	1.20	1.20	0.16

10. Determine the scale factor that relates the pair of trapezoids.

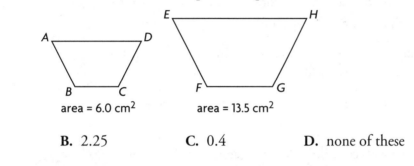

area = 6.0 cm²   area = 13.5 cm²

   A. 1.5   **B.** 2.25   **C.** 0.4   **D.** none of these

11. The diagram of a coffee shop and the attached parking lot was drawn with a scale of 1:250. On the diagram, the area of the coffee shop is 10 cm² and the area of the parking lot is 42 cm².

    Determine the areas of the actual coffee shop and the actual parking lot in square metres. Show your work.

8.5 Similar Objects: Scale Models and Scale Diagrams

Keep in Mind

▸ 3-D objects with proportional dimensions are said to be similar.

▸ A scale factor, k, compares linear measurements of a scale model to linear measurements, in the same units, of the actual object as a ratio:

$$k = \frac{\text{Linear measurement of scale model}}{\text{Corresponding linear measurement of object}}$$

▸ You can represent an object with a scale model or diagram. Scale choice depends on the size of both the original shape and the model or diagram.

▸ You can multiply any linear measurement of an object by the scale factor to calculate the measurement of a similar object.

▸ For a scale factor k between 0 and 1, the new object will be a reduction of the original.

▸ For k greater than 1, the new object will be an enlargement of the original.

Example 1

The plans for a bookend with a scale ratio of 1:6 are shown. Determine the dimensions (length, width, and height) of the actual bookend.

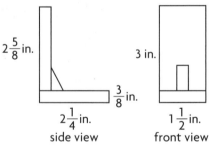

Solution

Step 1. I knew the 3-D scale diagram was similar to the real object, and its measurements were proportional to the actual measurements. I determined the actual measurements using the scale factor.

The scale factor is diagram : actual = 1:6. Since $\frac{1}{6}$ is less than 1, the diagram is a reduction of the actual bookend. This means that to get the dimensions of the actual bookend, I must enlarge the dimensions on the scale diagram, using the scale factor $\frac{6}{1}$, or 6.

Step 2. I multiplied each measurement by the scale factor of 6.

Base length $= \left(2\frac{1}{4} \text{ in.}\right)6$ Base width $= \left(1\frac{1}{2} \text{ in.}\right)6$

Base length $= 13\frac{1}{2}$ in.   Base width $= 9$ in.

Base thickness $= \left(\frac{3}{8} \text{ in.}\right)6$ Overall height $= (3 \text{ in.})6$

          Overall height $= 18$ in.

Base thickness $= 2\frac{1}{4}$ in.

The dimensions of the actual bookend are $13\frac{1}{2}$ in. by $2\frac{1}{4}$ in. by 18 in., with a base thickness of $2\frac{1}{4}$ in.

Example 2

A sewer pipe has an inner diameter of 1.2 m, a wall thickness of 0.1 m, and a length of 3.0 m. What measurements should be used to create a scale diagram of the pipe?

Solution

Step 1. I decided there should be two diagrams, a side view and a front view, instead of one diagram with perspective. This way, perspective would not distort the proportional measurements. I decided to put the side view on the top half of my sheet of paper, and the front view on the bottom half.

Step 2. I thought about what scale to use.

I have 200 mm of width to use on my sheet of paper and the pipe is 3000 mm long, so a good scale ratio to use is 1 : 15. I calculated each measurement.

length: 3000 mm ÷ 15 = 200 mm

inner diameter: 1200 mm ÷ 15 = 80 mm

wall thickness: 100 mm ÷ 15 = 6.666... mm

Practice

1. A 1 : 25 scale model of a tractor trailer is 0.4 ft tall, 0.3 ft wide, and 1.5 ft long. What are the dimensions of the actual trailer?

8.5 Similar Objects: Scale Models and Scale Diagrams **239**

2. A 1:35 scale model of a cabin is 18 cm tall, 20 cm wide, and 25.2 cm long. What is the volume of the actual cabin, in cubic metres? Round your answer to the nearest whole number.

3. A 1:8 scale model of a canoe is 36 in. long, with a beam (width) of 6.4 in. and a depth of 1.75 in. What are the dimensions of the actual canoe?

4. A 1:7 scale model of a snowmobile is 50 cm long, 19.0 cm wide, and 16.5 cm tall. What are the dimensions of the actual snowmobile?

5. Howard draws scale diagrams of artifacts discovered on archaeological digs. He draws a diagram of this artifact as shown, with a scale ratio of 1:12. Determine the length, width, and height of the actual artifact.

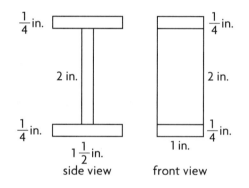

$\frac{1}{4}$ in.   2 in. $\frac{1}{4}$ in. $1\frac{1}{2}$ in.   side view

$\frac{1}{4}$ in.   2 in. $\frac{1}{4}$ in.   1 in.   front view

MULTIPLE CHOICE

6. Which of these cylinders is similar to a cylinder 10 cm long and 2.5 cm in diameter? Choose the best answer.

 A. a cylinder 16 cm long and 4 cm in diameter

 B. a cylinder 4 cm long and 1.5 cm in diameter

 C. a cylinder 12 cm long and 3.5 cm in diameter

 D. all of the above

7. Which of these right cones is similar to a right cone 20 cm high with a diameter of 10 cm? Choose the best answer.

 A. a right cone 30 cm high and 7.5 cm in radius

 B. a right cone 10 cm high and 5 cm in diameter

 C. a right cone 15 cm high and 7.5 cm in diameter

 D. all of the above

8. Which of these rectangular boxes is similar to a rectangular gift box 10 cm by 8 cm by 16 cm?

    A. a box 4 cm by 5 cm by 3 cm   **C.** a box 10 cm by 8 cm by 9 cm

    B. a box 15 cm by 13 cm by 21 cm   **D.** none of the above

9. Which of these rectangular boxes is similar to a rectangular gift box 14 cm by 6 cm by 12 cm?

    A. a box 4 cm by 5 cm by 3 cm   **C.** a box 6 cm by 3 cm by 7 cm

    B. a box 15 cm by 13 cm by 21 cm   **D.** a box 7 cm by 3 cm by 12 cm

WRITTEN RESPONSE

10. This flower planter with a regular hexagonal base has the dimensions indicated. Draw a scale diagram of the top and front views of the planter, using the grid provided. Explain what you did.

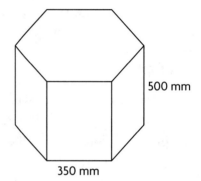

500 mm

350 mm

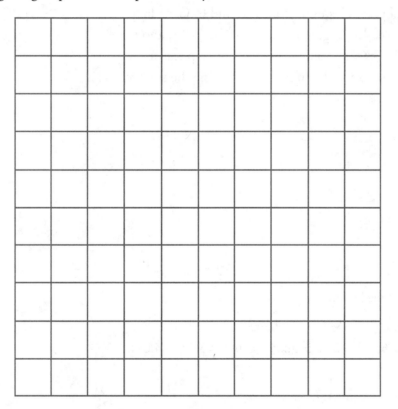

8.6 Scale Factors and 3-D Objects

YOU WILL NEED
• calculator

Keep in Mind

▶ If two 3-D objects are similar and their dimensions are related by a scale factor of k, then

- • Surface area of similar object $= k^2$(surface area of original object)
- • Volume of similar object $= k^3$(volume of original object)

▶ You can determine the surface area and volume of an enlarged or reduced object based on the dimensions of the original object.

Example 1

A Victorian train engine called "Vicky" was brought from England to Canada to "star" in the play *The Railway Children*. The engine was built in the 1890s and is about 16.5 m long. Toy replicas of Vicky were sold at the play. The replicas fit into boxes about 16.5 cm long, 2.6 cm wide, and 4.0 cm high. Determine the surface area of a shipping container that could hold Vicky.

Solution

Step 1. I determined what scale factor was used.

$$k = \frac{\text{Length of replica engine}}{\text{Length of original engine}}$$

$$k = \frac{16.5 \text{ cm}}{1650 \text{ cm}}$$

$$k = 0.01$$

Step 2. I determined the surface area of the box for the replica.

$$SA = 2(\text{area of base}) + 2(\text{area of side}) + 2(\text{area of front})$$

$$SA = 2(16.5 \text{ cm})(2.6 \text{ cm}) + 2(16.5 \text{ cm})(4.0 \text{ cm}) + 2(2.6 \text{ cm})(4.0 \text{ cm})$$

$$SA = 2831.4 \text{ cm}^2$$

Step 3. I determined the surface area of a shipping container for Vicky.

$$SA_{\text{replica}} = k^2(SA_{\text{original}})$$

$$2831.4 \text{ cm}^2 = (0.01^2)(SA_{\text{original}})$$

$$2831.4 \text{ cm}^2 \div (0.01^2) = SA_{\text{original}}$$

$$28\,314\,000 \text{ cm}^2 = SA_{\text{original}}$$

$$2831.4 \text{ m}^2 = SA_{\text{original}}$$

The surface area would be about 2831.4 m².

Example 2

Determine the volume of a shipping container that could hold Vicky, the train in Example 1.

Solution

Step 1. I determined the volume of the box for the replica.

$$\text{Volume}_{replica} = lwh$$

$$\text{Volume}_{replica} = (16.5 \text{ cm})(2.6 \text{ cm})(4.0 \text{ cm})$$

$$\text{Volume}_{replica} = 171.6 \text{ cm}^3$$

Step 2. I determined the volume of the shipping container for Vicky. I already knew the scale factor.

$$\text{Volume}_{replica} = k^3(\text{Volume}_{original})$$

$$171.6 \text{ cm}^3 = (0.01^3)(\text{Volume}_{original})$$

$$171.6 \text{ cm}^3 \div (0.01^3) = \text{Volume}_{original}$$

$$171\,600\,000 \text{ cm}^3 = \text{Volume}_{original}$$

$$171.6 \text{ m}^3 = \text{Volume}_{original}$$

The volume would be about 171.6 m³.

Practice

1. A stage director needs a large chess bishop for a scene. The bishop in her chess set is 78 mm tall. She wants the enlarged bishop to be 1.56 m tall.

    a) What scale factor must she apply to create the enlarged bishop?

    b) How many times greater will the surface area of the larger bishop be?

    c) How many times greater will the volume of the larger bishop be?

2. A director is filming *Alice in Wonderland* and needs a large mushroom for a scene. A normal mushroom is about 40 mm tall and has a volume of about 6.75 cm³. It will be enlarged by a scale factor of 120.

    a) How many times greater will the surface area of the larger mushroom be?

    b) What will the volume of the enlarged mushroom be?

3. Cylinders A and B are similar. By what factor is the surface area of cylinder B greater than the surface area of cylinder A?

20 mm

$r = 4$ mm $\boxed{A}$

100 mm

$r = 20$ mm

B

4. A right hexagonal prism is enlarged by a scale factor of 3.5.

a) Determine the value of $\dfrac{\text{Volume of large prism}}{\text{Volume of small prism}}$. Do not round.

b) Determine the value of $\dfrac{\text{Surface area of large prism}}{\text{Surface area of small prism}}$. Do not round.

5. Cylinders C and D are similar. By what factor is the volume of cylinder D greater than the volume of cylinder C?

$r = 10$ mm

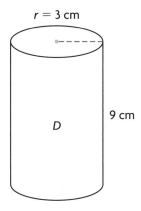

C 30 mm

$r = 3$ cm

6. A right cylinder is enlarged by a scale factor of 4.3.

a) Determine the value of $\dfrac{\text{Volume of large cylinder}}{\text{Volume of small cylinder}}$. Do not round.

b) Determine the value of $\dfrac{\text{Surface area of large cylinder}}{\text{Surface area of small cylinder}}$. Do not round.

D 9 cm

7. The surface area of an enlarged triangular prism is 6.25 greater than that of the original prism. How many times greater is the volume of the enlarged prism than the volume of the original?

8. A newly discovered solar system has two spherical planets. The volume of planet Alpha is 46.656 times that of planet Beta. How many times greater is the surface area of planet Alpha than that of planet Beta?

9. An orange has a diameter of 7 cm. A grapefruit has a diameter of 12 cm. How many times greater is the volume of a grapefruit than that of an orange?

10. A cook has a set of four mixing bowls. The bowls stack inside each other and are similar. The two largest diameters are 30 cm and 28 cm. The scale factor is the same from each bowl to the next smaller bowl.

a) To the nearest tenth of a centimetre, the diameters of the two smaller bowls are _____ cm and _____ cm.

b) To the nearest square centimetre, the surface areas of the two smaller bowls are _____ cm² and _____ cm².

11. The world's tallest building is the Burj Khalifa in Dubai, at 828 m tall. The Calgary Tower in Calgary is 191 m tall. Jermain wants to compare the Burj Khalifa and the Calgary Tower. He has decided to represent the Burj Khalifa with a rectangular prism that has a height of 50 cm. To the nearest tenth of a centimetre, the height of the rectangular prism Jermain should use to represent the Calgary Tower is _____ cm.

WRITTEN RESPONSE

12. For a woodwork project, Eldon made an alien battleship using 142 cubes.

a) How many cubes would he need to make an alien battleship with dimensions four times as large? Justify your answer.

b) Eldon used 56 mL of varnish to cover the battleship. How much varnish would he need to cover one with dimensions six times as large?

8 Test Prep

Complete the following to summarize the important ideas from this chapter.

Q: What methods and strategies can you use to compare rates?

A: • Write rates in the same _____, such as centimetres per second.

• Use unit _____, such as "/mL" (per millilitre).

• Graph information and use the fact that _____ represent rates

of _____.

NEED HELP?
• See Lessons 8.1, 8.2

Q: How does a scale factor relate a 2-D shape to a scale diagram of it?

A: • A scale _____ is _____ to the 2-D shape it represents.

The scale _____ is the ratio of a diagram _____ to

actual _____.

• Therefore, a _____ dimension is given by the corresponding

actual dimension, _____ by the scale factor.

• A scale factor k between ___ and ___ means that the scale diagram

is a(n) _____ of the original shape.

• A scale factor k greater than ___ means that the scale diagram is

a(n) _____ of the original shape.

• The ratio of area of _____ to _____ of actual

or original shape is given by ___.

NEED HELP?
• See Lessons 8.3, 8.4

Q: How does a scale factor relate a 3-D object to a scale model of it?

A: • A scale _____ is _____ to the 3-D object it represents,

meaning that the dimensions are _____. The scale _____

is the diagram-to-actual _____ ratio.

• Therefore, a _____ dimension is given by the corresponding

actual dimension, _____ by the scale factor.

• The ratio of surface _____ of model to surface _____

of actual or original object is given by ___.

• The ratio of _____ of model to _____ of actual or

original object is given by ___.

NEED HELP?
• See Lessons 8.5, 8.6

MULTIPLE CHOICE

1. The dosage of an antibiotic medicine for a person with a mass of 65 kg is 12 mL. Which equation determines the amount of medicine, P, in millilitres, needed for a person with a mass of 40 kg?

   A. $\dfrac{P}{65\text{ kg}} = \dfrac{12\text{ mL}}{40\text{ kg}}$

   B. $\dfrac{P}{12\text{ mL}} = \dfrac{65\text{ kg}}{40\text{ kg}}$

   C. $\dfrac{P}{40\text{ kg}} = \dfrac{12\text{ mL}}{65\text{ kg}}$

   D. $\dfrac{P}{40\text{ kg}} = \dfrac{65\text{ kg}}{12\text{ mL}}$

2. Data for triangle ABC is shown on the first line of the table. Triangle ABC is enlarged by a scale factor of 150%. Which triangle is the enlargement?

	Triangle	Length of Base (cm)	Height of Triangle (cm)	Area (cm², to nearest tenth)
	ABC	5.00	3.00	7.5
A.	DEF	7.50	4.50	16.9
B.	GHI	5.50	3.50	9.6
C.	JKL	15	9.00	67.5
D.	MNO	2.00	1.20	1.20

3. If a bat could fly at its top speed for 2.5 h, it would fly 62.5 km. If an elephant could run at its top speed for 15 min, it would run 10.0 km. Which animal is faster?

   A. A bat can fly at 25 km/h and an elephant can run at 40 km/h. The elephant is faster.

   B. A bat can fly at 40 km/h and an elephant can run at 25 km/h. The elephant is faster.

   C. A bat can fly at 25 km/h and an elephant can run at 40 km/h. The bat is faster.

   D. Both animals travel at the same speed.

NUMERICAL RESPONSE

4. It takes 3 h 20 min to fill a 5100 L water tank. Determine the time, to the nearest minute, it will take to fill a 6200 L tank.

5. Create a scale diagram of this garden, using a scale of 1 m : 200 m and the grid provided.

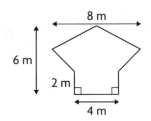

6. A chip truck sells french fries in two sizes of rectangular prism containers. The smaller container has a square base with 10 cm long sides and a height of 4 cm. The large container has a square base with 13 cm long sides and a height of 5.2 cm. Determine the factor by which the heights of the two containers differ. Answer to the nearest tenth.

7. A right hexagonal prism is enlarged by a scale factor of 5.7.

  a) Determine the value of $\dfrac{\text{Volume of large prism}}{\text{Volume of small prism}}$. Do not round.

  b) Determine the value of $\dfrac{\text{Surface area of large prism}}{\text{Surface area of a small prism}}$. Do not round.

8. A 1 : 30 scale model of a tractor is 0.3 ft tall, 0.2 ft wide, and 0.5 ft long. What are the dimensions of the actual tractor?

9. A 1 : 15 scale model of a statue is 13.5 cm tall, 11.2 cm wide, and 14.6 cm long. What are the dimensions of the actual statue?

10. Esther reduces this figure by a scale factor of $\dfrac{1}{3}$. Determine the area of the reduced figure, in square units. Round your answer to the nearest whole unit.

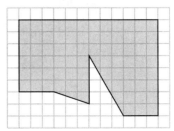

11. Joan works 30 h every two weeks. She works 50 weeks each year. At this rate, how many hours will she work in one year? Explain how you could solve this problem using two different strategies.

12. The gas tank of Angus's car holds about 90 L. He can either buy gas in his town at $1.39/L or travel across the U.S. border to fill up at US$3.23/gal (1 U.S. gallon = 3.79 L). The current exchange rate is US$1/C$1.04. Angus will use less than 2 L of gas to drive 15 min to his local gas station and one third of a tank to make the 1.5 h round trip to the nearest gas station across the border. Which option makes more sense? Justify your decision.

MULTIPLE CHOICE

1. Consider this linear inequality: $3x + 2y \geq 5$, $x \in I$, $y \in I$

   What type of boundary line is used for the graph of the solution set?

   A. solid   **B.** dashed   **C.** stippled   **D.** dashed and stippled

2. A system of linear inequalities is defined by

   $\{(x, y) \mid 3x - 2y < 12, x \in R, y \in R\}$

   $\{(x, y) \mid x + y \geq 5, x \in R, y \in R\}$

   Which of these points is in the solution set of the system?

   A. $(5, 2.5)$ **B.** $(5.5, -1)$ **C.** $(6, 3)$ **D.** $(1, 2)$

3. Which graph represents the solution set of the given system?

   $\{(x, y) \mid 3y + x \geq 6, x \in W, y \in W\}$

   $\{(x, y) \mid x < 5, x \in W, y \in W\}$

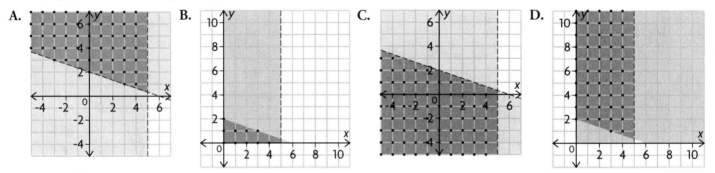

4. The quadratic function $f(x) = 2(x - 4)^2 - 8$ is in which form?

   A. factored form   **C.** partially factored form

   B. vertex form   **D.** standard form

5. What is the vertex of the parabola defined by $y = (3 - x)(x + 2)$?

   A. $(1, 3)$ **B.** $(-1, -4)$ **C.** $(-0.5, -6.25)$ **D.** $(0.5, 6.25)$

6. Which of these quadratic equations has one real root?

   A. $2x^2 + 6x - 5 = 0$ **C.** $x(x - 28) = 196$

   B. $3x^2 = 30x - 75$ **D.** $4(x + 2)^2 - 9 = 0$

7. Michael was solving the equation $x^2 + 2x + 1 = x - 1$. Where did he make an error?

$$x^2 + 2x + 1 = 1 - x$$

$$(x + 1)^2 = 1 - x \qquad \textbf{A.} \ \text{line 2}$$

$$(x + 1)^2 = 0 \quad \text{or} \quad 1 - x = 0 \qquad \textbf{B.} \ \text{line 3}$$

$$x + 1 = 0 \quad \text{or} \quad x - 1 = 0 \qquad \textbf{C.} \ \text{line 4}$$

$$x = -1 \quad \text{or} \quad x = 1 \qquad \textbf{D.} \ \text{line 5}$$

8. A quadratic equation has two real roots: $3 + \sqrt{5}$ and $3 - \sqrt{5}$. Which of the following could be the quadratic equation?

A. $x^2 - 3x = 5$ **C.** $x^2 + 6x + 4 = 0$

B. $x^2 = 6x - 4$ **D.** $x^2 - 6x - 5 = 0$

9. Which of the following gives the solutions of the quadratic equation $2x^2 - 7x = 11$?

A. $x = \dfrac{7 \pm \sqrt{49 - 44}}{2}$ **C.** $x = \dfrac{-7 \pm \sqrt{49 + 88}}{4}$

B. $x = \dfrac{-7 \pm \sqrt{49 + 44}}{2}$ **D.** $x = \dfrac{7 \pm \sqrt{49 + 88}}{4}$

10. The graph represents Debra's drive to work on a typical morning. What was Debra's speed on the fastest part of her journey?

A. 43 km/h   **B.** 120 km/h   **C.** 80 km/h   **D.** 60 km/h

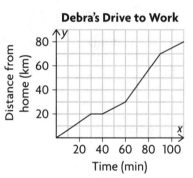

Debra's Drive to Work

11. Two similar objects have a scale factor of $1 : 2.5$ associated with them. The volume of the smaller object is 400 cm³. What is the larger object's volume?

A. 1000 cm³   **B.** 2500 cm³   **C.** 6250 cm³   **D.** none of these

NUMERICAL RESPONSE

12. Snappy Cards makes two types of greeting cards: scratch'n'sniff, or with a recorded tune that plays when the card is open. The company can make at most 250 scratch'n'sniff cards and at most 175 tune cards per day. However, they can make 300 or more cards in total per day. Scratch'n'sniff cards cost $1.25 to make, and tune cards cost $2.00 to make. Let s represent the number of scratch'n'sniff cards and t represent the number of tune cards.

a) State the restrictions: $s \in$ ___, $t \in$ ___

b) State the constraints: $s \geq$ ___, $s \leq$ ___, $t \geq$ ___, $t \leq$ ___, $s +$ ___ $\geq$ ___

c) Define the objective function: cost $C =$ _____

13. Verify that the point $(-3, 3)$ is a solution to this system:

$\{(x, y) \mid 5y - x \geq 7, x \in R, y \in R\}$

$\{(x, y) \mid x + 2y < 5, x \in R, y \in R\}$

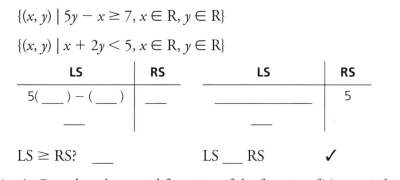

LS	RS		LS	RS
5(___) − (___)	___		_____	5
___			___	

LS ≥ RS? ___   LS ___ RS   ✓

14. a) Complete the partial factoring of the function $f(x) = -3x^2 + 24x - 18$:

$$f(x) = \underline{\ \ } x(x \ \underline{\ \ \ } \ \underline{\ \ \ } \ ) - \underline{\ \ }$$

b) Determine the y-intercept: $(0, \underline{\ \ })$.

c) Determine another point with the same y-coordinate as the y-intercept:
$(\underline{\ \ }, \underline{\ \ })$

d) Determine the equation of the axis of symmetry: $x = \underline{\ \ }$.
Determine the vertex: $(\underline{\ \ }, \underline{\ \ })$.

15. A quadratic function is given by $y = 4(x + 5)^2 - 35$. Determine

a) the coordinates of its vertex: $(\underline{\ \ }, \underline{\ \ })$

b) its y-intercept: $\underline{\ \ }$

c) its domain and range: $\{(x, y) \mid \underline{\hspace{2cm}}\}$

16. Solve the equation $2x^2 - 5x - 12 = 0$.

$x = \underline{\ \ }$ or $x = \underline{\ \ }$

17. Solve the equation $7x^2 - 2x + 1 = 3x + 2$. Give exact solutions.

$x = \underline{\hspace{2cm}}$ or $x = \underline{\hspace{2cm}}$

18. Nina and Franco are comparing their SUV and sedan fuel costs. On a 250 km trip, the SUV uses 45.3 L of gas. On a similar trip, of 180 km, the sedan uses 28.7 L of gas. Rounding to the nearest tenth, what is the fuel economy

a) of the SUV?   _____ L/100 km

b) of the sedan?   _____ L/100 km

c) By how much, to the nearest percent, is the sedan more fuel efficient? ___%

19. The scale diagram represents the net for a gift box. The base of the box is 15 mm wide on the diagram. The actual box will be 22.5 cm wide.

a) What is the scale ratio of the diagram? 1: ___

b) How many times larger is the surface area of the actual box than the area of the diagram? ___ times larger

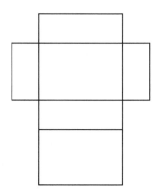

20. Consider the system of linear inequalities:

$\{(x, y) \mid 3x + y \geq 12, x \in R, y \in R\}$

$\{(x, y) \mid x < 2y - 6, x \in R, y \in R\}$

a) Determine the boundary of each inequality in slope−intercept form, and describe how to graph it (solid, dashed, or stippled).

b) For each inequality, determine which half plane (upper or lower) to shade.

c) Graph the solution set of the system on the grid provided. Identify two points in the solution set, and verify them as solutions.

21. Consider the system of linear inequalities:

$\{(x, y) \mid 2y - 5x < 7, x \in W, y \in W\}$

$\{(x, y) \mid x \geq 4, x \in W, y \in W\}$

a) Determine the boundary of each inequality, how it should be graphed, and which half plane (left or right) should be shaded.

b) Identify two points in the solution set, and validate them as solutions.

22. Lorel and Shaida are making shakes and smoothies for the drinks stand at their school fair. They can make a maximum of 280 drinks altogether, of which at most 120 can be shakes. They plan to sell shakes for $3.50 each and smoothies for $2.75 each.

a) Create an algebraic model of the situation.

b) Graph the system of inequalities in your model on the grid provided. State the vertices of the feasible region.

c) Predict which point in the feasible region maximizes the objective function. Explain.

d) Determine the maximum revenue that Lorel and Shaida can make. Verify that your solution satisfies the constraints of the original problem.

23. a) Describe how you can use a table of values to determine the vertex of the parabola defined by the quadratic function $y = 2x^2 - 10x + 7$.

b) Describe how to determine the vertex of the parabola by partial factoring.

c) Use either method to determine the vertex of the parabola.

d) Rewrite the function in vertex form.

24. A parabola has vertex $(3, -8.5)$ and y-intercept -4.

   a) Write the equation of the parabola in vertex form. Show your work.

   b) Write the equation of the parabola in standard form.

   c) Determine the exact values of the x-intercepts of the parabola.

25. Use graphing technology to determine the roots of the equation $3x^2 - 4x + 2 = 5x(2 - x)$, to the nearest thousandth. Verify your answers.

26. Determine a quadratic equation in the form $ax^2 + bx + 30 = 0$ that has roots $x = 5$ and $x = -3$.

27. Robert makes frames for his watercolours. He likes to design the border of each frame to be the same width all around and to have half the area of the watercolour. For a watercolour measuring 5 in. by 8 in., what overall dimensions should the frame have? Round to the nearest tenth.

28. Murray is wrapping a number of identical boxes for gifts for co-workers. Each box needs a length of 57 cm from a roll of gift wrap. There are two gift-wrap options, at different stores: 3 m rolls at $16.49 or 4 m rolls at $19.99. To save on shopping time, Murray wants to get only one kind of wrap.

a) If Murray has 15 gifts to wrap, should he buy 3 m or 4 m rolls?

b) If Murray has many extra gifts to wrap, which rolls should he buy?

29. An isosceles trapezoid has parallel sides measuring 6.4 cm and 4.0 cm and a height of 1.6 cm. Draw a 2 : 1 scale diagram of the trapezoid.

30. Marie is making table runners from a 1 : 12 scale plan. Her plan measures 2.4 cm by 28.2 cm. How much material, to the nearest tenth of a square metre, does Marie need for 8 runners?

31. The specifications for a picture frame are shown. Draw a scale diagram of the top, side, and front views of the picture frame, using a scale ratio of 1 : 5. The border of the frame is the same width left and right, and the same width top and bottom.

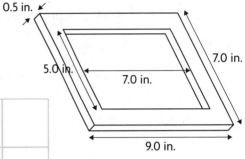

32. The scale factor for two similar cubes is 1:3. Their combined volume is 3500 cm³.

   a) Determine the volume of each cube. Show your work.

   b) Determine the side length of each cube.

   c) Determine the surface area of the smaller cube.

   d) Briefly describe two methods for determining the surface area of the larger cube. Use either method to determine this surface area.

1–8 Cumulative Test: Exam Prep

MULTIPLE CHOICE

1. Pierre is thinking about even numbers. He makes this conjecture: the sum of any 3 consecutive even integers is divisible by 4. Which of the following sets of numbers does NOT support the validity of Pierre's conjecture?

   A. 2, 4, 6   **B.** 8, 10, 12   **C.** 10, 12, 14   **D.** 14, 16, 18

2. Janet conjectures that the diagonals of a trapezoid always bisect each other. Which of these trapezoids is a counterexample to Janet's conjecture?

   A. an isosceles trapezoid

   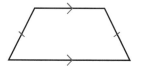

   C. a trapezoid with two right angles

   B. a parallelogram

   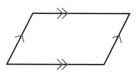

   D. None of these choices is a counterexample.

3. A regular polygon has internal angles measuring 165°. How many sides does the polygon have?

   A. 15   **B.** 24   **C.** 26   **D.** none of these

4. You are asked to solve this triangle. Which law, in which form, should you use first?

   A. sine law: $\dfrac{\sin A}{a} = \dfrac{\sin B}{b}$

   C. cosine law: $\cos C = \dfrac{a^2 + b^2 - c^2}{2ab}$

   B. sine law: $\dfrac{a}{\sin A} = \dfrac{b}{\sin B}$

   D. cosine law: $c^2 = a^2 + b^2 - 2ab \cos C$

   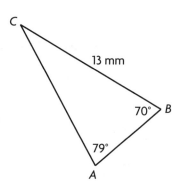

5. In $\triangle JKL$, $j = 38$ mm, $k = 32$ mm, and $\angle J = 107°$. How many triangles are possible with these dimensions?

   A. 0   **B.** 1   **C.** 2   **D.** not enough information to determine

6. Based on their standard deviations, which of these two sets of test scores (both out of 100) is more dispersed?

   A. Class A is significantly more dispersed.

   B. Class B is significantly more dispersed.

   C. The classes are about equally dispersed.

   D. The standard deviations do not give enough information to decide.

Class A	Class B
78, 69, 95, 65, 83, 87	51, 62, 68, 75, 88, 70, 59, 64, 77

7. Which of the following accurately describes how the solution set for the linear inequality $3x - 2y > 5$, $x \in I$, $y \in I$ should be graphed?

A. boundary dashed, upper half plane shaded

B. boundary solid, upper half plane shaded

C. boundary stippled, lower half plane shaded and stippled

D. boundary dashed, lower half plane shaded and stippled

8. Which of these quadratic functions corresponds to the parabola?

A. $y = 2x(6 - x) - 8$

B. $y = -2(x - 3)^2 + 10$

C. $y = 12x - 8 - 2x^2$

D. all of these choices

9. Which of these quadratic functions is equivalent to $y = 2x(x + 5) + 20$?

A. $y = 2(x + 5)^2 - 30$

B. $y = 2(x + 2.5)^2 + 7.5$

C. $y = 2(x + 2.5)^2 + 20$

D. $y = 2(x + 5)^2 + 7.5$

10. Which of these are approximate solutions of the quadratic equation $x^2 + 3x - 13 = 3x(x - 5)$?

A. 0.792, 8.208

B. −5.405, 2.405

C. −5.405, 0, 2.405, 5

D. −0.845, 3.845

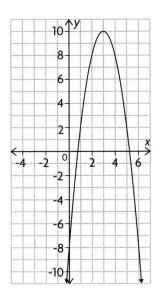

11. Helayne, Stuart, and Chloe are taking part in a 40 km run for charity. Helayne runs the first half of the run at a gentle 9 km/h, then completes it at 15 km/h. Stuart runs the first half at 18 km/h, but then has to walk the rest of the way at 6 km/h. Chloe completes the whole event at a steady 12 km/h. Who finishes first?

A. Helayne   **B.** Stuart   **C.** Chloe   **D.** Helayne and Chloe in a tie

12. Richard is roasting a chicken with a mass of 1.85 kg. His cookery book says to allow 15 min cooking time per pound plus an extra 15 min. Given that 2.2 lb $\doteq$ 1 kg, how long should Richard leave the chicken in the oven?

A. 1 h 1 min   **B.** 43 min   **C.** 1 h 11 min   **D.** 1 h 16 min

NUMERICAL RESPONSE

13. a) How many ways can you colour the edges of pentagon *ABCDE* so that each edge is either red, blue, or green, and two edges that meet at a vertex are different colours?   ___ ways

b) How many ways can you colour the edges of square *ABCD* in the same way as the pentagon in part a)?   ___ ways

14. Solve each Kakuro puzzle.

a)

b)

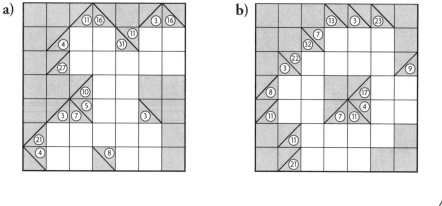

15. Determine each unknown angle in the figure shown.

$a =$ ___ ° $b =$ ___ ° $c =$ ___ ° $d =$ ___ °

$e =$ ___ ° $f =$ ___ ° $g =$ ___ ° $h =$ ___ °

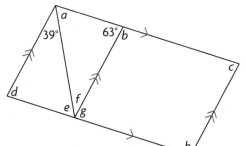

16. Solve $\triangle DEF$. Round to the nearest tenth of a centimetre or the nearest degree.

$\angle E =$ ___ ° $\angle F =$ ___ ° $e =$ ___ cm

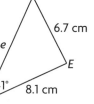

17. Solve $\triangle PQR$. Round to the nearest tenth of a metre or the nearest degree.

$q =$ ___ m $\angle P =$ ___ ° $\angle R =$ ___ °

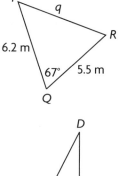

18. Martin determines the height of a pylon on the far side of a railway line by taking measurements from two positions, *A* and *B*. The base of the pylon is at *C*, and its top is directly above *C* at *D*. The diagram shows the positions of *A*, *B*, *C*, and *D*, as well as the measurements Martin took. Determine the following, to the nearest tenth.

a) What is the length of *AC*? _____ m

b) What is the height of the pylon? _____ m

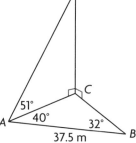

19. Art scores 87 on a chemistry test and 79 on a French test. The mean and standard deviation on both tests are shown. Determine Art's *z*-scores on each test, to the nearest hundredth:

Chemistry _____   French _____

	μ	σ
Chemistry	77.2	15.3
French	68.7	11.5

20. A telephone survey of 900 randomly selected respondents determined that 68% of Canadian adults watch at least one hockey game per month during the regular and post season. The results are accurate within 3 percent points, 19 times out of 20.

a) State the confidence level: ___%

b) State the margin of error: ___%

c) Determine the confidence interval: ___% to ___%

d) If the adult population of Canada is 24 986 000, what is the range of people that this survey predicts will watch at least one game per month?

between _____ and _____ Canadians

21. A system of linear inequalities is defined by:

$\{(x, y) \mid x > 3 - 2y, x \in W, y \in W\}$

$\{(x, y) \mid y \le 5, x \in W, y \in W\}$

LS	RS		LS	RS
___	3 − 2(___)		2	___

a) Determine whether (0, 2) is a solution of this system.

Solution? Yes/No   (circle one)

b) Is (0.1, 2.1) a solution of the system?

Yes/No   (circle one)

22. a) Complete this table of values for the function $f(x) = -0.5x^2 + 4.5x - 7$.

b) Determine the equation of the axis of symmetry: $x =$ ___

c) Determine the coordinates of the vertex: (___ , _____)

x	y
−1	
0	−7
1	
2	
3	
4	
5	
6	

23. A quadratic function has one x-intercept, $x = -4$, and one y-intercept, $y = 4$. Determine the factored form of the function:

$f(x) = a(x$ ___ ___ $)(x$ ___ ___ $)$

$f(x) = a(x$ ___ ___ $)^2$

$f(0) = a($ ___ $)^2$

_____ = _____ a

_____ = a

$f(x) =$ _____ $(x$ ___ ___ $)^2$

24. Solve the quadratic equation $3x^2 - 5x + 2 = 3 - 2x$. Give exact solutions and approximate solutions rounded to the nearest hundredth.

$3x^2$ ___ ___ x ___ ___ $= 0$

$x =$ _____   or $x =$ _____

$x \doteq$ _____   or $x \doteq$ _____

25. This floor plan was sketched at a scale ratio of 1 : 200. Not all the room measurements were recorded.

What is the actual area of the largest room? _____ m²

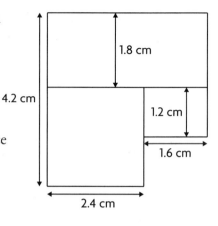

WRITTEN RESPONSE

26. Prove that the sum of two consecutive numbers is equal to the difference of the squares of those numbers.

27. Prove that *ABCD* is an isosceles trapezoid.

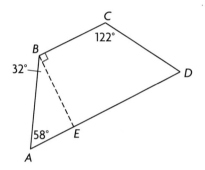

28. In △*ABC*, *AB* = 14 cm, *BC* = 15 cm, and *AC* = 16 cm.

a) Which is the smallest angle in △*ABC*? Which is the largest? Explain.

b) Determine the measure of the largest angle in △*ABC*, to the nearest degree.

29. In $\triangle XYZ$, $x = 1.1$ m, $y = 1.3$ m, and $\angle X = 52°$.

    a) Draw sketches of all possible triangles XYZ.

    b) Solve each possible $\triangle XYZ$. Round to the nearest degree or the nearest tenth of a metre.

30. Zenab and Krista set out on a canoe trip. Starting from the dock, they paddle northeast for 5.4 km until they reach Foggy Island, then turn due east, reaching Brousseau Township after another 2.6 km. Krista wonders how far it is from Brousseau back to the dock. Zenab remembers that the angle between the bearings from the dock to Foggy Island and to Brousseau is about 25°.

    a) Sketch the situation.

    b) Explain how the directions eliminate any ambiguity.

    c) Determine the return distance from Brousseau to the dock, to the nearest tenth of a kilometre.

31. a) Complete the frequency table for the following mass data for sea shells, in mg: 168, 290, 224, 254, 189, 268, 210, 156, 227, 254, 181, 193, 260, 303, 295, 259, 330, 217, 175, 284, 232, 205, 250, 172, 248, 278, 348, 317, 320, 193

Mass (mg)	Frequency
150–175	
175–200	

b) Draw a histogram for this data on the grid provided.

c) Describe the distribution.

d) Make a conjecture about why the distribution has this shape. How could you test your conjecture?

32. a) Based on the frequency distribution shown in the table, construct a frequency polygon for this height data on the grid provided.

b) Does the data approximate a normal distribution? Justify your answer.

c) Calculate the mean and median for the data. Do these values support your answer to part b)? Explain.

Student Height (cm)	Frequency
155–160	1
160–165	2
165–170	4
170–175	8
175–180	9
180–185	7
185–190	5
190–195	3
195–200	1

33. a) Graph the solution set for this system of linear inequalities on the grid provided.

$\{(x, y) \mid x \geq 0, y \geq 0, 2x + 5y \leq 10, x \in R, y \in R\}$

$\{(x, y) \mid x \geq 0, y \geq 0, x > y, x \in R, y \in R\}$

b) Based on your graph, is the point (3.5, 1) in the solution set for this system? Verify your answer numerically.

34. Zoë is creating party favours for her sister Janine's wedding. She can make little "travel totes" for $1.60 each and small "bling baskets" for $2.30 each. Janine has asked Zoë to make sure that

- there are at most 48 favours altogether
- there are at least 24 travel totes
- at least one-third of the favours are bling baskets

a) Create an algebraic model of the situation.

b) Graph the system of inequalities in your model on the grid provided, with travel totes on the horizontal axis. State the vertices of the feasible region.

c) Determine the minimum cost of producing an adequate supply of party favours, and the numbers of each type for this cost. Verify that your solution satisfies the constraints of the original problem.

35. Consider the quadratic equation $3x^2 - 5x - 2 = 0$.

a) Substitute the values for a, b, and c for this equation into the quadratic formula. Then, evaluate the radicand.

b) Based on the value of the radicand, is it necessary to use the quadratic formula to solve this equation? Explain.

c) Solve the equation.

36. The sum of the squares of three consecutive odd integers is 683.

a) Develop a quadratic equation to represent this situation.

b) What are the integers?

37. Brian uses a cookie dough recipe that calls for 250 mL of water per 400 mL of flour. Erin's cookie dough recipe calls for 200 mL of flour per 150 mL of water.

a) Which recipe uses the greater proportion of flour?

b) Brian and Erin agree to share a 1 kg bag of flour equally. How much water will each of them use?

38. The sketch shows a piece of staging for a concert, made up of three squares and a central triangle. The smaller squares have side lengths of 1.5 m. Draw a 1 : 50 scale diagram of the staging.

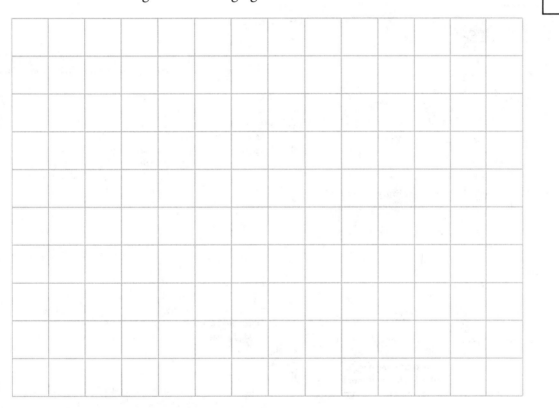

39. a) What is the ratio of the radii of the two cylinders?

b) Determine the ratio of the surface areas of the cylinders. Show your work.

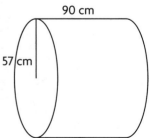

c) Based on your answers to parts a) and b), are the cylinders similar? Explain.

Answers

Chapter 1

Getting Started, page 2

1. **a)** vi)   **b)** ii)   **c)** iii)   **d)** i)   **e)** iv)   **f)** v)
2. d), b), a), c)
      a) 9   **b)** 6   **c)** 10   **d)** 3
3. **a)** e.g., 63   **b)** e.g., 25   **c)** e.g., 52
4. **a)** $x^2 + 3x + 4$; 44   **b)** $32 - 5x$; 7   **c)** $x^2 - 2$; 23
5. **a)** $8x - 2x^2$; -24 **b)** $(3x + 2)(3x - 2)$; 32   **c)** $(2x + 1)(x - 4)$; 18
6. **a)** $x = 15$ **b)** $x = 4.4$ **c)** $x = 4$ or -4
7. $\angle a = 102°$; $\angle b = 78°$; $\angle c = 102°$
8. **a)**

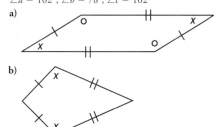

   b)

9. The next number will be $101010101^2 = 10203040504030201$.

Lesson 1.1, page 4

1. e.g., She conjectured that the number of customers ordering large coffees in February will be twice the number of customers who order a regular or medium coffee.
2. Her conjecture is reasonable. e.g., 66 and 165 are both multiples of 11.
3. e.g., The colours blue and yellow represent the sky and land. The star is the North Star that guides the people. The inukshuk is also a guide. The iglu is a traditional form of housing, while the caribou and narwhal are traditional sources of food. The crown is a reference to the Canadian government.
4. **a)** e.g., The largest angle in a triangle is opposite the longest side.
   b) e.g., The smallest angle in a triangle is opposite the shortest side.
5. e.g., When two lines intersect at a point, pairs of adjacent angles are supplementary.
6. **a)** e.g., When the factors are 9 and another factor containing only 7s, the product will begin with a 6 and end with a 3. The number of 9s in between the 6 and 3 will be one less than the number of 7s in the factor. $77777(9) = 699\ 993$
   b) e.g., The pattern seems the same for a different factor with repeated digits. $8(9) = 72$, $88(9) = 792$, $888(9) = 7992$, ...
7. e.g., The pattern can be expressed algebraically.
   $$\frac{1}{n} - \frac{1}{n+1} = \frac{1}{(n+1)^2 - (n+1)} \text{ or } \frac{1}{n^2 + n}$$
8. e.g., In general, Regina does not receive much precipitation per year, with the average about 320 mm. However, there are very few extremely dry years (precipitation <200 mm).
9. e.g., If every Canadian could text at the same time, the amount of time would be no more than 5 min. However, the Red Cross computer system would probably crash. It is not unreasonable for the task to be completed in at least 24 h.
10. A.
11. e.g., The statement is not a conjecture. The company making the claim may have tested only that one group; however, this group's opinion may not represent that of all juice drinkers across the country.

Lesson 1.2, page 8

1. e.g., I conjectured that the three horizontal lines are all the same length. I checked the validity of my conjecture by measuring each horizontal line.
2. e.g., The square root of the power of a number x, raised to the number of its divisors, is equal to the product of x's divisors. By gathering more evidence, I could validate my conjecture.
3. e.g., The angle created by the centre of a circle, the point of tangency of a tangent, and the tangent is 90°; Yes
4. e.g., There is a prime pair in every one of the intervals $1-50$, $51-100$, $101-150$, $151-200$; No; or, e.g., There is always a higher prime pair; Yes (probably!)

Lesson 1.3, page 10

1. **a)** e.g., Alberta shares a border with the United States.
   b) e.g., Emus, penguins, and ostriches have wings, but they cannot fly.
   c) e.g., Frogs, dolphins, and whales live in the water, but they are not fish.
   d) e.g., A rectangle is a quadrilateral that has four right angles.
   e) e.g., 2 is a prime number. 5 is a prime number. $2 + 5 = 7$
2. disagree; e.g., For an angle to be acute, it must be less than 90°. But an isosceles triangle could have angles of 35°, 35°, and 110°.
3. disagree; e.g., The graph continues into negative values of x. Belinda cannot see this because of the settings.
4. disagree; e.g., $7 \div 28 = 0.25 < 7$; When you divide a whole number by a lesser whole number, the quotient will be less than the dividend.
5. **a)** e.g., $6 + 6 = 12$
   b) e.g., $121 - 14 = 107$
   c) e.g., If people who live in New Zealand were to go north, toward the equator, the climate would get warmer.
   d) e.g., You can travel eastward, across the Atlantic, Europe, and Asia, to the Pacific.
6. **a)** e.g., $1 + 2 + 3 + 4 = 10$, and $2 \times 4 \neq 10$.
   b) no counterexample
   c) e.g., It is possible for snow to fall in May, so it may be snowing.
   d) no counterexample
7. e.g., Dolphins are mammals, and they are not raised on farms.
8. C.
9. A.
10. e.g., Disagree: $3 + (-4) = -1 < 3$.
    The sum of two positive numbers is greater than either number.
    The sum of two negative numbers is less than either number.

Lesson 1.4, page 14

1. **a)** e.g., Rain is not the only thing that falls from the sky.
   b) e.g., Franco may eat apples at other times of the day.
   c) e.g., Bradley may like to play other games besides video games.
   d) e.g., The results of the person in the commercial are likely caused by diet and regular exercise, not by the tonic.
2. Its square is also odd.
3. Its square root is also even.
4. The sum is divisible by 3.
5. e.g., The difference between the squares of two consecutive integers is 1 more than twice the lesser integer.
6. e.g., They are all equal.
7. e.g., The answer is always your birth year repeated three times.
8. e.g., The sum of 7 consecutive natural numbers is a multiple of 7.
9. e.g., They are not equal.
10. A.   **11.** B.   **12.** D.

13. e.g., Let $2x$ and $2y$ represent two even numbers, and let $2z + 1$ represent an odd number. Then

$2x + 2y + (2z + 1) = 2(x + y + z) + 1$

The term $2(x + y + z)$ must be even, since it is a multiple of 2. Since the sum is 1 more than an even number, it must be odd.

Lesson 1.5, page 18

1. a) a false assumption or generalization
   b) an error in reasoning: division by zero to get final line
   c) a false assumption or generalization
   d) an error in reasoning
   e) an error in calculation
   f) There is no error.
   g) an error in reasoning
   h) an error in reasoning

2. a) a false assumption: $2 + 2 = 4$, not 2
   b) an error in calculation: $7(2 + 1) = 21$, not 14
   c) an error in reasoning: the days are longer owing to the tilt of Earth's axis
   d) a false assumption: many other types of music are written today
   e) an error in reasoning: Pondthip could not give herself a hairdo, so there is no evidence she is a good hair dresser

3. C.   **4.** A.

5. e.g., In line 5, where Andrea divides both sides of the equation by $(x + y - z)$, she is dividing by 0.

6. In line 3, the "2" in "$n + 2$" was not multiplied by 2.

n	Use n to represent any number.
$n + 2$	Add 2.
$2n + 4$	Multiply by 2.
$2n + 10$	Add 6.
$n + 5$	Divide by 2.
n	Subtract 5.

7. e.g., In line 4, G'Shaw is ignoring the units. It does not make sense to square a tenth of a metre in this context, so the proof is meaningless.

Lesson 1.6, page 22

1. a) inductive reasoning   **d)** inductive reasoning
   b) deductive reasoning   **e)** inductive reasoning
   c) deductive reasoning   **f)** deductive reasoning

2. a)

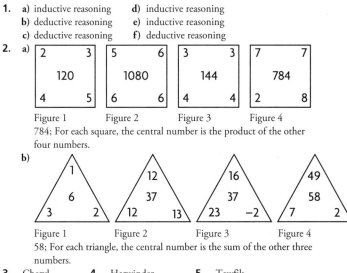

784; For each square, the central number is the product of the other four numbers.

b)

58; For each triangle, the central number is the sum of the other three numbers.

3. Cheryl   **4.** Harwinder   **5.** Tawfik

6. 14; e.g., The differences are 3, 4, ?, ?, and 7. Also, $(9 + 5) + 6 = 20$. So, the two missing differences are 5 and 6, and the missing term is $9 + 5 = 14$.

7. MATHEMATICS IS MADE OF FIFTY PERCENT FORMULAS, FIFTY PERCENT PROOFS, AND FIFTY PERCENT IMAGINATION

8. a) 405   **b)** 2.25   **c)** 10

9. a) $a = 2, b = 9$ **b)** 1

10. a) Neither true or false; e.g., If the sentence were true, it would also be false, which is impossible. If the sentence were false, then it would not be false, so it would be true, which is also impossible.
   b) e.g., Yes, because if the sentence had a meaning, it would either have to be true or false, and it cannot be either.

11. Neither true, false, nor meaningless; e.g., If the sentence were true, it would either also be false, which is impossible, or meaningless, which means it could not simply be true. If the sentence were false, then it would not be false and it would not be meaningless, so it would be true, which is also impossible. If the sentence were meaningless then it would be true, and therefore not meaningless.

12. The red bag contains the number 6. e.g., The total sum is 45, so the red bag sum is 30 and the white bag sum is 15. Red bag: There are only four numbers whose sum is 30: $6 + 7 + 8 + 9 = 30$. Therefore, all the other cards must be in the white bag.

13. 5; e.g., The total number of cards is 15. So, $15 \div 5 = 3$ cards are blue on both sides. Since yellow was seen 12 times in total, and there are no cards with yellow on both sides, 12 cards have yellow on one side. $12 + 3 = 15$, so each card must be either blue on both sides or yellow on one side. Before being flipped, 3 of the blue cards were blue on both sides, so there were $5 - 3 = 2$ blue and yellow cards. After being flipped, 3 of the blue cards were blue on both sides, so $6 - 3 = 3$ cards were blue and yellow.

Lesson 1.7, page 28

1. a)

6	3	2	7	5	9	8	4	1
1	8	4	6	3	2	7	9	5
5	9	7	4	8	1	6	2	3
2	7	6	1	9	5	4	3	8
9	5	8	2	4	3	1	6	7
3	4	1	8	7	6	2	5	9
4	1	9	5	6	8	3	7	2
8	6	3	9	2	7	5	1	4
7	2	5	3	1	4	9	8	6

b)

4	7	8	9	2	6	5	3	1
5	1	2	8	3	4	6	9	7
9	6	3	7	1	5	8	2	4
6	9	1	2	7	3	4	8	5
3	2	5	6	4	8	7	1	9
7	8	4	5	9	1	2	6	3
1	4	7	3	6	2	9	5	8
8	3	6	4	5	9	1	7	2
2	5	9	1	8	7	3	4	6

2. a)

(Kakuro-style grid with clues; filled answers)

b)

(Kakuro-style grid with clues; filled answers)

3. 20 routes

e.g., The driver can drive S, S, S, E, E, E in any order.
There are 10 possible orders starting with S: SSSEEE, SSESEE,
SSEEES, SESSEE, SESESE, SESEES, SEESSE, SEESES, SEEESS.
Similarly there are 10 orders starting with E. So, there are 20 routes
altogether.

4. a) e.g.,

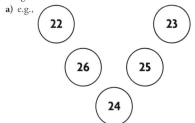

b) 24 solutions

5. a) e.g., Yes; Jenna risks getting grounded for 6 weeks if Kira defects, but
the next time, when Jenna defects, she will either get grounded for
3 weeks (as before) or will get no punishment. So the sisters are not
significantly worse off, and whenever they both happen to cooperate
they are much better off, being grounded for only 1 week each.

b) e.g., If both sisters play tit for tat, the worst that can happen is that
they will alternate cooperating and defecting, so that they take it in
turns to get the 6 weeks' grounding. However, it is more likely that
they will fall into the pattern of cooperating almost all the time, so
that they will generally be grounded for only 1 week each.

6. e.g., Case 1: Player 1 starts in the centre and player 2 then plays in a
corner. Whenever either player tries to form a row, column, or diagonal,
the other player can block. Case 2: Player 1 starts in the corner. The
only losing moves for player 2 are in the two adjacent corners; if player
2 avoids these, again the players can take turns blocking until stalemate.
Case 3: Player 1 starts in the middle of an edge. This plays out like
Case 1.

7. C.   **8.** D.   **9.** B.   **10.** C.

11. a)

2	7	4	8	1	5	9	3	6
5	3	6	2	7	9	1	8	4
1	8	9	3	6	4	7	2	5
3	9	2	1	5	8	4	6	7
4	1	8	7	2	6	3	5	9
7	6	5	4	9	3	2	1	8
8	2	7	6	4	1	5	9	3
6	5	1	9	3	7	8	4	2
9	4	3	5	8	2	6	7	1

b)

(Kakuro-style grid with clues; filled answers)

12. a) e.g.,

50   56
54   52
55   51
53

b) 216 solutions

13. a) 2   **b)** 4   **c)** 8   **d)** 6   **e)** 4   **f)** 3

Chapter 1 Test Prep, page 34

Q1:
- Inductive reasoning starts with specific <u>examples</u>.
- Identifying <u>properties</u> and observing <u>patterns</u> may lead to a general <u>conclusion</u>. This <u>conclusion</u> can then be stated as a <u>conjecture</u>.

Q2:
- Finding <u>more</u> evidence supporting a conjecture makes it <u>more</u> likely true.
- Evidence can also show a conjecture to be <u>false</u>, but can suggest ways to <u>modify</u> the conjecture.

Q3:
- A counterexample is an example that <u>disproves</u> a conjecture. This means that the conjecture is <u>invalid</u>.
- If you cannot find a counterexample, you <u>cannot</u> be certain a <u>counterexample</u> does not exist.
- If you do find a counterexample, the conjecture must be <u>false</u>. However, you may be able to <u>revise</u> the conjecture.

Q4:
- Deductive reasoning starts with general <u>assumptions</u> known to be true.
- <u>Logical</u> reasoning then leads to a specific <u>conclusion</u>.
- A <u>proof</u> of a conjecture must involve <u>general</u> cases.

Q5: • <u>Division</u> by zero can be an example of a(n) <u>error</u> in reasoning.
• A false <u>assumption</u> or <u>generalization</u> can lead to <u>circular</u> reasoning; that is, "proving" something that you began by assuming.

Chapter 1 Test, page 35

1. B. **2.** C. **3.** A. **4.** B.
5. B. **6.** C. **7.** A. **8.** B.
9. a) 768 **b)** 500 **c)** 224
10. a) 1 **b)** 5 **c)** 6 **d)** 2
11. a) disagree; e.g., $5 + 15 = 20$ **b)** disagree; e.g., $10 + 15 = 25$
12. e.g., If x represents any whole number, then the left side of the equation consists of any seven consecutive numbers. The sum of these numbers is equal to seven times the number plus 21. Each term of the right side, $7x + 21$, is divisible by 7. This equation proves that the sum of any seven consecutive numbers is divisible by 7. Example: $6 + 7 + 8 + 9 + 10 + 11 + 12 = 63$, and $63 \div 7 = 9$.
13. e.g., disagree; Television shows are not always realistic. At the scene of a real-life crime, there might not be enough evidence to prove a person's guilt.
14. e.g., Kangaroos have pouches; deductive reasoning
15. e.g., Each term is 9 more than the previous term, so the next two terms are 50 and 59; inductive reasoning

Chapter 2

Getting Started, page 38

1.

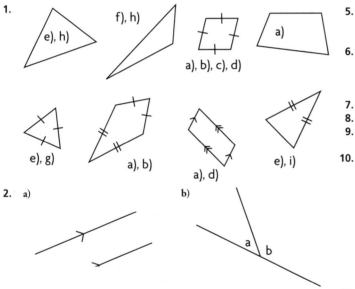

2. a)

b)

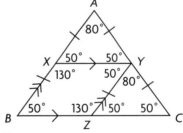

3. a) All corresponding angles are equal.
b) Corresponding sides are in the same ratio.
4. a) $\angle a = 65°$, $\angle b = 115°$, $\angle c = 65°$
b) $\angle d = 17°$, $\angle e = 73°$, $\angle f = 17°$
5. a) $\angle a = (180 - x)°$, $\angle b = x°$, $\angle c = (180 - x)°$
b) $\angle d = x°$, $\angle e = (180 - x)°$, $\angle f = (90 - x)°$
6. Triangles ABC and DEF are congruent.

Lesson 2.1, page 40

1. a) transversal: EF; corresponding angles:
b and f, d and h, a and e, c and g
interior angles: c, d, e, f
exterior angles: a, b, g, h

b) transversal: XY
corresponding angles: g and i, h and j, k and m, l and n
interior angles: h, i, l, m
exterior angles: a, b, g, h
2. a) Yes; TU and VW are parallel. **b)** No; PQ is not parallel to RS.
3. a) No; $\angle QVW \neq \angle SWU$ (corresponding angles)
b) Yes; $\angle RVU = \angle WVS$ (opposite angles); $\angle WVS = \angle TWQ$ (corresponding angles)
4. A.
5. e.g., No; a transversal can intersect two non-parallel lines.

Lesson 2.2, page 42

1. a) alternate exterior angles equal
b) corresponding interior angles equal
c) supplementary interior angles
d) alternate interior angles equal
2. a) $\angle x = 130°$; interior angles supplementary between parallel lines
$\angle y = 50°$; alternate interior angles equal between parallel lines
$\angle z = 50°$; vertically opposite angles equal
b) $\angle x = 60°$; corresponding angles equal between parallel lines
$\angle y = 120°$; supplementary angles
$\angle z = 60°$; alternate exterior angles equal between parallel lines
3. Angle b and the 40° angle are supplementary.
Angles c and b are vertically opposite angles.
Angles d and c are interior angles between parallel lines.
The sum of the interior angles in a triangle is 180°.
4. The errors are in line 4. The correct statement is $\angle AXY = \angle XYZ$ (alternate interior angles).
5. Yes. e.g., I measured $\angle B$ and $\angle C$ using a protractor. $\angle B = 70°$ and $\angle C = 110°$. The angles are supplementary interior angles. Also, $\angle A = \angle B$. Therefore, $AB \parallel CD$.
6. a) $\angle w = 30°$, $\angle x = 110°$, $\angle y = 70°$, $\angle z = 40°$
b) $\angle w = 35°$, $\angle x = 120°$, $\angle y = 25°$, $\angle z = 35°$
c) $\angle w = 32°$, $\angle x = 110°$, $\angle y = 38°$, $\angle z = 70°$
d) $\angle w = 135°$, $\angle x = 45°$, $\angle y = 75°$, $\angle z = 105°$
7. $\angle a = 120°$, $\angle b = 118°$, $\angle c = 62°$, $\angle d = 60°$, $\angle e = 118°$
8. $\angle m = 40°$, $\angle n = 90°$, $\angle o = 117°$, $\angle p = 63°$, $\angle q = 117°$, $\angle r = 23°$
9. $\triangle ADE$ is similar to $\triangle ABC$. Lee is correct. e.g., Corresponding angles are equal.
10.

11. Yes.
$\angle f = 135°$ Vertically opposite angles are equal.
$\angle g = 45°$ $\angle g$ and $\angle f$ are supplementary.
$\angle a = 45°$ angle vertically opposite $\angle g$
$\angle c = 100°$ The sum of interior angles in a triangle is 180°.
$\angle b = 15°$ The sum of interior angles in a triangle is 180°.
$\angle d = 15°$ $\angle b$ and $\angle d$ are alternate interior angles.
$30° + \angle c + 35° + \angle d = 30° + 100° + 35° + 15° = 180°$
Therefore, $WY \parallel XZ$.
$35° + \angle b + 30° + \angle c = 35° + 15° + 30° + 100° = 180°$
Therefore, $WX \parallel YZ$.
12. D.
13.
$\angle a = 44°$ alternate interior angles
$\angle a + \angle e + 53° = 180°$ sum of interior angles in a triangle
$\angle e = 83°$
$\angle e + \angle d = 180°$ supplementary angles
$\angle d = 97°$

Lesson 2.3, page 46

1. $\angle DCE = 45°$, $\angle CDE = 80°$, $\angle CED = 55°$
2. $\angle XAZ = 125°$, $\angle YBX = 80°$, $\angle YCZ = 135°$
3. e.g., $\angle b = 50°$ alternate interior angles between parallel lines
   $50° + 65° + \angle c = 180°$
              $\angle c = 65°$ supplementary angles
   $\angle a + \angle b + \angle c = 180°$
   $\angle a + 50° + 65° = 180°$ The interior angles in a triangle sum to 180°.
              $\angle a = 65°$
4. $\angle x = 115°$, $\angle y = 50°$
5. $\angle a = 30°$, $\angle b = 25°$, $\angle c = 105°$
6. $\angle OJK = 120°$, $\angle JKO = 30°$, and $\angle JOK = 30°$
7. $\angle DAC = 65°$
8. **a)** $EF \parallel GI$, since alternate interior angles are equal.
   b) $EF \parallel GI$, since corresponding angles are equal.
9. $\angle ECD + 105° = 180°$ supplementary angles
               $\angle ECD = 75°$
   $\angle CDE + \angle ECD + 40° = 180°$ Interior angles sum to 180°.
     $\angle CDE + 75° + 40° = 180°$
              $\angle CDE = 65°$
             $\angle ABD = \angle CDE$ corresponding angles
   Therefore, $AB \parallel CD$.
10. $\angle XAC + 70° = 180°$ supplementary angles
               $\angle XAC = 110°$
               $\angle ABC = \angle ACB$ property of isosceles triangle
    $\angle ABC + \angle ACB + 70° = 180°$ sum of the measures
              $2\angle ABC = 110°$ of interior angles in triangle
               $\angle ABC = 55°$
       $\angle YBA + \angle ABC = 180°$
               $\angle YBA = 125°$
       $\angle ZCA + \angle ACB = 180°$
               $\angle ZCA = 125°$

11. $AB \parallel DC$ given
    $AC \parallel DE$ given
    $\angle B = \angle DCE$ corresponding angles between parallel lines
    $\angle A = \angle ACD$ alternate interior angles between parallel lines
    $\angle D = \angle DCA$ alternate interior angles between parallel lines
    $\angle A = \angle D$ transitive property
    $\angle A + \angle B + \angle ACB = \angle D + \angle DCE + \angle E$ Both sides sum to 180°.
    $\angle D + \angle DCE + \angle ACB = \angle D + \angle DCE + \angle E$ substitution
    $\angle ACB = \angle E$
    Since three pairs of angles are equal, the triangles are similar.
12. D.
13. $40° + 45° + \angle z = 180°$ Interior angles sum to 180°.
              $\angle z = 95°$
    $60° + \angle x + 40° = 180°$ Interior angles sum to 180°.
              $\angle x = 80°$
    $60° + \angle x + \angle y = 180°$ Interior angles sum to 180°.
    $60° + 80° + \angle y = 180°$
              $\angle y = 40°$

Lesson 2.4, page 50

1. **a)** 900°   **b)** 128.6°   **c)** 51.4°
2. 2520°
3. No. e.g., The sum of the exterior angles of any polygon is 360°.
4. No. e.g., If the polygon is regular, interior angle measure =
   $\dfrac{180°(14 - 2)}{14}$, or 154.3°. The interior angle measure should be 154.3°.
5.

Regular Polygon	Measure of Interior Angle	360° Evenly Divisible by Measure of Interior Angle?
triangle	60°	Yes, so it will tessellate.
square	**90°**	**Yes, so it will tessellate.**
pentagon	**108°**	**no**
hexagon	**120°**	**Yes, so it will tessellate.**
heptagon	**128.6°**	**no**
octagon	**135°**	**no**

6. 145°, 130°, 125°, 120°, 100°, 100°
7. $\angle a = 36°$, $\angle b = 72°$, $\angle c = 108°$
8.

Regular Polygon	Measure of Interior Angle	360° Evenly Divisible by Measure of Interior Angle?
triangle	60°	yes
square	**90°**	yes
pentagon	**108°**	no

triangles and squares; e.g., To make a tessellation, the sum of the interior angles for a number of the two chosen polygons must equal 360°.
$60° + 90° + 60° + 90° + 60° = 360°$
$60° + 108° + 60° + 108° \neq 360°$
$90° + 108° + 90° + 90° \neq 360°$

9. B.   **10.** A.
11. $\angle a = \dfrac{180°(8 - 2)}{8}$ $2\angle d + 135° = 180°$
        $\angle a = 135°$ $2\angle d = 45°$
                             $\angle d - 22.5°$
      $\angle a + \angle b = 180°$
    $135° + \angle b = 180°$ $\angle b + \angle c + \angle d = 135°$
             $\angle b = 45°$ $45° + \angle c + 22.5° = 135°$
                                $\angle c = 67.5°$

Chapter 2 Test Prep, page 54

Q1: • If the intersected lines are <u>parallel</u>,
    … corresponding angles are <u>equal</u>.
    … alternate exterior angles are <u>equal</u>.
    … alternate interior angles are <u>equal</u>.
    … same-side interior angles are <u>supplementary</u>.
 • If corresponding angles are equal, the intersected lines are <u>parallel</u>.

Q2: • The <u>sum</u> of the <u>interior</u> angle measures of a triangle is <u>180°</u>.
    … $\angle A + \angle B + \angle C = \underline{180°}$
 • The measure of an <u>exterior</u> angle is the sum of the measures of the two <u>non</u>-adjacent <u>interior</u> angles.
    … $\angle DBA = \underline{\angle A + \angle C}$

Q3: • The <u>interior</u> angle sum of an *n*-sided <u>convex</u> polygon is $\underline{180°(n - 2)}$.
 • The measure of each <u>interior</u> angle of a <u>regular</u> polygon is
    $\dfrac{\underline{180°(n - 2)}}{\underline{n}}$
 • In the diagram, $\angle a + \angle b + \angle c + \angle d = \underline{180°}(4 - 2)$.
 • The sum of the <u>exterior</u> angle measures of any <u>convex</u> polygon is 360°.
  In the diagram, $\underline{\angle w} + \underline{\angle x} + \underline{\angle y} + \underline{\angle z} = 360°$.

Chapter 2 Test, page 55

1. C. **2.** D. **3.** B. **4.** A.
5. C. **6.** A. **7.** D. **8.** B.
9. C. **10.** C. **11.** B.
12. $\angle a = 115°$, $\angle b = 30°$, $\angle c = 35°$, $\angle d = 35°$
13. $\angle a = 45°$, $\angle b = 55°$, $\angle c = 110°$,
$\angle d = 70°$, $\angle e = 110°$, $\angle f = 25°$
14. **a)** 2880° **b)** 160° **c)** 40°
15.
$\angle q = 30°$ corresponding interior angles
$\angle t = 65°$ corresponding interior angles
$\angle r + 30° = 180°$ interior angles
$\angle r = 150°$
$\angle s + \angle t = 180°$ interior angles
$\angle s = 115°$
$\angle p + \angle q + 65° = 180°$ Interior angles sum to 180°.
$\angle p = 85°$
16.
$\angle RST + 110° = 180°$ supplementary angles
$\angle RST = 70°$
$\angle SRT + \angle RST + 30° = 180°$ Interior angles sum to 180°.
$\angle SRT = 80°$
$\angle QPT = 80°$ given
$\angle QPT = \angle SRT$ transitive property
Therefore, $PQ \parallel RS$.   Corresponding angles are equal.
17. 23
18.
$AB = AE$ given
$\angle B = \angle E$ property of isosceles triangle
$\angle BAC = \angle EAD$ given
$\therefore \triangle ABC \cong \triangle AED$ ASA
$AC = AD$ corresponding sides
$\therefore \triangle ACD$ is isosceles.

1–2 Cumulative Test, page 58

1. B. **2.** C. **3.** D. **4.** C.
5. A. **6.** C. **7.** D.
8. **a)** 15 **b)**

8	3	4
1	5	9
6	7	2

c)

2	9	4
7	5	3
6	1	8

d) 8

9. **a)** 2 **b)** 1 **c)** 2 **d)** 1
10. $\angle a = 72°$ $\angle b = 82°$ $\angle c = 98°$
$\angle d = 88°$ $\angle e = 72°$ $\angle f = 72°$
11. $\angle EAB = 108°$ $\angle AEF = 36°$ $\angle EAF = 72°$ $\angle FAB = 36°$
$\angle EFA = 36°$
$\angle AFB = 108°$ $\angle EBA = 36°$ $\angle DAC = 36°$ $\angle ADC = 72°$
$\angle ACD = 72°$
$\triangle ACD \sim \triangle EAF$ $\triangle ABE \sim \triangle FAB$
12. **a)** e.g., No. If it mattered, you might not be able to escape, as you would have to know already which guard to question.
b) e.g., "If I asked the other guard which door he was guarding, what would he say?"
13. **a)** e.g., The sum of two consecutive perfect squares is always an odd number.
b) e.g., $2^2 + 3^2 = 4 + 9$, or 13; $3^2 + 4^2 = 9 + 16$, or 25; $100^2 + 101^2 = 10\ 000 + 10\ 201$, or 20 201
c) $S = x^2 + (x + 1)^2$
$S = x^2 + x^2 + 2x + 1$
$S = 2x^2 + 2x + 1$
$S = 2(x^2 + x) + 1$, which is always an odd number.
14. $\angle DAB = \angle B + \angle C$ given
$\angle BAC + \angle DAB = 180°$ supplementary angles
$\angle BAC + \angle B + \angle C = 180°$ substitution
15. Yes. e.g., The internal angles of squares are 90°.
Equilateral triangle internal angles are 60°.
Two squares can fit together, forming an angle of $2(90°) = 180°$.
This leaves $360° - 180° = 180°$, which equals $3(60°)$, so three equilateral triangles can fit at the same vertex.

Chapter 3

Getting Started, page 62

1. **a)** ii) **b)** v) **c)** vi) **d)** iv) **e)** i) **f)** iii)
2. **a)** $x = 2.5$ **b)** $a = 68$ **c)** $p = \dfrac{30}{7}$
3. **a)** AC, BC; opposite largest (90°) and smallest (38°) angles
b) EF, DF; opposite largest (80°) and smallest (30°) angles
c) LN, LM; opposite largest (75°) and smallest (40°) angles
4. **a)** $\angle X$, $\angle Y$; opposite longest (9 cm) and shortest (5 cm) sides
b) $\angle Q$, $\angle R$; opposite longest (13 cm) and shortest (5 cm) sides
c) $\angle K$, $\angle L$; opposite longest (2.0 cm) and shortest (1.2 cm) sides
5. $\angle a = 77°$ (corresponding angles), $\angle b = 103°$ (supplementary angles), $\angle c = 61°$ (sum of angles in triangle), $\angle d = 61°$ (sum of angles in triangle), $\angle e = 119°$ (supplementary angles)
6. **a)** 0.3746 **b)** 0.5 **c)** 1
7. **a)** 24° **b)** 68° **c)** 68°
8. $AB = 7.3$ cm, $BC = 3.9$ cm, $\angle B = 62°$
9. **a)** Yes. e.g., Since $PQ \parallel ST$ and $PR \parallel ST$, corresponding angles are equal.
b) Yes. e.g., $\dfrac{PQ}{SR}$ and $\dfrac{PR}{ST}$ are both equivalent to $\dfrac{QR}{RT}$.

Lesson 3.1, page 64

1. **a)**

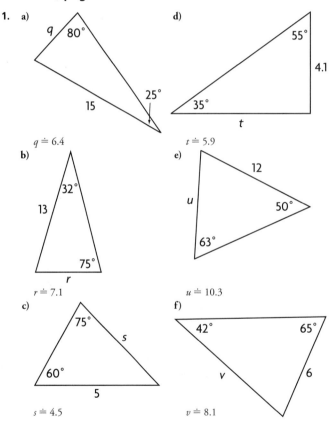

$q \doteq 6.4$
$t \doteq 5.9$
$r \doteq 7.1$
$u \doteq 10.3$
$s \doteq 4.5$
$v \doteq 8.1$

2. a)

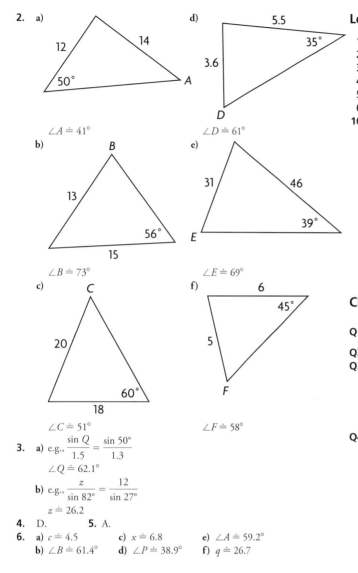

$\angle A \doteq 41°$

b)

$\angle B \doteq 73°$

c)

$\angle C \doteq 51°$

d)

$\angle D \doteq 61°$

e)

$\angle E \doteq 69°$

f)

$\angle F \doteq 58°$

3. a) e.g., $\dfrac{\sin Q}{1.5} = \dfrac{\sin 50°}{1.3}$

$\angle Q \doteq 62.1°$

b) e.g., $\dfrac{z}{\sin 82°} = \dfrac{12}{\sin 27°}$

$z \doteq 26.2$

4. D.   **5.** A.

6. a) $c \doteq 4.5$ **c)** $x \doteq 6.8$ **e)** $\angle A \doteq 59.2°$
   b) $\angle B \doteq 61.4°$ **d)** $\angle P \doteq 38.9°$ **f)** $q \doteq 26.7$

Lesson 3.2, page 68

1. a) Yes. e.g., Two sides and angle opposite known side are given.
   b) No. e.g., Missing side length is opposite only known angle.
   c) Yes. e.g., Two angles and any side are given.

2. a) $r \doteq 47.8$ m   **c)** $\angle D \doteq 41°$ **e)** $x \doteq 42.3$ km
   b) $\angle H \doteq 88°$ **d)** $m \doteq 23.4$ m   **f)** $\angle M \doteq 53.9°$

3. a) $e \doteq 16.8$ cm   **b)** $t \doteq 102.0$ cm

4. Let a be the longer side length, and let h be the height.
   The gorge is $\doteq 28.8$ m deep.

5. The wires are $\doteq 77.7$ m and $\doteq 85.0$ m in length,
   and the mast is $\doteq 75.0$ m tall.

6. C.   **7.** $\angle L \doteq 42°, \angle N \doteq 88°, n \doteq 14.6$ cm

8. The crew travelled $\doteq 21.4$ km.

Lesson 3.3, page 72

1. a) Yes. e.g., Three sides are given.   **b)** No. e.g., Given angle is not
   contained.   **c)** Yes. e.g., Two sides and contained angle are given.

2. a) $f \doteq 11.2$ cm   **b)** $j \doteq 1.3$ m

3. a) $\angle N \doteq 73°$ **b)** $\angle U \doteq 52°$

4. a) $\angle F \doteq 81°$ **b)** $z \doteq 16.4$ cm
   c) $a \doteq 20.6$ cm   **d)** $\angle S \doteq 42°$

5. B.   **6.** $v \doteq 13.1$ cm; $\angle U \doteq 89°$; $\angle T \doteq 36°$

7. The pendulum swings through an angle of $\doteq 17.5°$.

Lesson 3.4, page 76

1. a) yes; sine law   **b)** yes; cosine law   **c)** no   **d)** yes; sine law
2. a) $\angle L \doteq 57°$ **b)** $\angle Y \doteq 73°$ **d)** $\angle O \doteq 52°$
3. a) yes; sine law   **b)** no   **c)** yes; e.g., sine law and cosine law
4. a) $\doteq 35.2$ m   **c)** $\doteq$ N49°W
5. a) $\doteq 112.4$ m   **b)** $\doteq 72.9$ m
6. $\doteq 1.7$ km   **7.** $\doteq 32°$ **8.** B.   **9.** A.
10.

$h \doteq 60.0$ m

Chapter 3 Test Prep, page 80

Q1: $\dfrac{a}{\sin A} = \boxed{\dfrac{b}{\sin B}} = \boxed{\dfrac{c}{\sin C}}$ or $\dfrac{\sin A}{a} = \boxed{\dfrac{\sin B}{b}} = \boxed{\dfrac{\sin C}{c}}$

Q2: $a^2 = \underline{b^2 + c^2 - 2bc \cos A}$

Q3: • You can either rearrange and then <u>substitute</u>, or <u>substitute</u> and then
   <u>rearrange</u>.
   • If you <u>rearrange</u> first, you will then be using the cosine law in the form
   $\underline{\cos} A = \boxed{\dfrac{b^2 + c^2 - a^2}{2bc}}$

Q4: • Given three <u>sides</u>, <u>SSS</u>, to determine an angle: use the <u>cosine</u> law in the
   form $\cos A = \boxed{\dfrac{b^2 + c^2 - a^2}{2bc}}$.
   • Given two <u>sides</u> and the <u>angle</u> opposite one of the sides, <u>SSA</u>, to
   determine another <u>angle</u>: use the <u>sine</u> law in the form $\boxed{\dfrac{\sin A}{a}} = \boxed{\dfrac{\sin B}{b}}$.
   • Given two <u>sides</u> and the included <u>angle</u>, <u>SAS</u>, use the <u>cosine</u> law in the
   form $\underline{a^2 = b^2 + c^2 - 2bc \cos A}$.
   • Given two <u>angles</u> and a <u>side</u>, <u>ASA</u> or <u>AAS</u>, to determine another side:
   use the sine law in the form $\boxed{\dfrac{a}{\sin A}} = \boxed{\dfrac{b}{\sin B}}$.

Chapter 3 Test, page 81

1. D.   **2.** B.   **3.** C.   **4.** A.
5. B.   **6.** D.   **7.** D.
8. a) $a = \underline{13.3}$ m.   **b)** $w = \underline{35.2}$ cm.   **c)** $\angle D = \underline{51°}$.
9. $\underline{3.4}$ km   **10.** $\underline{67°}$ **11.** $\underline{1429}$ m.   **12.** $\underline{968}$ km
13. $\doteq 82°$ **14.** $\doteq 3171$ m, $\doteq 2983$ m
15. a) $\doteq 153$ m   **b)** $\doteq 76°$

Chapter 4

Getting Started, page 84

1. a) iv)   **b)** vi)   **c)** ii)   **d)** iii)   **e)** i)   **f)** v)
2. a) $AC \doteq 2.6$ cm, $BC \doteq 1.8$ cm, $\angle A \doteq 35°$
   b) $\angle D \doteq 33.0°, \angle F \doteq 57.0°, DF \doteq 9.5$ cm
3. a) $SAS, x \doteq 37.9$ mm   **b)** $SSS, \theta \doteq 69.8°$
4. a) $SSA, \theta \doteq 50.2°$ **b)** $ASA, x \doteq 5.2$ m
5. a) $x \doteq 34.8$ **b)** $x \doteq 75.7°$
6. a) $x \doteq 2.1$ cm   **b)** $x \doteq 13.7$ km
7. $\angle X \doteq 81°, y \doteq 6.1$ cm, $z \doteq 3.0$ cm

Lesson 4.1, page 86

1. a) No; tan 48° = −tan 132°
   b) Yes; 20° and 160° are supplementary angles.
   c) No; 60° is not the supplement of 30°.
   d) No; sin 100° = sin 80°
2. sin 62° = 0.8829…; 118°
3. −9.5144…; 84°
4. a) ≐ 28°   b) ≐ 152°
   c) 0.47; since the sine ratios of supplementary angles are equal, sin 28° = sin 152°.
5. C.   6. D.   7. ≐ 7° and ≐ 173°

Lesson 4.2, page 88

1. a) e.g., We do not have the right information to use the cosine law. We are given *ASA*, so we need to determine the measure of the third angle in the triangle, and then use the sine law.
   b) e.g., The triangle is not a right triangle, so we cannot use the primary trigonometric ratios. We need to determine the measure of the third angle in the triangle, and then use the sine law.
2. a) e.g., both   b) the cosine law   c) the sine law   d) neither
3. a) x = 3.7 cm   b) x = 5.4 cm
4. a) x = 84°   b) x = 63°
5. e.g., They are the same in that you write two different expressions for one of the altitudes of the triangle. They are different because for one of these expressions, you have to use the fact that the sine of the obtuse angle is equal to the sine of its supplement.
6. e.g., They are the same in that you use the Pythagorean theorem in two triangles to write two different expressions for *h²*. They are different because for one of these expressions, you have to use the fact that the cosine of the obtuse angle has the opposite value of the cosine of its supplement.
7. ∠A ≐ 62.2°, ∠B ≐ 84.3°, ∠C ≐ 33.6°
8. ∠M ≐ 32.6°, ∠N ≐ 22.4°, n ≐ 12.1 m
9. ≐ 5880 m

Lesson 4.3, page 92

1. a) *SSA*   b) *SSA*   c) not *SSA*
2. a) ∠A is acute and h < a < b, so two triangles are possible.
   b) ∠D is acute and d > f, so one triangle is possible.
3. a) h = 8.8 cm; ∠R is obtuse and r > s, so one triangle is possible.
   b) h = 5.4 cm; ∠X is acute and x < h, so no triangle is possible.
   c) h = 27.8 cm; ∠A is acute and h < a < b, so two triangles are possible.
4. a) no triangle   b) one right triangle

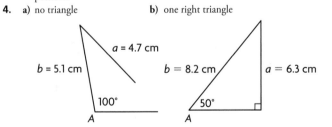

5. In △XYZ, ∠X = 67°, x = 3.2 m, and y = 3.4 m.
   a) ≐ 78°   b) ≐102°; e.g., ∠X is acute, so ∠Y could be obtuse.
   c) e.g., h < x < y, so there are two possible triangles. In one of these triangles, ∠Y is acute; in the other, ∠Y is obtuse. So, both values for ∠Y correspond to possible triangles.
6. C.   7. B.   8. B.
9. ∠A ≐ 30° or 150°; There are two possible triangles; e.g., ∠B is acute, so ∠A could be either acute or obtuse.
10. ∠E ≐ 64°; This is the only possible answer; e.g., ∠D is obtuse, so ∠E must be acute.

11. a) e.g.,

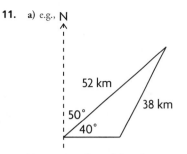

   b) e.g., 38 > 52 sin 40°, so the situation could be ambiguous; however, the fact that the second leg is southwest means that the flight creates an obtuse triangle, removing one possibility.
   c) ≐ 21.8 km

Lesson 4.4, page 98

1. lighthouse A: ≐ 8.2 km; lighthouse B: ≐ 20.3 km
2. ≐ 84.2 m   3. ≐ 11.1 m
4. ≐ 5.2 km   5. ≐ 6.8 m
6. a) ∠ACB = 60°   b) AC = 114.350… m   c) CD = 183 m
7.

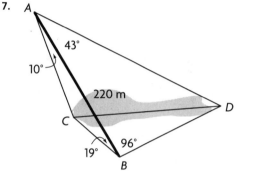

≐ 353.4 m

8. bearing of ship A from station C ≐ 30.733…° west of south, or S31°W
   bearing of ship B from station C ≐ 14° west of south, or S14°W

Chapter 4 Test Prep, page 103

Q1: • The sine ratios are related by <u>sin</u> θ = + <u>sin</u> (180° − θ).
   • The cosine and tangent ratios are related by <u>cos</u> θ = −<u>cos</u> (180° − θ) and <u>tan</u> θ = −<u>tan</u> (180° − θ).

Q2:

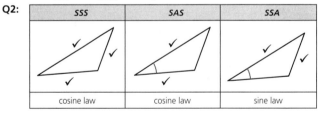

SSS	SAS	SSA
cosine law	cosine law	sine law

ASA	AAS
sine law	sine law

Q3: • If ∠A, the given angle, is obtuse, the unknown ∠B (opposite b) must be <u>acute</u>, so at most one <u>triangle</u> is possible.
   • If ∠A is <u>acute</u>, you can compare the given sides a and b with the triangle's <u>height</u>, h, to determine how many <u>triangles</u> are possible.
   • The only <u>ambiguous</u> case, where two triangles are possible, is when ∠A is acute and a, b, and h are related by <u>h < a < b</u>.

acute triangle   obtuse triangle   right triangle

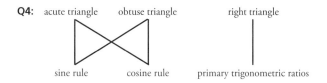

sine rule   cosine rule   primary trigonometric ratios

Chapter 4 Test, page 104

1. A. **2.** B. **3.** C. **4.** D.
5. A. **6.** D. **7.** D. **8.** B.
9. a) $x = \underline{10.0}$ cm   b) $x = \underline{9.4}$ cm
10. $\theta = \underline{53°}$
11. $x = \underline{14.0}$ cm; $\theta = \underline{48°}$
12. No triangle is possible.

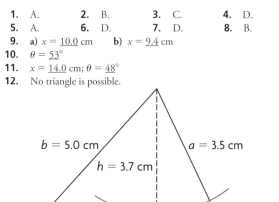

13. $\doteq 1.6$ m.
14. a) Since $\angle P$ is acute and $h < p < r$, two triangles are possible.
    b) $\angle R$ acute: $\doteq 1604$ mm²; $\angle R$ obtuse: $\doteq 583$ mm²
15. a) e.g., The support beam is too short to reach the ground with the main beam at the given angle.
    b) e.g., The support beam is long enough to reach the ground, but it could form either an obtuse or an acute triangle with the main beam and the ground. This problem could be fixed by stating which direction the support beam must lean.

Chapter 5

Getting Started, page 108

1. 143.9, 144.2, 144.7, 144.7, 145.0, 145.3, 145.5, 145.8, 146.3, 148.0
2. a) vi)   b) iv)   c) iii)   d) vii)   e) v)
3. a) mean $\doteq 44.25$ cm, median $= 44$ cm, mode $= 43$ cm
   b) 37 cm
   c) mean $\doteq 45.29$ cm, median $= 45$ cm, mode $= 43$ cm
   d) e.g., The mean is most affected, because a single unusual value can change it significantly. The mode is least affected, because an outlier would almost certainly not be the mode.
4. a) median   b) mean   c) mode
5. a) 24   b) 4   c) 8   d) 8   e) 4
6. e.g., Perhaps there were some lower days due to construction, which Ravi discarded as outliers, while Kumiko kept them in her calculation.
7. a) e.g., Jaycee's jumps are more variable in length than Gary's.
   b) Jaycee. e.g., His personal best is likely further from their common mean value.
8. a) **Duration of Calls**

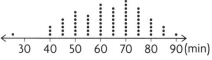

   b) e.g., The data is fairly evenly distributed around the mode of 70 min; outlier: 25 min

Lesson 5.1, page 110

1. a) Brand A: 6.0, 6.5, 6.9, 7.0, 7.3, 7.5, 7.8, 8.0
      Brand B: 6.0, 6.1, 6.5, 7.2, 7.5, 7.5, 7.5, 7.5
   b) Brand A: range $= \underline{2.0 \times 10^3}$ h
      mean $= \dfrac{\boxed{57.0 \times 10^3 \text{ h}}}{8}$, or $\doteq \underline{7.1 \times 10^3}$ h
      median $= \underline{7.15 \times 10^3}$ h
      mode $= \underline{\text{none}}$
      Brand B: range $= \underline{1.5 \times 10^3}$ h
      mean $= \dfrac{\boxed{55.8 \times 10^3 \text{ h}}}{8}$, or $\doteq \underline{7.0 \times 10^3}$ h
      median $= \underline{7.35 \times 10^3}$ h
      mode $= \underline{7.5 \times 10^3}$ h
   c) Which brand of bulbs has the greater range in lifespan? $\underline{A}$
      the greater median lifespan? $\underline{B}$ the greater mean lifespan? $\underline{A}$
   d) e.g., Based on the range, brand B seems the more reliable choice.
2. e.g., The means are almost the same for both groups, and the mode is undefined for group B. However, the median is lower for group B, so this group likely has the lower average age. Group B probably contains the youngest students, as its range is greater.

Lesson 5.2, page 112

1. a) $1.0-1.5$ h
   b)

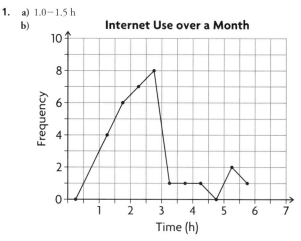

Internet Use over a Month

e.g., Jerry spent 1.5–3.0 h on the Internet for 21 out of 31 days. He spent about half of the month on the Internet for 2.0–3.0 h per day. Jerry mostly logged the longer Internet times for only one day in the month.

2. a)

Height (m)	Frequency
1.0–1.3	4
1.3–1.6	4
1.6–1.9	6
1.9–2.2	8
2.2–2.5	8
2.5–2.8	6
2.8–3.1	2
3.1–3.4	2

b)

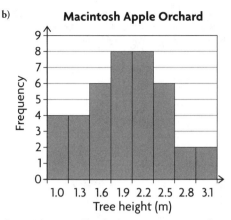

Macintosh Apple Orchard

c) e.g., The range of heights between 1.9–2.2 m and 2.5–2.8 m occur most frequently, with eight trees. The least frequent heights fall in the ranges of 2.8–3.1 m and 3.1–3.4 m, with two trees.

3. a) e.g., 7 intervals of 1 h

b)

Time (h)	Frequency
1.0–2.0	5
2.0–3.0	13
3.0–4.0	5
4.0–5.0	3
5.0–6.0	1
6.0–7.0	2
7.0–8.0	1

c)

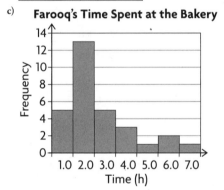

Farooq's Time Spent at the Bakery

d) e.g., For about half of the month, Farooq spends 2.0–3.0 h per day at the bakery.
There are very few days when he spends more than 4 h at the bakery.
For most of the month, Farooq works 1.0–4.0 h per day at the bakery.

4. a) e.g., Use 1-h intervals. These are appropriate because they divide the data into 8 equal intervals.

b) e.g., The midpoint will be the half-hour point of each 1-h interval.

c)

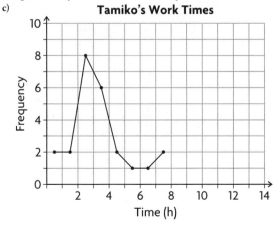

Tamiko's Work Times

5. a)

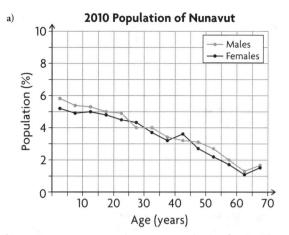

2010 Population of Nunavut

b) e.g., For most age groups, there are more males than females. The only two age groups where females outnumbered males were 25−29 and 40−44. The number of males and females in each age group decreases with age.

6. A.

7. e.g., They should be used to represent large sets of data that have been systematically organized into intervals. Frequency polygons work best when graphically comparing two or more data sets.

8. a) 10%

b) e.g., No. The data was grouped, so Kara can be certain only that the greatest number of test scores were between 71% and 80%.

Lesson 5.3, page 116

1. a)

Store	Jean A ($)	$(x - \bar{x})^2$	Jean B ($)	$(x - \bar{x})^2$
1	45.99	0.0144	46.59	0.7569
2	46.49	0.3844	45.99	0.0729
3	44.99	0.7744	45.29	0.1849
4	45.99	0.0144	44.99	0.5329
$\sum x$	183.46	1.1876	182.86	1.5476
$\bar{x}$	45.87	—	45.72	—
$\sqrt{\dfrac{\sum(x - \bar{x})^2}{n}}$	—	0.5449	—	0.6220

standard deviation for jean A $\doteq$ 54¢; standard deviation for jean B $\doteq$ 62¢

b) e.g., Since the standard deviation for Jean A is lower, the prices for Jean A were more consistent.

2. a) $\bar{x} = 635\,870$ points; $\sigma \doteq 151\,387$ points

b) e.g., The standard deviation is large. This means the players vary greatly in their abilities.

3. a) Group 1: $\bar{x} \doteq 11.1$, $\sigma \doteq 2.2$; Group 2: $\bar{x} \doteq 9.9$, $\sigma \doteq 1.4$; Group 3: $\bar{x} \doteq 10.2$, $\sigma \doteq 1.8$

b) e.g., Group 1 had the greatest mean number of books read, but their standard deviation was 2.2 books, so the range of books read within one standard deviation of the mean was from 8.9 to 13.3.
Group 2 had the lowest mean number of books read, and their standard deviation was lower than group 1, so the range of books read within one standard deviation of the mean was from 8.5 to 11.3.
Group 3 had a lower mean and a lower standard deviation than group 1.
So, group 1 performed the best, because they had the highest mean and also the highest number of books at one standard deviation above the mean.

4. a) Jordan

b) e.g., The standard deviation is lower for Brendan (0.7) than for Jordan (1.2). Brendan is more consistent.

5. a) mean: $\bar{x} \doteq 73.6$ points   standard deviation: $\sigma \doteq 18.3$ points
   b) mean: $\bar{x} \doteq 79.3$ points   standard deviation: $\sigma \doteq 12.7$ points
   e.g., The mean is increased and the standard deviation is decreased. This signifies Jarome Iginla's point production is more consistent when the two point totals for the lowest seasons are removed.

6. Brand A: $\bar{x} \doteq 88.1$ kg, $\sigma \doteq 0.16$ kg; Brand B: $\bar{x} \doteq 88.1$ kg, $\sigma \doteq 0.11$ kg
   e.g., The means are approximately the same, but the standard deviation is slightly lower for B's bags. So, the masses of B's bags are more consistent. Mario should order Brand B. However, the standard deviations are low for each supplier, so Mario could order from either supplier.

7. a) Ever Study: $\bar{x} \doteq 13.3$ h, $\sigma \doteq 4.6$ h; Elite Education: $\bar{x} \doteq 13.7$ h, $\sigma \doteq 4.3$ h
   b) e.g., The standard deviation for Elite Education is lower, so their clients are more consistent in their studying times.

8. C.

9. e.g., The mean test scores were approximately the same. However, the standard deviation for Class A was lower. This means that the test scores for class A were more consistent and closer to the mean than those for Class B. So, Class A performed better, in this sense.

10. a) $\bar{x} \doteq \$37$, $\sigma \doteq \$12$
   b)

Tips ($)	Frequency, f	Midpoint of Interval, x	$f \cdot x$
10–20	3	15	45
20–30	4	25	100
30–40	6	35	210
40–50	6	45	270
50–60	1	55	55
	20		680

   $\bar{x} \doteq \$34$, $\sigma \doteq \$32$
   c) e.g., The mean for the ungrouped data was higher than the mean for the grouped data. The standard deviation for the ungrouped data was much lower than the standard deviation for the grouped data. So, the mean and standard deviation for the grouped data are not accurate representations of the actual mean and standard deviation for the data.

Lesson 5.4, page 122

1. a) 47.5%   **b)** 15.85%   **c)** 0.15%

2. a) e.g., Test 1 and test 2 have equal means, but test 2's standard deviation is almost twice that of test 1. So, the test 2 graph would be flatter than the test 1 graph.
   b) e.g., Test 1 and test 3 have different means but the same standard deviation. So, the widths of the graphs are the same.
   c)

Test	Jasmine's Mark	Jasmine's Mark (%)
1	$\mu + 2\sigma$	90
2	$\mu - 1.5\sigma$	78
3	$\mu + 3.5\sigma$	84

3. a)

Interval	11–15	16–20	21–25	26–30	31–35	36–40
Frequency	4	6	15	18	9	4
Midpoint	13	18.0	23.0	28.0	33.0	38.0

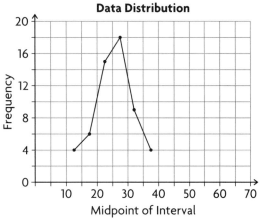

e.g., The two middle intervals represent 60% of the data. The four middle intervals represent 86% of the data. Therefore, the data is normally distributed, since the intervals are close to 68% and 95% of the data. Also, the graph of the data approximates a bell shape.

b)

Interval	20–24	25–29	30–34	35–39	40–44	45–49
Frequency	1	5	5	2	3	4
Midpoint	22	27	32	37	42	47

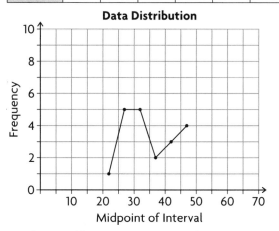

e.g., The two middle intervals represent 35% of the data. The four middle intervals represent 75% of the data. Therefore, the data is not normally distributed, since the intervals are not close to 68% and 95% of the data. The graph of the data confirms this.

c)

Interval	1–6	7–12	13–18	19–24	25–30	31–36
Frequency	1	8	5	8	4	4
Midpoint	3.5	9.5	15.5	21.5	27.5	33.5

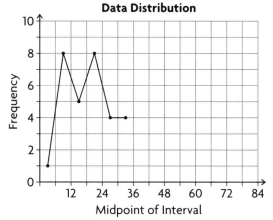

e.g., The two middle intervals represent 43% of the data. The four middle intervals represent 83% of the data. Therefore, the data is not normally distributed, since the intervals are not close to 68% and 95% of the data. The graph of the data confirms this.

4. a) $\mu \doteq 18.5$ goals, $\sigma \doteq 11.3$ goals
   b)

Left Boundary (years)	Interval (years)	Midpoint (years)	Frequency
$\mu - 4\sigma = -25.2$	-25.2–(-14.4)	-19.8	0
$\mu - 3\sigma = -14.4$	-14.4–(-3.6)	-9.0	0
$\mu - 2\sigma = -3.6$	-3.6–7.2	1.8	4
$\mu - 1\sigma = 7.2$	7.2–18.0	12.6	7
$\mu = 18.0$	18.0–28.8	23.4	7
$\mu + 1\sigma = 28.8$	28.8–39.6	34.2	6
$\mu + 2\sigma = 39.6$	39.6–50.4	45.0	0
$\mu + 3\sigma = 50.4$	50.4–61.2	55.8	0

c)

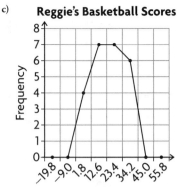
Reggie's Basketball Scores
(Frequency vs Points, x-axis labels: −19.8, −9.0, 1.8, 12.6, 23.4, 34.2, 45.0, 55.8)

d) e.g., The two middle intervals represent 58% of the data. The four middle intervals represent 100% of the data. Therefore, the data is normally distributed, since the intervals are close to 68% and 95% of the data. The graph of the data confirms this, because it is approximately bell-shaped.

5. 5 years

Lesson 5.5, page 126

1. a) $z \doteq 1.9685$ **b)** $z \doteq 2.32$ **c)** $z \doteq -0.4545$ **d)** $z \doteq -1.6667$

2. a) 97.64% **b)** 98.98% **c)** 32.64% **d)** 4.80%

3. a) 7.48% **b)** 9.02%

4. a) $z \doteq 1.04$ **b)** $z \doteq -1.035$ **c)** $z \doteq -0.175$

5. $\doteq 82\%$

6. a) $\doteq 94.4\%$ **b)** 1.3%

7. D.

8. a) accounting: $z = 2.884\ldots$; chemistry: $z = 2.295\ldots$
b) accounting: over 99.8%; chemistry: 98.9%
c) accounting

Lesson 5.6, page 130

1. a) 95% **b)** $65\% \pm 2.9\%$, or 62.1% to 67.9% **c)** 20 630 to 22 556

2. a) $1.1\ \text{L} \pm 0.1\ \text{L}$, or 1.0 L to 1.2 L
b)

Sample Size (cartons)	Margin of Error (L) (mixed up)	Margin of Error (L) (correct)
75	± 0.15	**± 0.20**
150	± 0.05	**± 0.15**
500	± 0.20	**± 0.05**

e.g., As the sample size increases, the margin of error decreases.

3. a) 80% **b)** $80\% \pm 3.5\%$, or 76.5% to 83.5% **c)** 1913 to 2088

4. a) 90%; $95\% \pm 3.7\%$, or 91.3% to 98.7% **b)** 7 760 500 to 8 389 500

5. car A

6. a) 6.65 cm to 6.75 cm **b)** ±0.05 cm

7. B.

8. $34\% \pm 3.2\%$, or 30.8% to 37.2%

9. a) 95% **b)** $28\% \pm 3.2\%$, or 24.8% to 31.2%
c) 8 367 520 to 10 526 880

Chapter 5 Test Prep, page 135

Q1: A1: Graph the frequency <u>polygons</u> for both data sets on the same graph and visually compare their distributions.

A2: Calculate the <u>standard</u> <u>deviation</u> of each data set. A high (or low) <u>standard</u> <u>deviation</u> indicates a <u>more</u> (or <u>less</u>) dispersed set.

Q2: • If the data set is well approximated, you can make <u>predictions</u> based on properties of <u>normal</u> curves.
• A normal distribution is <u>symmetric</u> about its mean, which also equals the <u>median</u> and the mode. About <u>68%</u> of the data is within one <u>standard</u> <u>deviation</u> of the mean, and about <u>95%</u> is within two <u>standard</u> <u>deviations</u> of the mean.

• A z-score indicates how many <u>standard</u> <u>deviations</u> a data value is above or below the <u>mean</u>. The z-score for a data value x is $z = \dfrac{x - \boxed{\mu}}{\boxed{\sigma}}$.

Q3: • The sample size is $n = \underline{1023}$. The margin of error is <u>3.2%</u>.
• The <u>confidence</u> level, based on the phrase "19 times out of 20", is <u>95%</u>.
• The <u>95%</u> confidence interval for support for the Conservative party is 29.9% to <u>36.3%</u>.

Chapter 5 Test, page 136

1. B.   **2.** B.   **3.** D.   **4.** A.   **5.** C.

6. A.   **7.** C.   **8.** D.   **9.** B.   **10.** C.

11. Brand A: <u>1875</u> km   Brand B: <u>1738</u> km

12. Which range of trunk widths occurs most frequently?   <u>6.0−6.5</u> m
Which ranges of trunk widths occur least frequently?   <u>4.5−5.0</u> m and <u>7.0−7.5</u> m

13. <u>7</u> intervals of width <u>1 h</u>

14. <u>16.35%</u>

15. The confidence interval is $76\% \pm \underline{3.4}\%$, or from <u>72.6</u>% to <u>79.4</u>%.

16. a) What is the mean price and standard deviation for each brand?

Store	DVD A ($)	$(x - \bar{x})^2$	DVD B ($)	$(x - \bar{x})^2$
1	32.94	5.06	34.59	9.30
2	31.97	10.37	38.99	1.82
3	35.92	0.53	36.99	0.42
4	39.93	22.47	39.99	5.52
Σ	140.76	38.43	150.56	17.06
$\bar{x}$	**35.19**	—	**37.64**	—
$\sqrt{\dfrac{\Sigma(x - \bar{x})^2}{n}}$	—	**3.10**	—	**2.07**

b) e.g., Brand A is cheaper, but Brand B is more consistently priced.

17. a)

Time (h)	Frequency
1.0−2.0	2
2.0−3.0	6
3.0−4.0	9
4.0−5.0	4
5.0−6.0	1
6.0−7.0	1
7.0−8.0	1

b)

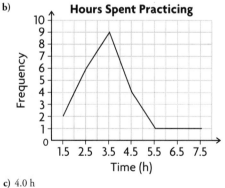
Hours Spent Practicing
(Frequency vs Time (h), x-axis: 1.5, 2.5, 3.5, 4.5, 5.5, 6.5, 7.5)

c) 4.0 h
d) 1.5 h
e) e.g., The frequency polygon is not bell-shaped, so the data is not normally distributed.

18. a) $\doteq 82\%$ **b)** $\doteq 0.13\%$

19. e.g., A 2.5% repair rate means that 97.5% of the burners do not need repairs. This represents three standard deviations from the mean, which is 5.5 years. The warranty should be for 5 years.

20. a) 90% **b)** $75\% \pm 3.3\%$ or 71.7% to 78.3% **c)** 717 to 783

1. D. **2.** A. **3.** B. **4.** A. **5.** B.
6. B. **7.** B. **8.** C. **9.** B. **10.** B.
11. C. **12.** C. **13.** B. **14.** C. **15.** B.
16. C. **17.** A.
18. $q \doteq 4.4$ cm, $r \doteq 2.4$ cm, $\angle R = 30°$
19. $\angle U \doteq 48°$, $\angle V \doteq 60°$, $w \doteq 6.7$ m
20. **a)** $\doteq 77°$ **b)** $\doteq 42°$
21. **a)** $x = \underline{15}$ cm; $y = \underline{11}$ cm **b)** $\angle Y = \underline{34}°$; $\angle Z = \underline{96}°$; $z = \underline{19.5}$ cm
22. Shorter diagonal $= \underline{24}$ mm; Longer diagonal $= \underline{30}$ mm
23. **a)** 1.07, 1.28 **b)** 1.33, 1.17 **c)** Basil
24. **a)** store A: 45.1; store B: 45.3 **b)** store A: 4.1; store B: 4.5
  c) store B **d)** store B
25. $\doteq 45$ m
26. **a)** $\doteq 240$ m **b)** $\doteq 65°$
27. **a)** $\doteq 12$ mm **b)** $\doteq 11$ mm
28. **a)** $\doteq 52.4$ cm **b)** $\doteq 24.1$ cm **c)** $\doteq 966$ cm² **d)** $A = ab \sin \theta$
29. **a)**

Height (cm)	Tally	Frequency
20–24	|	1
25–29	|||	3
30–34	||||	4
35–39	||||	4
40–44	|||	3
45–49	|	1
50–54	|	1
55–59	||	2
60–64	|||||	5
65–69	||	2
70–74	||||	4

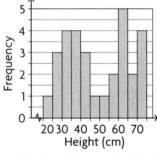

Heights of Bean Plants

b) e.g., Most bean plants are either short (around 30–40 cm high) or tall (around 60–65 cm high).
30. **a)** e.g., Data is not very close to a normal distribution.
  b) e.g., Data is reasonably close to a normal distribution.
31. **a)** 299.9 g to 301.1 g; ± 0.6 g **b)** 164 cartons; 82 cartons
  c) The sample size increases when the confidence level increases. e.g., A larger sample must be taken to be more certain that samples have a mean mass in the acceptable range.

Chapter 6

Getting Started, page 146

1. **a)** vii) **b)** iv) **c)** v) **d)** i) **e)** iii) **f)** vi) **g)** ii)
2. e.g., **a)** $(3.5, 2.75)$ **b)** $(0, 15)$ **c)** $(-3, 7)$
3. **a)** $x = 6$ **b)** $w = -11$ **c)** $b < 1$
4. **a)** $y = \dfrac{2}{3}x - 3$ **b)** $y \geq \dfrac{1}{2}x + 4$ **c)** $y > 2x + 4$
5. **a)** $17 - 2x$; 9 **b)** $2 - \dfrac{7y}{12}$; $\dfrac{15}{4}$ **c)** $-\dfrac{1}{6x} + \dfrac{1}{3y}$; $-\dfrac{5}{3}$

6. **a)** LS = 13, RS = 13 **b)** LS = 12, RS = 12
  c) 1st equation: LS = -3, RS = -3; 2nd equation: LS = 0, RS = 0
7. **a)**

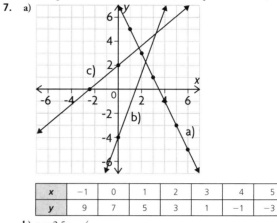

x	−1	0	1	2	3	4	5	6
y	9	7	5	3	1	−1	−3	−5

b) $y = 2.5x - 4$
c) x-intercept: $(-1.5, 0)$, y-intercept: $(0, 2)$
8. $(5.5, 2.5)$
9. 5 mints and 10 toffees or 6 mints and 12 toffees
10. **a)** whole numbers, or W **b)** discrete

Lesson 6.1, page 148

1. **a) i)** $y - x = 10$ **ii)** solid **iii)** $(0, 0)$ is not a solution.
   iv) above
  b) i) $y = x + 3$ **ii)** dashed **iii)** $(0, 0)$ is a solution.
   iv) below
  c) i) $y = -3$ **ii)** dashed **iii)** $(0, 0)$ is a solution. **iv)** above
2. **a)**

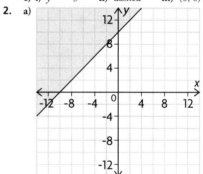

b)

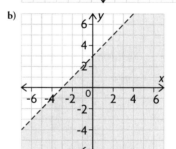

c)

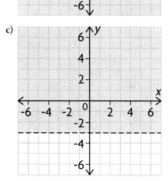

3. **a)** The boundary line is not shown, but is stippled where points have integer coordinates. The half plane is covered by a series of points.
   b) The boundary line is a dashed line. The half plane is covered by a series of points.
   c) The boundary line is a dashed line. The half plane is covered by a series of points.
4. The graph looks the same as described in question 3, but the graphs are now restricted by $x \geq 0$ and $y \geq 0$, so the graph occurs only in the first quadrant.
5. **a)** solution   **b)** solution   **c)** not a solution
6. **a)**

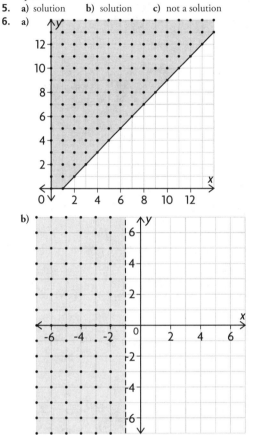

   b)

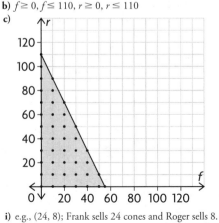

7. **a)** e.g., Let x represent the width of the hall; let y represent height.
   b) e.g., $x \leq 10 + 3y$
   c) not stippled; e.g., because the context is continuous
   d) solid; e.g., because the boundary is included in the solution region for $\leq$ type inequalities
8. **a)** e.g., Let f represent the number of cones Frank sells and r represent the number Roger sells; $2f + r \leq 110$, with $f \in \mathbb{W}$, $r \in \mathbb{W}$.
   b) $f \geq 0, f \leq 110, r \geq 0, r \leq 110$
   c)

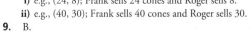

   i) e.g., (24, 8); Frank sells 24 cones and Roger sells 8.
   ii) e.g., (40, 30); Frank sells 40 cones and Roger sells 30.
9. B.

10. **a)** Let b represent the number of beaded bracelets sold and r represent the number of rubber bands sold; $10b + 2r \leq 278$, where $b \in \mathbb{W}$, $r \in \mathbb{W}$.
    b)

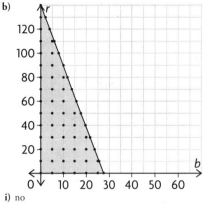

    i) no
    ii) 15 beaded bracelets and 25 rubber bands, but not 25 beaded bracelets and 15 rubber bands

Lesson 6.2, page 154

1. **a)** i)   **b)** ii)
2. e.g., $(-2, 4)$, $(0, 2)$, $(1, 4)$
3. **a)**

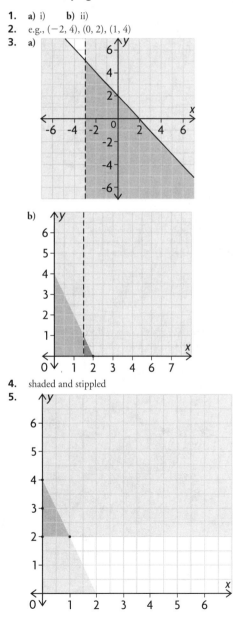

   b)

4. shaded and stippled
5.

Lesson 6.3, page 156

1. **a) i)** $(-1, 1)$ **ii)** open dot
   b) i) $(-1, 5)$ **ii)** solid dot

2. **a)**

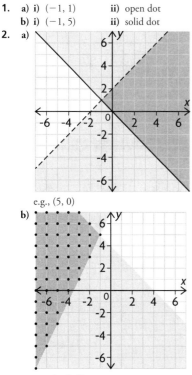

e.g., $(5, 0)$

   b)

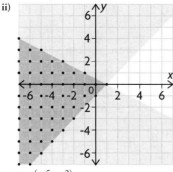

e.g., $(-5, 0)$

3. **a) i)** The boundary line $-2y - x = 1$ is included. The boundary line $x - 1 = y$ is included. So, the intersection point is included.

   ii)

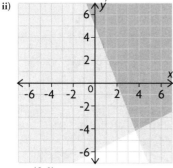

e.g., $(-5, -2)$

   b) i) The boundary line $x - 2y = 12$ is not included. The boundary line $2y + 5x = 10$ is included. So, the intersection point is not included.

   ii)

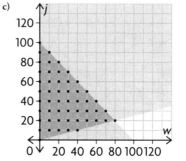

e.g., $(6, 0)$

4. **a)** Let x represent the width of the banner. Let y represent its length.
   $\{(x, y) \mid x > 0, y > 0, y < 200, x \in R, y \in R\}$
   $\{(x, y) \mid x > 0, y > 0, 2x + 2y \le 500, x \in R, y \in R\}$

   b)

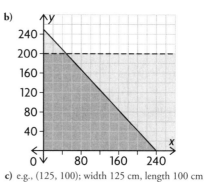

   c) e.g., $(125, 100)$; width 125 cm, length 100 cm

5. B.

6. The boundary line $3x - y = 4$ is not included in the solution. The boundary line $2x + y = 6$ is included in the solution. So, the intersection point is not included in the solution region.

7. **a)** Let x represent the number of white shells.
   Let y represent the number of mottled shells.
   $\{(x, y) \mid x + y \le 200, x \in W, y \in W\}$
   $\{(x, y) \mid x \le 4y, x \in R, y \in R\}$

   b)

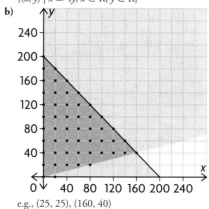

e.g., $(25, 25)$, $(160, 40)$

Lesson 6.4, page 162

1.

Statements	Part of Model
Let V represent the total volume. $V = 500b + 250t$	objective function
Let b represent the number of bottles. Let t represent the number of drink cartons.	defining statement
$b \ge 0$ (from restriction) and $b \le 6$ $t \ge 0$ (from restriction) and $t \le 8$	constraints
$b \in W$ and $t \in W$	restrictions

2. **a)** The two variables are the number of water bottles and number of juice bottles. They both must be whole numbers.
   b) Let w represent the number of <u>water bottles</u> and j the number of <u>juice bottles</u>.
   i) the number of <u>water bottles</u>: $\{(w, j) \mid w \le \underline{100}, w \in \underline{W}, j \in \underline{W}\}$
   ii) the number of <u>juice bottles</u>: $\{(w, j) \mid j \le 100, w \in \underline{W}, j \in \underline{W}\}$
   iii) the number of bottles of each type of drink sold:
   $\{(w, j) \mid \underline{w \le 3j}, w \in \underline{W}, j \in \underline{W}\}$
   $\{(w, j) \mid \underline{w + j \le 100}, w \in \underline{W}, j \in \underline{W}\}$
   c)

d) (0, 0), (0, 100), and (75, 25)
e) The objective function is $R = 1.00w + 1.25j$.
3. Let x represent the number of lower-deck tickets.
Let y represent the number of upper-deck tickets.
Let R represent the revenue.
$\{(x, y) \mid x \le 45\ 000, x \in \mathbb{W}, y \in \mathbb{W}\}$
$\{(x, y) \mid y \le 15\ 000, x \in \mathbb{W}, y \in \mathbb{W}\}$
$\{(x, y) \mid x + y \ge 40\ 000, x \in \mathbb{W}, y \in \mathbb{W}\}$
objective function: $R = 100x + 60y$

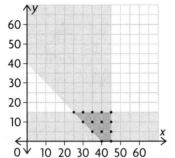

4. Let k represent the number of hours Kathy works.
Let r represent the number of hours Ravi works.
Let B represent the total number of boxes filled.
$k \ge 0$
$r \ge 0$
$\{(k, r) \mid k \le 10, k \in \mathbb{R}, r \in \mathbb{R}\}$
$\{(k, r) \mid r \le 12, k \in \mathbb{R}, r \in \mathbb{R}\}$
$\{(k, r) \mid k + r \le 18, k \in \mathbb{R}, r \in \mathbb{R}\}$
objective function: $B = 10k + 12r$

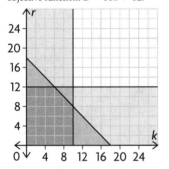

5. **a)** Let x represent the number of apple trees.
Let y represent the number of pear trees.
Let R represent the revenue.
constraints: $x \ge 0, y \ge 0$
$\{(x, y) \mid x + y \le 500, x \in \mathbb{W}, y \in \mathbb{W}\}$
$\{(x, y) \mid x \ge 4y, x \in \mathbb{W}, y \in \mathbb{W}\}$
objective function: $R = (8.75)4x + (9.50)3y$
b) (0, 0), (500, 0), (400, 100)
c) objective function: $R = (9.00)4x + (9.50)3y$

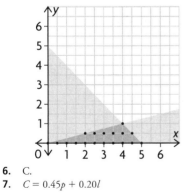

6. C.
7. $C = 0.45p + 0.20l$

Lesson 6.5, page 166

1. **a)** (−2, 4), (−2, −3.5), and (4, −2)
   b) (4, −2) **c)** (−2, −3,5)
2. **a)** (30, 55), (45, 40), and (45, 55)
   b) (45, 55) **c)** (45, 40)
3. (−4, −8)

Lesson 6.6, page 168

1. **a)** (−2, 1), (1, 4), and (4, 1)
   b) (−2, 1) **c)** (1, 4)
2. (−4, 1), (4, −3), and (4, 5); (−4, 1) represents a minimum value of −10; (4, −3) represents a maximum value of 14; (4, 5) represents a value of −2.
3. (0, 1) **4.** (2, 2)
5. **a)** Let s represent the number of stamps and let c represent the number of baseball cards.
   restrictions: $s \in \mathbb{W}, c \in \mathbb{W}$
   constraints: $s \ge 1, c \ge 1, s \le 100, c \le 75, s + c \le 150$
   objective function: $C = 0.10s + 0.50c$
   b) (100, 1); Yanni spent a minimum of $10.50 on his collection of 100 stamps and 1 baseball card.
6. **a)** Let V represent the total number of vehicles.
   Let c represent the number of cars.
   Let m represent the number of minivans.
   restrictions: $c \in \mathbb{W}, m \in \mathbb{W}$
   constraints: $c \ge 0, m \ge 0, 4c + 6m \le 44, c \le 6, m \ge 3$
   objective function to maximize: $V = c + m$
   b) The maximum number of vehicles is 6 cars and 3 minivans.
   c) 42
7. B.
8. **a)** Let w represent the number of wallets and let b represent the number of belts.
   restrictions: $w \in \mathbb{W}, b \in \mathbb{W}$
   constraints: $w \ge 0, b \ge 0, w \le 4, b \ge 10, w + b \le 20$
   objective function: $C = 2.25w + 1.50b$
   b) $15

Chapter 6 Test Prep, page 173

Q1: • First, determine the <u>boundary</u> by turning the inequality <u>sign</u> into an ≡ sign.
• To determine which half <u>plane</u> is included in the solution set, use the inequality to test a <u>point</u> on either side of the <u>boundary</u>.
• If the inequality type is < or >, the boundary <u>is not</u> included. Use a <u>dashed</u> line for the boundary.
• If the inequality type is ≤ or ≥, the boundary <u>is</u> included. Use a <u>solid</u> line for the boundary with a continuous <u>solution</u> set, and a stippled line with a <u>discrete</u> <u>solution</u> set.

Q2: • In the <u>continuous</u> case, the optimal solutions will be at the <u>vertices</u> of the <u>feasible</u> region.
• In the <u>discrete</u> case, the optimal solutions may not be at the <u>vertices</u> of the <u>feasible</u> region. However, they will be near to the <u>vertices</u>.

Q3: • Create an <u>algebraic</u> model with a <u>defining</u> statement, <u>restrictions</u>, constraints, and an <u>objective</u> function.
• Create a <u>graphical</u> model of the system of <u>inequalities</u>; locate the <u>vertices</u> of the <u>feasible</u> region.
• Evaluate the <u>objective</u> function at (or near) the <u>vertices</u>.
• Choose the desired <u>solution</u>. Verify that each <u>solution</u> satisfies the <u>constraints</u> for the problem.

Chapter 6 Test, page 174

1. C. **2.** B. **3.** A. **4.** D. **5.** D. **6.** C.
7. e.g., **a)** (0, −2) **b)** (0, 0)
8. **a)** (2.4, 1.8) **b)** an <u>open</u> dot

9. **a)**

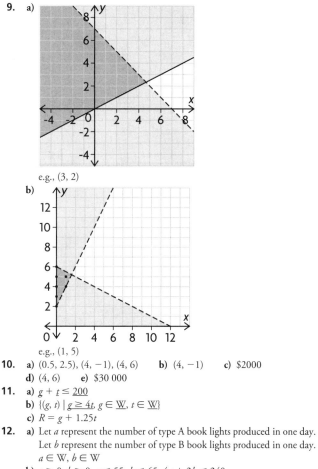

e.g., (3, 2)

b)

e.g., (1, 5)

10. **a)** (0.5, 2.5), (4, −1), (4, 6)   **b)** (4, −1)   **c)** $2000
  d) (4, 6)   **e)** $30 000

11. **a)** $g + t \leq 200$
  b) $\{(g, t) \mid g \geq 4t, g \in \mathbb{W}, t \in \mathbb{W}\}$
  c) $R = g + 1.25t$

12. **a)** Let a represent the number of type A book lights produced in one day.
    Let b represent the number of type B book lights produced in one day.
    $a \in \mathbb{W}, b \in \mathbb{W}$
  b) $a \geq 0, b \geq 0, a \leq 55, b \leq 65, 4a + 2b \leq 240$
  c)

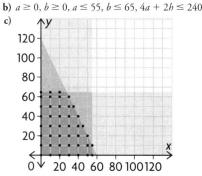

  d) (0, 0), (0, 65), (27.5, 65), and (60, 0)
  e) (55, 65) and (45, 50) are not solutions. (25, 25) is a solution. So, the company can make 25 of type A lights and 25 of type B lights.

13. Let t represent the number of tacos that can be made in a day.
  Let b represent the number of burritos that can be made in a day.
  Let C represent the cost of making the goods.
  restrictions: $t \in \mathbb{W}, b \in \mathbb{W}$
  constraints: $t \geq 0, b \geq 0, t \leq 50, b \leq 75, t + b \leq 125$
  objective function to maximize: $C = 0.75t + 1.25b$

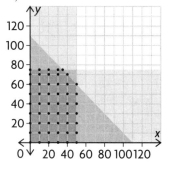

Their minimum cost will be $0, if they make no tacos or burritos. Their maximum cost will be $120, if they make 35 tacos and 75 burritos.

Chapter 7

Getting Started, page 178

1. **a)** iv)   **b)** i)   **c)** iii)   **d)** ii)
2. **a)** function   **b)** function   **c)** not a function
3. **a)** function   **b)** not a function
4. **a)** $x = 8$ **b)** $x = 3$ **c)** $x = 4$ or -4
5. **a)**   **b)**

  c)

6. **a)** $(x - 4)(x + 6)$ **b)** not possible   **c)** $3(x + 2)(x - 7)$
7. **a)** $x = 5$ or -5 **b)** $x = 8.5$ **c)** $x = 1$
8. **a)** $x = 0$ or $x = 3$ **b)** $p = 0$ or $p = -\dfrac{2}{3}$ **c)** $b = -4$ or $b = 2.5$
  d) $x = -\dfrac{1}{3}$ or $x = 1.4$

Lesson 7.1, page 180

1. **a)** $y = 4 - x^2 + 2x$ **b)** $y = 2(5x - 3)$ **c)** $y = (2x - 1)(x + 3)$
    $y = \underline{-x^2 + 2x + 4}$ $y = \underline{10x - 6}$ $y = \underline{2x^2 + 5x - 3}$
    yes   no   yes
2. **a)** opens down, y-intercept 4   **b)** opens up, y-intercept -3
3. The line of symmetry does not change. The lowest point shifts up or down as c increases or decreases.
4. **a)** -2 **b)** 0   **c)** 4
5. **a)** -2; neither   **b)** upward

Lesson 7.2, page 182

1. **a)** e.g., (0, 2), (2, 12)   **b)** e.g., (0, 0), (−1, 7)
2. **a)** maximum; -1 **b)** minimum; -1
3. maximum; 9
4. **a)** minimum; $a > 0$ **b)** maximum; $a < 0$
5. **a)**

x	0	1	2	3	4	5	6	7
f(x)	13	−11	−27	−35	−35	−27	−11	13

  b) $x = 3.5$
  c) (3.5, −36); minimum

d)

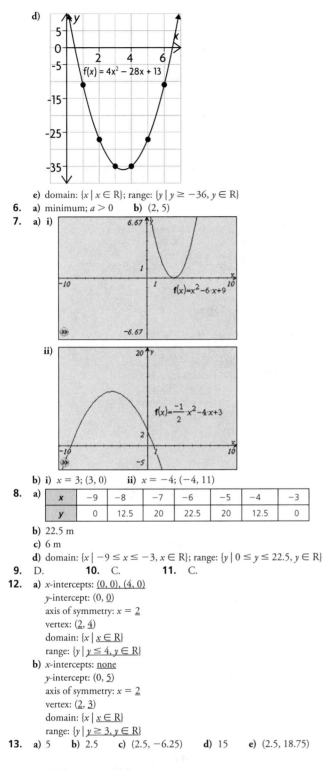

$f(x) = 4x^2 - 28x + 13$

e) domain: $\{x \mid x \in R\}$; range: $\{y \mid y \geq -36, y \in R\}$

6. **a)** minimum; $a > 0$ **b)** $(2, 5)$

7. **a) i)**

ii)

$f(x) = x^2 - 6 \cdot x + 9$

$f(x) = \dfrac{-1}{2} \cdot x^2 - 4 \cdot x + 3$

b) i) $x = 3$; $(3, 0)$ **ii)** $x = -4$; $(-4, 11)$

8. **a)**

x	−9	−8	−7	−6	−5	−4	−3
y	0	12.5	20	22.5	20	12.5	0

b) 22.5 m
c) 6 m
d) domain: $\{x \mid -9 \leq x \leq -3, x \in R\}$; range: $\{y \mid 0 \leq y \leq 22.5, y \in R\}$

9. D. **10.** C. **11.** C.

12. **a)** x-intercepts: $\underline{(0, 0), (4, 0)}$
  y-intercept: $(0, \underline{0})$
  axis of symmetry: $x = \underline{2}$
  vertex: $(\underline{2}, \underline{4})$
  domain: $\{x \mid \underline{x \in R}\}$
  range: $\{y \mid \underline{y \leq 4, y \in R}\}$
  b) x-intercepts: $\underline{\text{none}}$
  y-intercept: $(0, \underline{5})$
  axis of symmetry: $x = \underline{2}$
  vertex: $(\underline{2}, \underline{3})$
  domain: $\{x \mid \underline{x \in R}\}$
  range: $\{y \mid \underline{y \geq 3, y \in R}\}$

13. **a)** 5 **b)** 2.5 **c)** $(2.5, -6.25)$ **d)** 15 **e)** $(2.5, 18.75)$

Lesson 7.3, page 186

1. **a)** yes **b)** no **c)** yes **d)** no **e)** yes **f)** no
2. **a)** yes **b)** no; $0.6x^2 + 3x - 2 = 0$ **c)** yes
  d) no; $2x^2 - 4x - 2 = 0$
3. **a)** e.g., $x = -0.75$ and $x = 3.5$ **b)** LS = 0, RS = 0; LS = 0, RS = 0
4. **a)** e.g., $x = -0.12$ and $x = 1.8$
  b) e.g., LS = −2.289…, RS = −2.246…; LS = 12.84, RS = 12.96
5. **a)** e.g., $x = -0.325$ and $x = 1.754$
  b) e.g., LS = −4.333…, RS = −4.322…; LS = 8.737…, RS = 8.741…

6. **a)** Jenna determined the values that make the expression on the left equal to 0, not the values that make the left and right sides equal each other.
  b) e.g., about $x = -0.15$ and about $x = 1.35$
7. D. **8.** B.
9. Fred must have been driving more than 90 km/h; e.g., At 90 km/h the skid mark would have been only about 65 m long.

Lesson 7.4, page 190

1.

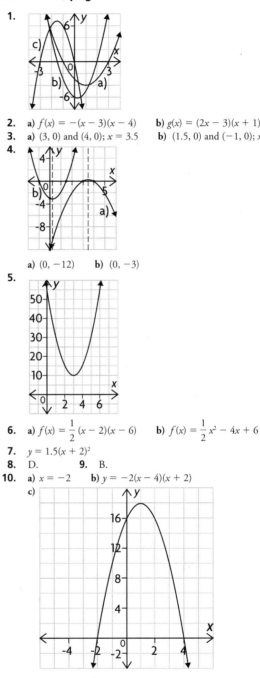

2. **a)** $f(x) = -(x - 3)(x - 4)$ **b)** $g(x) = (2x - 3)(x + 1)$
3. **a)** $(3, 0)$ and $(4, 0)$; $x = 3.5$ **b)** $(1.5, 0)$ and $(-1, 0)$; $x = 0.25$
4.

a) $(0, -12)$ **b)** $(0, -3)$

5.

6. **a)** $f(x) = \dfrac{1}{2}(x - 2)(x - 6)$ **b)** $f(x) = \dfrac{1}{2}x^2 - 4x + 6$
7. $y = 1.5(x + 2)^2$
8. D. **9.** B.
10. **a)** $x = -2$ **b)** $y = -2(x - 4)(x + 2)$
  c)

Lesson 7.5, page 194

1. **a)** $x = -6$ or $x = 3$ **b)** $x = -2$ or $x = -10$
  c) $x = \dfrac{2}{3}$ or $x = -\dfrac{2}{3}$
2. **a)** $x = 5$ **b)** $x = -6$

3. **a)** $x = 3$ or $x = 1$

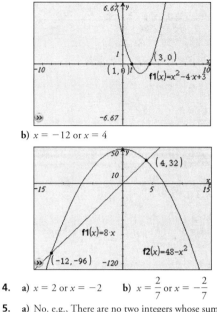

b) $x = -12$ or $x = 4$

4. **a)** $x = 2$ or $x = -2$ **b)** $x = \dfrac{2}{7}$ or $x = -\dfrac{2}{7}$

5. **a)** No. e.g., There are no two integers whose sum is 6 and whose product is -3.

b) $x = 2$

6. $x = 6$ or $x = -4$ **7.** e.g., $x^2 - 2x - 48 = 0$

8. **a)** $x = \dfrac{1}{3}$ or $x = -\dfrac{2}{5}$

b) e.g., He might have had the wrong signs in the factors.

9. \$4.70

10. C.

11. **a)** $x = -4$ or $x = 7$

b) Factors should be $x + 4$ and $x - 7$, because the roots are $x = -4$ and $x = 7$.

Lesson 7.6, page 198

1. **a)** **i)** down   **ii)** $(1, 4)$

b) **i)** up   **ii)** $(-2, 7)$

2. **a)** $(-3, 12)$ **b)** $x = -3$ **c)** -6 **d)** $(-6, -6)$

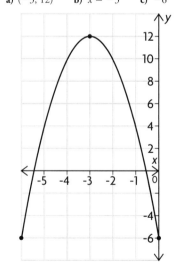

3. C.

4. **a)** e.g., $y = 2(x - 1)^2$, $y = 2(x - 1)^2 - 5$, $y = 2(x - 1)^2 + 3$,...

b) e.g., $y = -(x - 3)^2 - 1$, $y = 3(x - 3)^2 - 1$,
$y = 0.2(x - 3)^2 - 1$,...

5. **a)** vertex: $(2, 3)$ y-intercept: $(0, 5)$

b) $g(x) = \dfrac{1}{2}(x - 2)^2 + 3$

6. **a)**

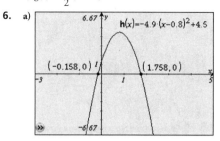

b) The zero at $t = -0.158...$ has no meaning, as time cannot be negative. The zero at $t = 1.758...$ is when the ball hits the ground.

7. **a)** $f(x) = -0.32(x - 7.5)^2 + 18$

b) domain: $\{x \mid 0 \le x \le 15, x \in \mathbb{R}\}$ range: $\{y \mid \in 0 \le y \le 18, y \in \mathbb{R}\}$

8. A.   **9.** A.

10. vertex: $(6, -1)$; y-intercept: -10

11. $y = \dfrac{1}{3}(x + 3)^2 - 1$

Lesson 7.7, page 202

1. Ryan made the error. He used "5" instead of "-5" for b.

2. **a)** $a = 3$, $b = -2$, $c = 1$ **b)** $a = -2$, $b = 4$, $c = -3$

3. **a)** No. The radicand is not a perfect square.

b) No. The radicand is not a perfect square.

c) Yes. The radicand is a perfect square.

d) Yes. The radicand is a perfect square.

4. **a)** $x = 1.5$ or $x = -1$

b) $x = \dfrac{3 - \sqrt{19}}{5}$ or $x = \dfrac{3 + \sqrt{19}}{5}$

c) no real roots

d) $x = \dfrac{4 - \sqrt{10}}{2}$ or $x = \dfrac{4 + \sqrt{10}}{2}$

5. $\doteq 0.4$ m

6. on Mars: $t = \underline{3.713...}$
on Neptune: $t = \underline{1.452...}$
The ball would fall to the base of the spacecraft $\underline{2.26\ s}$ earlier on Neptune.

7. $\doteq 6.7$ s

Lesson 7.8, page 206

1. The numbers are -13 and 15.

2. **a)** $\doteq 5.0$ cm.

b)

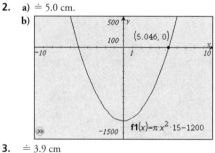

3. $\doteq 3.9$ cm

4. $\doteq 1.15$ s

5. 15 and 16 or -15 and -16

6. $\doteq 33$ cm, $\doteq 54$ cm

7. D.

8. $\doteq 34$ cm square

Chapter 7 Test Prep, page 210

Q1: • The degree is <u>2</u>.
• The graph is a <u>parabola</u> with a single vertical <u>axis of symmetry</u>.
• The <u>vertex</u> of a parabola is its highest or lowest point and lies on its <u>axis of symmetry</u>.
• A parabola can have <u>zero</u>, <u>one</u>, or <u>two</u> x-intercepts.

Q2: • standard form: $\underline{y = ax^2 + bx + c}$, where $a \neq 0$
$a \geq 0$, parabola opens <u>up</u>
$a \leq 0$, parabola opens <u>down</u>
c is the <u>y-intercept</u>.
• factored form: $\underline{y = a(x - r)(x - s)}$, where $a \neq 0$
r and s are the <u>x-intercept(s)</u>.
• vertex form: $\underline{y = a(x - h)^2 + k}$, where $a \neq 0$
(h, k) is the <u>vertex</u>.

Q3: • standard form: Use a <u>table</u> of values to determine the <u>vertex</u> and <u>axis</u> of symmetry; or use <u>partial</u> factoring; plot the <u>y-intercept</u>.
• factored form: Plot the <u>x-intercepts</u>; also determine the axis of <u>symmetry</u> and <u>vertex</u>.
• vertex form: Plot the <u>vertex</u>, determine the <u>y-intercept</u>, and use the <u>axis of symmetry</u> to determine the other symmetric point.

Q4: • The number of roots is determined by the <u>number of times</u> the corresponding parabola intersects the <u>x-axis</u>.
• There can be <u>zero</u>, <u>one</u>, or <u>two</u> roots.

Q5: • Solution values are <u>approximate</u>.
• The number of <u>solutions</u> is obvious.
• The solution process is relatively <u>quick</u>.

Q6: • Solution values are <u>exact</u>.
• The number of <u>solutions</u> is not always obvious.
• The solution process involves solving <u>linear</u> equations.

Q7: • The quadratic formula is $x = \dfrac{\underline{-b \pm \sqrt{b^2 - 4ac}}}{2a}$.
• It applies to the quadratic equation $\underline{ax^2 + bx + c = 0}$, where $\underline{a \neq 0}$.

Q8: • Solution values are <u>exact</u>.
• If the radicand, $\underline{b^2 - 4ac}$, simplifies to a perfect square, then the equation can be solved by <u>factoring</u>.
• If the <u>radicand</u> is negative, then the equation has no real solution.

Q9: • A problem may have only one <u>admissible</u> solution, even though the quadratic equation that represents it has two <u>real</u> solutions. Solutions that do not make sense in the context of the problem are <u>inadmissible</u>.

Chapter 7 Test, page 212

1. D.   2. C.   3. D.   4. C.
5. D.   6. B.   7. C.   8. C.
9. B.   10. A.   11. A.   12. C.
13. **a)** x-intercepts: $(\underline{-3}, 0)$, $(\underline{1}, 0)$; y-intercept: $(0, \underline{2})$;
axis of symmetry: $x = \underline{-1}$; vertex: $\underline{(-1, 3)}$
b) range: $\{y \mid y \leq \underline{3}, y \in \mathbb{R}\}$
14. $x = 2$ and $x = -19$
15. $x = -17$ and $x = 19$
16. **a)** $x = -2$ **b)** $(-2, 27)$ **c)** $y = -5(x + 2)^2 + 27$
17. **a)** $a = 3, b = -2, c = 1$ **b)** $a = -2, b = 4, c = -3$
18. **a)** $x = \dfrac{-3 + \sqrt{65}}{14}, x = \dfrac{-3 - \sqrt{65}}{14}$
b) $x = \dfrac{-1 + \sqrt{13}}{4}, x = \dfrac{-1 - \sqrt{13}}{4}$
19. 13 and 14 or -14 and -13
20. 40 cm; 17 cm

21.

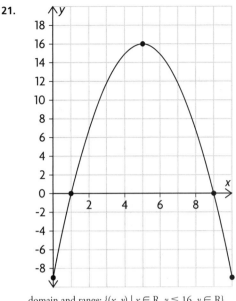

domain and range: $\{(x, y) \mid x \in \mathbb{R}, y \leq 16, y \in \mathbb{R}\}$
22. $\doteq 78$ km/h
23. $y = \dfrac{1}{3}(x + 3)^2 - 2$
24. **a)** $x = \dfrac{3.1 + \sqrt{30.41}}{5.2}$ or $\dfrac{3.1 - \sqrt{30.41}}{5.2}$
$x = 1.66...$ or $x = -0.46...$
b) no real roots; The radicand is negative.
25. **a)** $H(t) = -5(t - 2.5)^2 + 76.25$ **b)** 31.25 m

Chapter 8

Getting Started, page 216

1. **a)** iii)   **c)** ii)   **e)** vi)   **g)** v)
b) iv)   **d)** viii)   **f)** i)   **h)** vii)

2. **a)** 4   **b)** 2.75   **c)** -0.4, or $-\dfrac{2}{5}$

3. **a)** $SA = 166$ m², $V = 140$ m³   **b)** $SA \doteq 259.2$ cm², $V \doteq 274.9$ cm³
c) $SA = 864$ mm², $V = 1728$ mm³

4. **a)** 5   **b)** 45   **c)** 21

5. **a)** 0.375   **b)** 0.3125   **c)** 4.25   **d)** 3.2

6. **a)** 2.45 m   **b)** 450 s   **c)** 38 000 cm²

7. **a)** $8x + 6$ **b)** $5k^2 - 10k$ **c)** $-28 + 4t - 8t^2$

8. **a)** $\dfrac{25}{3}$ **b)** $\dfrac{1}{11}$ **c)** $-\dfrac{17}{2}$ **d)** $\dfrac{x}{48}$

9. **a)** x^5 **b)** x^4 **c)** x^{12} **d)** $\dfrac{1}{x^3}$

10. **a)** 25   **b)** $\doteq 13.4$ **c)** 0.3   **d)** $\doteq 2.5$

11. **a)** $x = 44.8$ **b)** $t \doteq 1.93$ **c)** $w = 67.2$

12. AB and KL, BC and LG, CD and GH, DE and HI, EF and IJ, FA and JK

Lesson 8.1, page 218

1. $\doteq 0.92$ L/km   2. $\doteq 9.6$ km/h   3. $2.13/L
4. $\doteq \$0.27$/egg   5. The 10 lb sack is the better buy.
6. The butcher charges less per kilogram.
7. The farmers' market charges the lower price.
8. The peregrine falcon can travel faster.
9. Coloura paint will cover a greater surface area.
10. They paved the road faster on Wednesday.
11. Plan B costs less.

12. a) *BC*   **b)** yes; *CD* and *FG*   **c)** 10 km/h
    d) The cyclist is travelling faster in *FG*.
13. e.g., These rates are speedy: they could represent a car driving. It could
    be that a police officer in a patrol car is driving at the speed limit, when
    he sees a speeding car. He speeds up to catch the speeder, and then stops
    the speeder to give a ticket. Then the officer drives off at a slower speed.
14. B.   **15.** B.
16.

Year	Attendance	Rate of Change (visitors/year)
1950	600 000	—
1960	930 000	$\dfrac{930\ 000 - 600\ 000}{1960 - 1950} = 33\ 000$
1975	1 290 000	$\dfrac{1\ 290\ 000 - 930\ 000}{1975 - 1960} = 24\ 000$
1980	1 290 000	$\dfrac{1\ 290\ 000 - 1\ 290\ 000}{1980 - 1975} = 0$
1995	1 010 000	$\dfrac{1\ 010\ 000 - 1\ 290\ 000}{1995 - 1980} = -18\ 667$
1997	900 000	$\dfrac{900\ 000 - 1\ 010\ 000}{1997 - 1995} = -55\ 000$
2001	952 000	$\dfrac{952\ 000 - 900\ 000}{2001 - 1997} = 13\ 000$
2002	902 000	$\dfrac{902\ 000 - 952\ 000}{2002 - 2001} = -50\ 000$
2006	959 000	$\dfrac{959\ 000 - 902\ 000}{2006 - 2002} = 14\ 250$
2009	855 000	$\dfrac{855\ 000 - 959\ 000}{2009 - 2006} = -34\ 667$

The attendance decreased at the greatest rate from 1995 to 1997 and
increased at the greatest rate from 1950 to 1960.

Lesson 8.2, page 224

1. $\doteq$ 2 h 47 min   **2.** $\doteq$ $3.58   **3.** $\doteq$ 51 turns
4. a) $105   **b)** 35 lb
5. a) e.g., 5 000 000 ha   **b)** e.g., $240 000 000
6. C.   **7.** A.   **8.** $3740.42   **9.** $505.45

Lesson 8.3, page 228

1. B.   **2.** C.   **3.** e.g., 1 cm : 20 cm
4. e.g., 5 cm : 1 cm   **5.** e.g., 25 mm : 1 mm
6. 9 cm by 16.5 cm   **7.** 10.5 cm by 15 cm
8. The lot should be 15 cm long and 10 cm wide.
    The house should be 7.5 cm long and 5 cm wide.
    The house should be 2.5 cm from the left end of the lot.
9. $\doteq$ 14 cm
10.

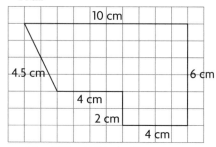

11. e.g., 1 in. : 150 in.; 11.2 in. by 4 in.
12. a) area of studio #1: 93.75 m²
    area of studio #2: 156.25 m²
    area of studio #3: 187.5 m²
    area of supplies closet: (15)(5) = 75 m²
    b) 237.5 m²

Lesson 8.4, page 234

1. 800 cm²   **2.** 250 cm²   **3.** $\doteq$ 30 cm²
4. $\doteq$ 7 cm²   **5.** $\doteq$ 48 unit²   **6.** $\doteq$ 20 unit²
7. a) 0.6   **b)** triangle *A*: 240 cm²; triangle *B*: 86.4 cm²   **c)** 1
8. $\doteq$ 236.6 unit²   **9.** D.   **10.** A.
11. coffee shop: 62.5 m²; parking lot: 262.5 m²

Lesson 8.5, page 238

1. 10 ft tall, 7.5 ft wide, 37.5 ft long   **2.** $\doteq$ 389 m³
3. 288 in. long, 51.2 in. wide, 14 in. deep
4. 350 cm long, 133 cm wide, 115.5 cm high
5. length: 18 in., width: 12 in., height: 30 in.
6. A.   **7.** D.   **8.** D.   **9.** C.
10. e.g., I used scale 1:20.

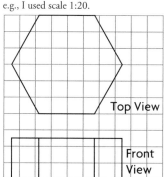

Lesson 8.6, page 242

1. a) 20   **b)** 400 times   **c)** 8000 times
2. a) 14 400 times   **b)** 11 664 000 cm³
3. 25
4. a) 42.875   **b)** 12.25
5. 27
6. a) 79.507   **b)** 18.49
7. 15.625 times   **8.** 12.96 times
9. e.g., about 5 times greater
10. a) 26.1 cm, 24.4 cm   **b)** 1070 cm², 935 cm²
11. 11.5 cm
12. a) 9088 cubes   **b)** 2016 mL

Chapter 8 Test Prep, page 246

Q1: • Write rates in the same <u>units</u>, such as centimetres per second.
    • Use unit <u>rates</u>, such as "/mL" (per millilitre).
    • Graph information and use the fact that <u>slopes</u> represent rates of
      <u>change</u>.
Q2: • A scale <u>diagram</u> is <u>similar</u> to the 2-D shape it represents. The scale
      <u>factor</u> is the ratio of diagram <u>measurements</u> to actual <u>measurements</u>.
    • Therefore, a <u>diagram</u> dimension is given by the corresponding actual
      dimension, <u>multiplied</u> by the scale factor.
    • A scale factor *k* between <u>0</u> and <u>1</u> means that the scale diagram is a(n)
      <u>reduction</u> of the original shape.
    • A scale factor *k* greater than <u>1</u> means that the scale diagram is a(n)
      <u>enlargement</u> of the original shape.
    • The ratio of <u>area</u> of diagram to <u>area</u> of actual or original shape is given
      by <u>*k²*</u>.
Q3: • A scale <u>model</u> is <u>similar</u> to the 3-D object it represents, meaning that
      the dimensions are <u>proportional</u>. The scale <u>factor</u> is the diagram-to-
      actual <u>measurement</u> ratio.
    • Therefore, a <u>model</u> dimension is given by the corresponding actual
      dimension, <u>multiplied</u> by the scale factor.
    • The ratio of surface <u>area</u> of model to surface <u>area</u> of actual or original
      object is given by <u>*k²*</u>.
    • The ratio of <u>volume</u> of model to <u>volume</u> of actual or original object is
      given by <u>*k³*</u>.

Chapter 8 Test, page 247

1. C.　　**2.** A.　　**3.** A.　　**4.** 4 h 3 min

5.

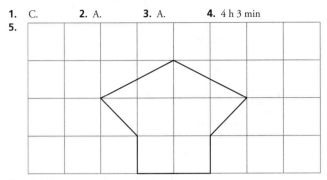

6. $\doteq 1.3$

7. **a)** 185.193　　**b)** 32.49

8. 9 ft tall, 6 ft wide, 15 ft long

9. 202.5 cm tall, 168 cm wide, 219 cm long

10. $\doteq 9$ unit²

11. strategy 1: Determine the unit rate, then multiply by 50 weeks/year.
strategy 2: Use equivalent ratios to solve for the number of hours worked, x, in 50 weeks.
750 h

12. Filling up in Canada: unit rate is C$1.39/L
Filling up in the U.S.: C$79.77 for 60 L of gas, or unit rate of about $1.33/L
e.g., $1.33/L is a little less than $1.39/L, but buying gas at home would take less time, waste less fuel, and be more convenient. So, buying gas at home makes more sense.

6–8 Cumulative Test, page 250

1. C.　　**2.** A.　　**3.** D.　　**4.** B.
5. D.　　**6.** B.　　**7.** B.　　**8.** B.
9. D.　　**10.** C.　　**11.** C.

12. **a)** $s \in \underline{W}$, $t \in \underline{W}$
b) $s \geq \underline{0}$, $s \leq \underline{250}$, $t \geq \underline{0}$, $t \leq \underline{175}$, $s + \underline{t} \geq \underline{300}$
c) cost $C = \underline{1.25s + 2t}$

13.

LS	RS		LS	RS
$5(\underline{3}) - (\underline{-3})$ $\underline{18}$	$\underline{7}$		$\dfrac{(\underline{-3}) + 2(\underline{3})}{\underline{3}}$	5
LS ≥ RS? ✓			LS $\underline{\leq}$ RS ✓	

14. **a)** $f(x) = \underline{-3x(x - 8)} - 18$　　**b)** $(0, \underline{-18})$　　**c)** $(8, \underline{-18})$
d) axis of symmetry: $x = \underline{4}$; vertex: $(\underline{4}, \underline{30})$

15. **a)** the coordinates of its vertex: $(\underline{-5}, \underline{-35})$
b) its y-intercept: $\underline{65}$
c) its domain and range: $\{(x, y) \mid \underline{x \in R}, \underline{y \geq -35}, \underline{y \in R}\}$

16. $x = \underline{-1.5}$ or $x = \underline{4}$

17. $x = \dfrac{5 + \sqrt{53}}{14}$ or $x = \dfrac{5 - \sqrt{53}}{14}$

18. **a)** $\doteq 18.1$ L/100 km　　**b)** $\doteq 15.9$ L/100 km　　**c)** $\doteq 12\%$

19. **a)** $1 : \underline{15}$　　**b)** 225 times larger

20. **a)** The boundary of $3x + y \geq 12$ is $y = -3x + 12$; draw a solid line with y-intercept 12 and slope -3. The boundary of $x < 2y - 6$ is $y = 0.5x + 3$. Draw a dashed line with y-intercept 3 and slope 0.5.
b) $3x + y \geq 12$: shade upper half plane; $x < 2y - 6$: shade upper half plane

c)

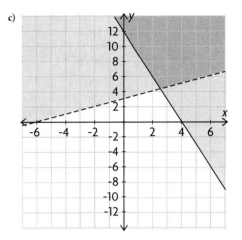

e.g., (0, 12), (3, 7)

21. **a)** The boundary of $2y - 5x < 7$ is $y = 2.5x + 3.5$; draw a dashed line, y-intercept 3.5 and slope 2.5; shade right half plane. The boundary of $x \geq 4$ is $x = 4$; draw a stippled vertical line through 4 on the x-axis; shade right half plane.

b)

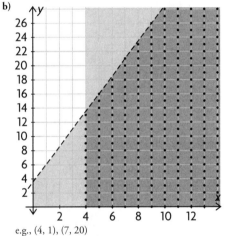

e.g., (4, 1), (7, 20)

22. **a)** Let x represent the number of shakes and y represent the number of smoothies.
Restrictions: $x \in W$, $y \in W$
Constraints: $x \geq 0$, $y \geq 0$
$x + y \leq 280$
$x \leq 120$
Objective function: revenue, $R = 3.5x + 2.75y$

b)

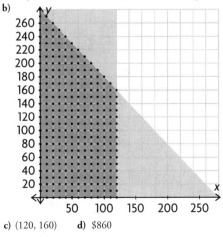

c) (120, 160)　　**d)** $860

23. **a)** e.g., Create a table of values and look for two points that have the same y-values. Use the corresponding x-value(s) to determine the equation of the axis of symmetry and the x-coordinate of the vertex. Calculate the corresponding y-value to determine the y-coordinate of the vertex.

b) e.g., Factor the $2x^2 - 10x$ part as $2x(x - 5)$. This tells you that the parabola has a y-intercept of $(0, 7)$ and another point at the same y-coordinate, $(5, 7)$. The axis of symmetry must lie midway between these points, giving the x-coordinate of the vertex. You can substitute this to determine the x-coordinate of the vertex.

c) $(2.5, -5.5)$

d) $y = 2(x - 2.5)^2 - 5.5$

24. **a)** $y = a(x - 3)^2 - 8.5$
$-4 = a(-3)^2 - 8.5$
$-4 = 9a - 8.5$
$4.5 = 9a$
$0.5 = a \qquad y = 0.5(x - 3)^2 - 8.5$

b) $y = 0.5x^2 - 3x - 4$

c) $3 + \sqrt{17}, 3 - \sqrt{17}$

25. $0.157, 1.593 \qquad LS = RS$

26. $-2x^2 + 4x + 30$

27. 6.4 in. by 9.4 in.

28. **a)** Murray should buy 3 m rolls.
b) Murray should buy 4 m rolls in this case.

29.

30. $\doteq 7.8 \text{ m}^2$

31.

32. **a)** $125 \text{ cm}^3, 3375 \text{ cm}^3$ **b)** 5 cm, 15 cm **c)** 150 cm^2
d) e.g., Multiply the surface area of the smaller cube by the square of the scale factor, $32 = 9$; or substitute 15 cm into the formula $SA = 6s^2$; 1350 cm^2

1–8 Cumulative Test: Exam Prep, page 258

1. B. **2.** C. **3.** B. **4.** B. **5.** B.
6. C. **7.** C. **8.** D. **9.** B. **10.** A.
11. C. **12.** D.
13. **a)** 30 ways **b)** 18 ways
14. **a)**

b)

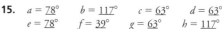

15. $a = \underline{78}° \qquad b = \underline{117}° \qquad c = \underline{63}° \qquad d = \underline{63}°$
$e = \underline{78}° \qquad f = \underline{39}° \qquad g = \underline{63}° \qquad h = \underline{117}°$

16. $\angle E = \underline{87}° \qquad \angle F = \underline{52}° \qquad e = \underline{10.2} \text{ cm}$

17. $q = \underline{6.5} \text{ m} \qquad \angle P = \underline{51}° \qquad \angle R = \underline{62}°$

18. **a)** 20.9 m **b)** 25.8 m

19. Chemistry $\underline{0.64}$ French $\underline{0.90}$

20. **a)** 95% **b)** 3% **c)** 65% to 71%
d) between 16 240 900 and 17 740 060 Canadians

21. **a)** yes **b)** no

22. **a)**

x	y
−1	−12
0	−7
1	−3
2	0
3	2
4	3
5	3
6	2

b) $x = 4.5$ **c)** $(4.5, 3.125)$

23. $f(x) = a(x \underline{+ 4})(x + 4)$
$f(x) = a(x \underline{+ 4})^2$
$f(0) = a(\underline{4})^2$
$\underline{4} = \underline{16}a$
$\underline{0.25} = a$
$f(x) = \underline{0.25}(x \underline{+ 4})^2$

24. $x = \dfrac{3 + \sqrt{21}}{6}$ or $x = \dfrac{3 - \sqrt{21}}{6}$
$x = \underline{1.26}$ or $x = \underline{-0.26}$

25. 28.8 m^2

26. e.g., Let n and $n + 1$ represent the numbers.
$(n + 1)^2 - n^2 = n(n + 1) + 1(n + 1) - n^2$
$(n + 1)^2 - n^2 = n^2 + 2n + 1 - n^2$
$(n + 1)^2 - n^2 = 2n + 1$
$(n + 1)^2 - n^2 = n + (n + 1)$

27. $\angle ABC = 32° + 90°$, or $122°$
$\angle ABC + \angle BAD = 180°$
$BC \parallel AD$ Corresponding angles are equal.
So, $ABCD$ is a trapezoid.
$\angle ADC + \angle BCD = 180°$ co-interior angles between parallel lines
$\angle ADC + 122° = 180°$
$\angle ADC = 58°$
$\angle BAD = 58°$
$\angle ADC = \angle BAD$ transitive property
So, $ABCD$ is isosceles.

28. **a)** $\angle C; \angle B$ **b)** $\doteq 67°$

29. a)

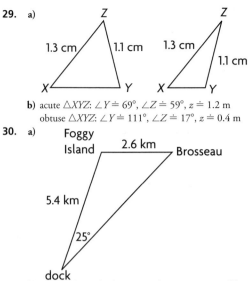

b) acute $\triangle XYZ$: $\angle Y \doteq 69°$, $\angle Z \doteq 59°$, $z \doteq 1.2$ m
obtuse $\triangle XYZ$: $\angle Y \doteq 111°$, $\angle Z \doteq 17°$, $z \doteq 0.4$ m

30. a)

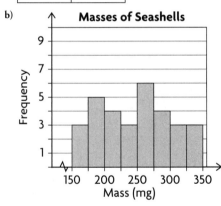

b) e.g., Without the directions, there are two possible triangles, with either an obtuse or an acute angle at Foggy Island. Going northeast first and then east means there must be an obtuse angle at Foggy Island.

c) $\doteq 6.1$ km

31. a)

Mass (mg)	Frequency
150–175	3
175–200	5
200–225	4
225–250	3
250–275	6
275–300	4
300–325	3
325–350	2

b)

Masses of Seashells

c) e.g., The distribution has two peaks, one between 175 mg and 200 mg, and one between 250 mg and 275 mg.

d) e.g., There are two categories of seashells in this sample, one larger than the other. Test by collecting more seashells.

32. a)

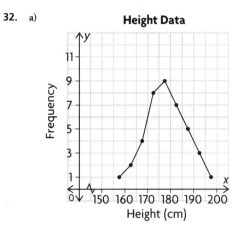

Height Data

b) e.g., Yes. The frequency polygon is bell-shaped and more or less symmetrical.

c) mean $=$ 178 cm
median $=$ 177.5 cm
Yes. The mean and median are approximately the same.

33. a)

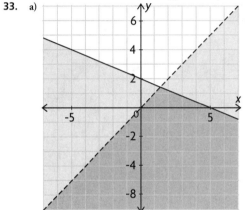

b) no

34. a) e.g., Let t represent the number of travel totes and b the number of bling baskets.
restrictions: $t \in \mathbb{W}$, $b \in \mathbb{W}$
constraints: $t \geq 0$, $b \geq 0$
$t + b \leq 48$ $t \geq 24$ $b \geq \frac{1}{3}(b + t)$ or $2b \geq t$
objective function: $C = 1.6t + 2.3b$

b) (24, 12), (24, 24), (32, 16)

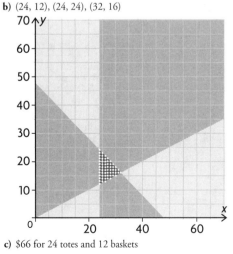

c) $66 for 24 totes and 12 baskets

35. a) $x = \dfrac{5 \pm \sqrt{25 - 4(3)(-2)}}{2(3)}$; radicand = 49

b) No. e.g., The radicand is a perfect square, so the solutions will be rational. This means the equation must be factorable.

c) $x = -\dfrac{1}{3}$ or $x = 2$

36. a) e.g., $n^2 + n - 56 = 0$

b) The integers are 13, 15, 17 or $-17, -15, -13$.

37. a) Brian's recipe uses the greater proportion of flour.

b) Brian: 312.5 mL; Erin: 375 mL

38.

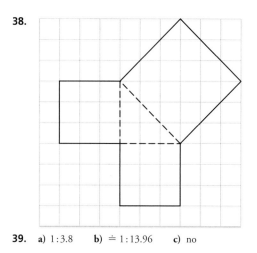

39. a) 1 : 3.8   **b)** $\doteq$ 1 : 13.96   **c)** no

14498

Z-Score Table

To determine the percent of data with a z-score equal to or less than a specific value, locate the z-score on the left side of the table and match it with the appropriate second decimal place at the top of the table.

For example, when

$z = -1.15$

the percent of data that is 1.15 standard deviations below the mean is 0.1251, or 12.51%.

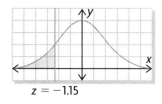

$z = -1.15$

z	0.09	0.08	0.07	0.06	0.05	0.04	0.03	0.02	0.01	0.00
−2.9	0.0014	0.0014	0.0015	0.0015	0.0016	0.0016	0.0017	0.0018	0.0018	0.0019
−2.8	0.0019	0.0020	0.0021	0.0021	0.0022	0.0023	0.0023	0.0024	0.0025	0.0026
−2.7	0.0026	0.0027	0.0028	0.0029	0.0030	0.0031	0.0032	0.0033	0.0034	0.0035
−2.6	0.0036	0.0037	0.0038	0.0039	0.0040	0.0041	0.0043	0.0044	0.0045	0.0047
−2.5	0.0048	0.0049	0.0051	0.0052	0.0054	0.0055	0.0057	0.0059	0.0060	0.0062
−2.4	0.0064	0.0066	0.0068	0.0069	0.0071	0.0073	0.0075	0.0078	0.0080	0.0082
−2.3	0.0084	0.0087	0.0089	0.0091	0.0094	0.0096	0.0099	0.0102	0.0104	0.0107
−2.2	0.0110	0.0113	0.0116	0.0119	0.0122	0.0125	0.0129	0.0132	0.0136	0.0139
−2.1	0.0143	0.0146	0.0150	0.0154	0.0158	0.0162	0.0166	0.0170	0.0174	0.0179
−2.0	0.0183	0.0188	0.0192	0.0197	0.0202	0.0207	0.0212	0.0217	0.0222	0.0228
−1.9	0.0233	0.0239	0.0244	0.0250	0.0256	0.0262	0.0268	0.0274	0.0281	0.0287
−1.8	0.0294	0.0301	0.0307	0.0314	0.0322	0.0329	0.0336	0.0344	0.0351	0.0359
−1.7	0.0367	0.0375	0.0384	0.0392	0.0401	0.0409	0.0418	0.0427	0.0436	0.0446
−1.6	0.0455	0.0465	0.0475	0.0485	0.0495	0.0505	0.0516	0.0526	0.0537	0.0548
−1.5	0.0559	0.0571	0.0582	0.0594	0.0606	0.0618	0.0630	0.0643	0.0655	0.0668
−1.4	0.0681	0.0694	0.0708	0.0721	0.0735	0.0749	0.0764	0.0778	0.0793	0.0808
−1.3	0.0823	0.0838	0.0853	0.0869	0.0885	0.0901	0.0918	0.0934	0.0951	0.0968
−1.2	0.0985	0.1003	0.1020	0.1038	0.1056	0.1075	0.1093	0.1112	0.1131	0.1151
−1.1	0.1170	0.1190	0.1210	0.1230	0.1251	0.1271	0.1292	0.1314	0.1335	0.1357
−1.0	0.1379	0.1401	0.1423	0.1446	0.1469	0.1492	0.1515	0.1539	0.1562	0.1587
−0.9	0.1611	0.1635	0.1660	0.1685	0.1711	0.1736	0.1762	0.1788	0.1814	0.1841
−0.8	0.1867	0.1894	0.1922	0.1949	0.1977	0.2005	0.2033	0.2061	0.2090	0.2119
−0.7	0.2148	0.2177	0.2206	0.2236	0.2266	0.2296	0.2327	0.2358	0.2389	0.2420
−0.6	0.2451	0.2483	0.2514	0.2546	0.2578	0.2611	0.2643	0.2676	0.2709	0.2743
−0.5	0.2776	0.2810	0.2843	0.2877	0.2912	0.2946	0.2981	0.3015	0.3050	0.3085
−0.4	0.3121	0.3156	0.3192	0.3228	0.3264	0.3300	0.3336	0.3372	0.3409	0.3446
−0.3	0.3483	0.3520	0.3557	0.3594	0.3632	0.3669	0.3707	0.3745	0.3783	0.3821
−0.2	0.3859	0.3897	0.3936	0.3974	0.4013	0.4052	0.4090	0.4129	0.4168	0.4207
−0.1	0.4247	0.4286	0.4325	0.4364	0.4404	0.4443	0.4483	0.4522	0.4562	0.4602
−0.0	0.4641	0.4681	0.4721	0.4761	0.4801	0.4840	0.4880	0.4920	0.4960	0.5000

z	0.00	0.01	0.02	0.03	0.04	0.05	0.06	0.07	0.08	0.09
0.0	0.5000	0.5040	0.5080	0.5120	0.5160	0.5199	0.5239	0.5279	0.5319	0.5359
0.1	0.5398	0.5438	0.5478	0.5517	0.5557	0.5596	0.5636	0.5675	0.5714	0.5753
0.2	0.5793	0.5832	0.5871	0.5910	0.5948	0.5987	0.6026	0.6064	0.6103	0.6141
0.3	0.6179	0.6217	0.6255	0.6293	0.6331	0.6368	0.6406	0.6443	0.6480	0.6517
0.4	0.6554	0.6591	0.6628	0.6664	0.6700	0.6736	0.6772	0.6808	0.6844	0.6879
0.5	0.6915	0.6950	0.6985	0.7019	0.7054	0.7088	0.7123	0.7157	0.7190	0.7224
0.6	0.7257	0.7291	0.7324	0.7357	0.7389	0.7422	0.7454	0.7486	0.7517	0.7549
0.7	0.7580	0.7611	0.7642	0.7673	0.7704	0.7734	0.7764	0.7794	0.7823	0.7852
0.8	0.7881	0.7910	0.7939	0.7967	0.7995	0.8023	0.8051	0.8078	0.8106	0.8133
0.9	0.8159	0.8186	0.8212	0.8238	0.8264	0.8289	0.8315	0.8340	0.8365	0.8389
1.0	0.8413	0.8438	0.8461	0.8485	0.8508	0.8531	0.8554	0.8577	0.8599	0.8621
1.1	0.8643	0.8665	0.8686	0.8708	0.8729	0.8749	0.8770	0.8790	0.8810	0.8830
1.2	0.8849	0.8869	0.8888	0.8907	0.8925	0.8944	0.8962	0.8980	0.8997	0.9015
1.3	0.9032	0.9049	0.9066	0.9082	0.9099	0.9115	0.9131	0.9147	0.9162	0.9177
1.4	0.9192	0.9207	0.9222	0.9236	0.9251	0.9265	0.9279	0.9292	0.9306	0.9319
1.5	0.9332	0.9345	0.9357	0.9370	0.9382	0.9394	0.9406	0.9418	0.9429	0.9441
1.6	0.9452	0.9463	0.9474	0.9484	0.9495	0.9505	0.9515	0.9525	0.9535	0.9545
1.7	0.9554	0.9564	0.9573	0.9582	0.9591	0.9599	0.9608	0.9616	0.9625	0.9633
1.8	0.9641	0.9649	0.9656	0.9664	0.9671	0.9678	0.9686	0.9693	0.9699	0.9706
1.9	0.9713	0.9719	0.9726	0.9732	0.9738	0.9744	0.9750	0.9756	0.9761	0.9767
2.0	0.9772	0.9778	0.9783	0.9788	0.9793	0.9798	0.9803	0.9808	0.9812	0.9817
2.1	0.9821	0.9826	0.9830	0.9834	0.9838	0.9842	0.9846	0.9850	0.9854	0.9857
2.2	0.9861	0.9864	0.9868	0.9871	0.9875	0.9878	0.9881	0.9884	0.9887	0.9890
2.3	0.9893	0.9896	0.9898	0.9901	0.9904	0.9906	0.9909	0.9911	0.9913	0.9916
2.4	0.9918	0.9920	0.9922	0.9925	0.9927	0.9929	0.9931	0.9932	0.9934	0.9936
2.5	0.9938	0.9940	0.9941	0.9943	0.9945	0.9946	0.9948	0.9949	0.9951	0.9952
2.6	0.9953	0.9955	0.9956	0.9957	0.9959	0.9960	0.9961	0.9962	0.9963	0.9964
2.7	0.9965	0.9966	0.9967	0.9968	0.9969	0.9970	0.9971	0.9972	0.9973	0.9974
2.8	0.9974	0.9975	0.9976	0.9977	0.9977	0.9978	0.9979	0.9979	0.9980	0.9981
2.9	0.9981	0.9982	0.9982	0.9983	0.9984	0.9984	0.9985	0.9985	0.9986	0.9986